"Hill and Plitnick deliver a thoughtful and incisive analysis of how progressive commitments to racial and social justice are undermined by the 'Palestinian exception.' Building the civil rights movement for the twenty-first century in America requires an international intersectionality that necessarily includes advocating for the rights and dignity of Palestinians and Israelis alike. *Except for Palestine* is timely and vital."

—Congresswoman Rashida Tlaib,
Michigan's 13th Congressional District

"Hill and Plitnick have produced a timely and powerful indictment of decades of U.S. policy exceptionalizing Israel at the expense of progressive values. Their thorough examination of American progressives' intellectual and moral hypocrisy when it comes to defending Palestinians' human rights, civil rights, and right to challenge Israeli occupation is a valuable resource."

—Lara Friedman, president of
the Foundation for Middle East Peace

"This book explores some of the most fundamental contradictions confronting liberal spaces in the U.S. and makes a powerful case for the progressive core values of humanity, justice, and dignity to finally include the Palestinian people."

—Ahmad Abuznaid, executive director of
the U.S. Campaign for Palestinian Rights

"*Except for Palestine* cogently explores the reasons for the silence of so many progressives and liberals when it comes to the unceasing violations of the rights of the Palestinian people. Hill and Plitnick dismantle one by one the arguments used to justify this shameful silence, and in doing so provide an eloquent, balanced, and hard-hitting analysis of why ending an egregious exception to accepted norms of justice and equality is so imperative."

—Rashid Khalidi, author of *Brokers of Deceit: How the U.S. Has Undermined Peace in the Middle East*

"A timely and compelling treatise on the moral failings of U.S. policy and American politics in relation to Israel/Palestine."

—Khaled Elgindy, Responsible Statecraft

EXCEPT FOR PALESTINE

The Limits of Progressive Politics

Marc Lamont Hill
and
Mitchell Plitnick

THE
NEW
PRESS

NEW YORK
LONDON

Requests for permission to reproduce selections from this book should
be made through our website: https://thenewpress.com/contact.

First published in the United States by The New Press, New York, 2021
This paperback edition published by The New Press, 2022
Distributed by Two Rivers Distribution

ISBN 978-1-62097-592-3 (hc)
ISBN 978-1-67097-725-5 (pb)
ISBN 978-1-62097-593-0 (ebook)
CIP data is available

The New Press publishes books that promote and enrich public discussion and
understanding of the issues vital to our democracy and to a more equitable world.
These books are made possible by the enthusiasm of our readers; the support
of a committed group of donors, large and small; the collaboration of our many
partners in the independent media and the not-for-profit sector; booksellers, who
often hand-sell New Press books; librarians; and above all by our authors.

www.thenewpress.com

Composition by dix!
This book was set in Fairfield LH

Contents

To the loving memory of Teo Hunt Surasky, who left this world in 2020 much too soon. And to his mothers, Carolyn Hunt and Cecilie Surasky, who have enriched and strengthened Mitchell's life in more ways than they can imagine.

To Ahmed Erekat (الله يرحمه), a beautiful spirit stolen from the world two weeks before his wedding. May his grave be made spacious, filled with light, and placed in paradise.

Preface

As this book was going to press, Joe Biden had just defeated Donald Trump in the 2020 presidential election. Despite Trump's defiant protests to the contrary, Biden garnered a decisive popular and electoral college victory. In doing so, the election effectively ended four years of the greatest corruption, mismanagement, and hateful leadership that the United States had seen in many years.

Still, Biden's victory was a qualified one. Although he lost the popular vote by nearly 6 million votes, Trump still scored the support of more than 73 million Americans, hardly an overwhelming rebuke of his proto-fascist presidency. While significantly better than Trump on several key matters, Biden won by running on a platform that offered no radical vision of the future and promised no fundamental social change. Rather, the Biden presidency promised a return to the status quo ante that proved such fertile ground for Trump's authoritarian hucksterism.

This is not to suggest that Trump's defeat was a small matter. To the contrary, Biden's presidency offered, to borrow a phrase from James Baldwin, "a means of buying time." By removing the immediate threat of fascism, white nationalism, and extraordinary incompetence, the American people cleared a little bit of space to better fight the perennial threats of white supremacy, capitalism, and empire.

Embracing such a sober analysis of president-elect Biden's platform enables us to set aside any illusions about the current political moment. We recognize that the effects of Trump's reign will not magically disappear in the wake of the 2020 election. We also understand that President Biden is incapable, and in some cases unwilling, to repair the damage wielded by the previous administration. With such reduced expectations, we have little reason to believe that the Biden presidency will properly attend to the systemic issues that preceded and, indeed, helped produce the Trump phenomenon. This analysis applies not only to domestic matters, but also to U.S. foreign policy.

During the Trump presidency, American policy toward Palestine and Israel dropped all pretense of even-handedness. Many of the normal diplomatic niceties and policy charades deployed by previous presidents were simply abandoned. Trump's agenda was driven openly and unabashedly not just by pro-Israel forces, but by the most radical of those forces: the religious-nationalist settler movement. Trump's administration came together with an Israeli government that had been moving further and further to the right with each election, and a compromised and divided Palestinian leadership consumed by its own internal squabbles over the crumbs of authority Israel tossed it. The purpose of this collaboration was to create a final status solution in the region that forever excluded the possibility of a free, functional, and self-determined Palestinian state that included Palestinian citizens of Israel, residents of the West Bank and Gaza, and those currently living as refugees around the world. Given this relationship, it is no surprise that Israel received many gifts from the United States, including recognition of Western Jerusalem as its capital and Israel's annexation of the Golan Heights; a U.S. plan for permanent Israeli control of the West bank dubbed, in the best Orwellian tradition, "the Deal of the Century"; the ending of funding for basic services to Palestinian refugees; and other large concessions. Even more telling is that the Israeli government was not asked to give anything in return, even as a token exchange.

In the three months prior to the election, as he rushed to score more diplomatic "victories," the Trump administration forged agreements for normalization of relations between Israel and Arab states Bahrain, the United Arab Emirates, and Sudan. These agreements often required the forceful stifling of dissent against them.[1] This was a sharp departure from the recent past, when there was an Arab consensus that backed an exchange of normal relations with Israel for the creation of a Palestinian state, with uniform support for the Arab Peace Initiative of 2002, which promised just such an arrangement.[2] The shift in the United States' position and its heavy pressure on Israel's behalf made it possible to break that Arab state consensus. In so doing, they further diminished what little bargaining leverage Palestinians had.

President Biden almost certainly would not have made the decisions Trump did, some of which we explore in this book. But as we enter the dawn of his presidency, he has also made it clear that he has no intention of reversing them. Known during his time as vice president as Obama's "salesman" to the pro-Israel community,[3] Biden is not as enamored as he once was of Israeli Prime Minister Benjamin Netanyahu. Still, he is absolutely committed to, as his presidential campaign website stated, ". . . urge Israel's government and the Palestinian Authority to take steps to keep the prospect of a negotiated two-state outcome alive and avoid actions, such as unilateral annexation of territory and settlement activity, or support for incitement and violence, that undercut prospects for peace between the parties."[4] Such goals are nearly identical to those of the Barack Obama administration, whose failures occurred before Trump gave Israel all it requested for four years, raising Israeli expectations of Washington and destroying what little Palestinian faith remained in the United States.

This book, written in the age of Trump, carries an even more powerful message as we enter the age of Biden. We must remember that nearly nothing that Trump did—as ill-advised, cruel, or reckless as it may have been—was an original idea. His decisions were all based on long-held policy positions of various sectors within the pro-Israel community. Many were bipartisan, such as the move of the American embassy from Tel Aviv to Jerusalem, which, as we explain in detail, was based on a law passed during the Clinton administration with an overwhelming majority of Democrats and Republicans.

Long before Trump came along, Israel's occupation of the West Bank and siege on the Gaza Strip had become a part of the background of the American media landscape. Although it occasionally flared up and appeared in the headlines, it was nonetheless understood as a part of the violent tapestry of daily life in the Middle East. That Orientalist perception, along with the normalization of the occupation and dispossession of the Palestinian people, was cemented within the public imagination during the Obama-Biden years. Those are the "good old days" to which Biden promises to return us.

In the United States, we are struggling to reckon with a legacy of structural injustice that has defined our history. American policy in Palestine and Israel has always been hopelessly intertwined with our own longstanding struggles with white supremacy, Islamophobia, anti-Semitism, and ethnocentrism. As we've come to understand that racism, sexism, religious bigotry, anti-LGBTQIA hate, and other prejudices are intersectional, we must also recognize how these systems of oppression inform our foreign policy. We cannot truly grapple with our history if we ignore how it has also affected the rest of the world. If we are to adopt a progressive political outlook—one rooted in anti-racist, anti-imperialist, humanistic, and intersectional values—we must begin to prioritize the freedom, dignity, and self-determination of Palestinians.

As with Barack Obama's tenure, we will be tempted to view Palestine through a relative lens during the Biden presidency. Rather than analyzing policies on their own terms, we will feel compelled to compare them to those of his Republican predecessor, just as we did with Obama in relation to George W. Bush. While such an approach can serve as a pragmatic measuring stick, it cannot be permitted to shape our values, nor determine the boundaries of our advocacy.

The imbalance of power between Israel and the Palestinians, a circumstance reinforced by the overwhelming political, economic, and military influence of the United States, can never be ignored or understated as we develop workable analyses and principled solutions. This means that any hope for a future in which all people of the region can live in peace, security, freedom, and hope requires the involvement of other states. It is up to us, as Americans, to ensure that our involvement is based on universal humanistic values that are applied in a consistent manner. Such an approach has not historically been part of U.S. policy. As we enter the Biden era, we must change direction. We must no longer render Palestine exceptional.

EXCEPT FOR
PALESTINE

Introduction

Palestine Cannot Be an Exception

"I don't care what they say. I don't care what the fake media says. That's an invasion of our country."

These words were uttered by President Donald Trump in advance of the fall 2018 midterm elections. Trump had taken to Twitter and the campaign trail to warn the nation of what he portrayed as a growing immigrant threat stemming from the southern U.S. border. In his remarks, the president not only referred to a caravan of immigrants coming from Central America as an "invasion," but suggested that the majority of the incoming refugees were criminals and terrorists.

Trump's harsh words were coupled with unprecedented action, as he deployed thousands of troops to the border. Although his words and actions sparked considerable outrage from voices across the political spectrum, the response to Trump was nearly universal among those Americans who politically identified as "progressives." As expected, American progressives expressed sympathy for those fleeing persecution, who were desperately pursuing a better life for themselves and their families.[1] Their response to Trump's draconian immigration views, as well as the policy proposals reflected and foreshadowed by those views, stood in stark contrast to another major announcement that the White House made just weeks earlier.[2]

In the summer of that same year, the Trump administration decided to cut off funding for the United Nations Relief and Works Agency (UNRWA), the agency that provides emergency food, shelter, medication, supplies, and education to millions of Palestinian refugees living in the West Bank, Gaza, and camps in neighboring countries.[3] As a result of this decision, fewer people would have access to proper schooling, health care, and basic life-saving services. This time, rather than outrage, progressives offered little more than silence or apparent indifference.

Of course, these two situations are not exactly the same. After all, the idea of Honduran and Guatemalan refugees heading slowly up to the U.S. border to seek asylum would be expected to cause anxieties, however racist, among nativist Americans. With regard to UNRWA, however, the goal was simply to meet the basic needs of a vulnerable population. And with a cost of around $200 million for that fiscal year, support for UNRWA was a drop in the ocean of the U.S. budget. American taxpayers would incur no other costs to substantially relieve the threat of starvation, lack of shelter, absence of education, and shortages of medicine to millions of refugees. For most people, but especially those who identify with liberal or progressive values, this should have been an easy call. Sadly, it was not.

In response to the migrant caravan controversy, many in the United States uttered the familiar American refrain: "This is not who we are." Such claims, often made at moments of national tragedy or moral crisis, appeal to both a singular American identity and a coveted set of collective social values. For liberals, the idea that America could turn its back on people running from dictatorships, women escaping abuse, or racial and ethnic minorities fleeing persecution was morally outrageous. It not only contradicted core political values stemming from our notions of democracy, but our very conception of self. In contrast, such questions were not raised about the UNRWA cuts. Indeed, there was little policy debate at all. Supporters of Palestinian rights complained, of course, that the cuts were needlessly cruel to innocent people. And their voices were joined by some of the more liberal supporters of Israel, who added that President Trump's decision would make the Palestinians more desperate, and thus undermine Israel's security concerns. But these were largely minority positions. Even when Trump went a step further and eliminated $25 million in funding for Palestinian hospitals in East Jerusalem and another $10 million that funded people-to-people exchanges between Israel and the Palestinians, the larger liberal community in the United States was silent, if not apathetic.

This double standard was thrown into even sharper relief when Trump suggested that U.S. troops respond with live fire against anyone from the Central American caravan throwing rocks.[4] Most Americans, and virtually all liberals, were outraged that the president would call for such disproportionate use of force against unarmed people. Yet Israel has responded for many years in this very manner. Recent years in the Gaza Strip have seen hundreds of Palestinians shot with both rubber-coated bullets (which can be lethal) and live ammunition, despite presenting no immediate threat to any Israeli soldier or civilian. Such actions have a long history and have been well documented by Israeli, Palestinian, and international human rights groups. Still, even when American citizens have been in the line of fire while protesting alongside Palestinians, there has been no widespread outcry for a debate on U.S. policy regarding these incidents, much less the broader policies that have failed to deliver freedom, justice, equality, or peace in the region.

Why Is Palestine the Exception?

It is tempting to view the ethical and political contradictions of American policy on Israel-Palestine as a result of the current political moment. Such an approach allows us to frame Donald Trump as a political outlier whose policies were out of step with both the global community and his political predecessors. While this was true on many fronts—from his denialist approach to climate change, to his desire to build a wall along the Southern border, to his inhumane and market-centered response to the COVID-19 pandemic—it was far less true regarding Israel-Palestine. Rather than introducing a radically different policy agenda, Trump was simply the most aggressive and transparent articulation of long-standing bipartisan policies.

Through his approach, Donald Trump removed the veneer of even-handedness that prior administrations worked hard to maintain. For example, cutting funds to UNRWA was an idea that had been floated in Washington for years, dating back at least to the George W. Bush administration. Trump's decision to move the U.S. embassy in Israel from Tel Aviv to Jerusalem caused enormous controversy in the U.S. In so doing, he fulfilled a promise that one presidential candidate after another, Democrat and Republican, had campaigned on, only to backtrack once in office. By recognizing Jerusalem as Israel's undivided capital, Trump altered the status quo on which the international community based its support for a two-state solution. To accomplish this, however, he did not need to fight for new legislation. Rather, he merely invoked a law that was created in 1995, with overwhelming bipartisan support, during the presidency of liberal Democrat Bill Clinton.

It was during the comparatively progressive presidency of Barack Obama—seen by many as the most sympathetic U.S. president to the Palestinian cause since Jimmy Carter more than three decades earlier—that negotiations toward a two-state solution collapsed under the weight of years of collective frustration. The Palestinians had become fed up with a quarter century of talks that always prioritized Israeli concerns over their own. As these talks dragged on with no end in sight, Israeli settlement construction increased exponentially, and the occupation became ever more repressive. The leaders of the Palestinian Authority and the Palestine Liberation Organization could no longer make the case to their people that there was hope in negotiations with Israel. Meanwhile, Israeli prime minister Benjamin Netanyahu was declaring that there would be no Palestinian state on his watch, even while his government's official stance was to support the two-state solution.[5] Netanyahu squared this circle by claiming to support Palestinian "self-rule" while also making clear his stance that Israel's security required that it maintain full control of the strategic Jordan Valley, a long-contested area that makes up some 30 percent of the West Bank, as well as other key parts of the occupied land.[6]

This is not to suggest that Obama was responsible for the lack of a legitimate peace deal, nor that he offered full-throated support of Israeli policy. In fact, Obama's disagreements with Netanyahu over illegal settlement expansion, the 2015 nuclear agreement with Iran, and the United States' role in the wider Middle East have been well documented. Still, despite the disagreements with Netanyahu, the Obama administration continued the bipartisan U.S. practice of extending extraordinary financial and military support to Israel. President Obama's $38 billion aid package to Israel, finalized in 2016 as he was leaving office, marked the "largest military aid package from one country to another in the annals of human history."[7] Such resources, which were offered without any concrete policy demands regarding Palestinian human rights or self-determination, provided Israel the financial security and "qualitative military edge" necessary to resist compliance with international law or earnest engagement with the peace process.[8] Obama's relative progressivism offered a distinction without a difference in the lives of Palestinians.

U.S. policy in Israel-Palestine rests upon decades of decisions that have been supported, either through active endorsement or silent complicity, by the American Left. No American president has been an exception in this regard. Rather, it is Palestine itself that has been rendered morally, ethically, and politically exceptional. The impact of this exceptionalism can be seen in the United States and in Israel-Palestine, where conditions continue to worsen.

Much like in the United States, the political climate in Israel has become increasingly right-wing and authoritarian in recent years. The growing influence of religious nationalism has manifested in violent actions against both non-Jews and Jewish Israelis who are seen as "assimilating" with non-Jews,[9] as well as more recent controversies over legislation regarding parental rights for same-sex couples, which have become more pronounced as religious nationalist groups become more intertwined with Benjamin Netanyahu's Likud party.[10] More clearly, the intense and ongoing public battle over the status of African refugees in Israel revealed a deep xenophobia that extended well beyond the Palestinians.[11] Still, the bulk of Israeli authoritarianism has been directed at the Palestinians and their supporters. Opposition to the occupation from Israeli Jews has never been a very safe option, as activists supporting peace or Palestinian rights have long been the targets of harassment, physical attacks, and even murder.[12] In recent years, however, we have seen a dramatic rise in barely veiled and overt support from leading government officials for the idea that peace and human rights groups in Israel—whether Jewish, Palestinian, or mixed—were seditious and their employees, volunteers, and supporters were "moles" trying to undermine the state from within. This is classic totalitarian stuff, and it has led to physical attacks on people working in those organizations as well as legislation selectively aimed at blocking their funding and their ability to disseminate information.

As alarming as those trends are, the situation for Palestinians has gotten much worse. The ongoing siege of Gaza has led to unemployment rates that are routinely over 40 percent and often rise to over 50 percent. Its economy has collapsed due to tight restrictions on exports enforced by both Israel and Egypt. A United Nations report estimated that Gaza would be uninhabitable by 2020 and that 95 percent of the water there was already unfit for human consumption. Although these predictions have come to pass, two million Gazans continue to live under these conditions. Life is only a little better in the West Bank, as settlements (and the extra land allocated for them), closed military zones, and other restrictions make it impossible for Palestinian towns to grow. Palestinians cannot get permits to build necessary extensions on existing homes in areas under Israeli military control, forcing them to build without them in order to meet basic demographic needs. This results in a steady stream of demolitions of so-called "illegal" structures. Unemployment in the West Bank is generally around 18 percent, and Palestinian workers frequently suffer a loss of income because Israeli military closures make it impossible for them to get to their jobs.

In Israel, the assault on Palestinian identity has intensified. The highly controversial "Nation-State Bill" that Israel passed into law in July 2018 epitomized this attack. The law states plainly that only Jews can exercise national self-determination in Israel, downgrades Arabic from an official language to one of "special status," and explicitly states that Jewish settlement of the "Land of Israel" (a phrase that includes the West Bank) is to be encouraged. The bill was controversial when it was passed, even in Israel. Although it has few directly actionable provisions, as a stipulation in the Basic Laws underpinning the country's legal system, it has the force of what Americans would think of as constitutional law. Therefore, it is likely to be used as the basis for other laws and as a guide for Supreme Court decisions that pertain to the relative rights of Jewish and Palestinian citizens of Israel. Outside of Israel, the law has drawn widespread scorn, including from American Jewish groups such as the American Jewish Committee and the Anti-Defamation League, which have a long history of antipathy to Palestinian rights.

The conditions mentioned here should be profoundly disturbing to American liberals and progressives, as they are clearly out of step with the values they claim to hold most dear. Yet year after year, Israel is by far the leading recipient of U.S. foreign aid, with little resistance from progressive voices. The United States repeatedly isolates itself on the world stage in order to shield Israel as much as possible from any consequences that it might face as a result of its policies and actions. Questioning this lockstep support in any but the mildest terms has long been seen as a political third rail and is often greeted by charges of bias against the world's only Jewish state, or even allegations of outright anti-Semitism. Against the backdrop of these realities, the American political left has normalized a world in which it is acceptable, through words and policies, to embrace the ethical and political contradiction of being "progressive except for Palestine."

In this book, we challenge this status quo. We examine the various ways that Palestine is often positioned as exceptional among those who identify as liberal, as well as "center-left," "progressive," and sometimes even "radical." While these communities generally endorse ideologies, policies, practices, and protests that reflect their worldview, they often become notably silent about the plight of Palestinians. When the topic turns to Palestine, the same people who consistently advocate for freedom and justice fail to live up to their professed ideals. Through an analysis of key policies and debates directly related to Israel and Palestine, we spotlight these contradictions and offer insights into possible solutions.

Although this book is written from a place of radical hope, it is nonetheless informed by a sober pragmatism about the opportunistic basis of U.S. policy in the Middle East. For example, America's ongoing partnership with Saudi Arabia, despite the Saudis' devastation of Yemen, the murder of *Washington Post* journalist Jamal Khashoggi, and even suspicions that parts of the royal family funded Osama bin Laden, makes it clear that human rights are not the primary predicate for U.S. policy in the region. Still, our public discourse has recently featured a more robust public debate over this partnership and whether it truly serves our political interests and ethical ideals. In a democracy, such discourse must be vigorous and ongoing. For this reason, it is now time to widen the opening for discussion on the U.S. policy toward Israel, especially regarding the treatment of the Palestinians.

We also write this book with a clear understanding of the realities of modern anti-Semitism. In the current moment, systematic inequality and anti-Jewish rhetoric and violence are not only persistent but spreading across the globe, and the United States has not been at all immune from this scourge. For this reason, it is important to explicitly stress that the exceptional nature of the liberal engagement with Palestine is not the product of Jewish cabals of power, political conspiracies, or any of the other centuries-old anti-Semitic tropes that have been used to dehumanize, isolate, and otherwise harm Jewish people. This is not to deny the remarkable success that the pro-Israel Jewish community and some of its allies have had in advocating both for a certain view of Israel in mainstream discourse and for legislation that favors Israeli interests. But the ability to successfully play the American political game is hardly unique to the Jewish community, and certainly not attributable to the sort of nefarious characteristics and anti-Semitic stereotypes that are becoming all too popular again in this age of resurgent white nationalism.

While this book powerfully contradicts such narratives by examining the material policy conditions and institutional arrangements that led to the current conditions, we nonetheless feel morally and politically compelled to explicitly reject these and all other anti-Semitic narratives. At the same time, we also stress that a commitment to Palestinian freedom does not, cannot, and must not reflect hatred or harm toward Jewish people. On the contrary, the realization of Palestinian rights cannot be fully attained without the realization of Jewish rights, and vice versa.

In this book, we also argue that recent efforts to stigmatize, and potentially even illegalize the growing dissent over U.S. policy on Israel and Palestine reflects a growing authoritarianism in both Israel and the United States. By looking at multiple dimensions of the struggle over Israel and Palestine, we show why a change in policy is urgently needed. More importantly, we demonstrate that if liberal-minded Americans truly believe our foreign and domestic policies should reflect the values of freedom, justice, and equality, it is impossible to be satisfied with the current state of affairs. This dissatisfaction must prompt them to argue forcefully for change. Just as progressives opposed the Trump administration's policies on immigration, racial justice, gender equality, LGBTQI* rights, and many other issues, we must recognize that we cannot enjoy particular freedoms in the United States if our government is helping to deny those same rights to others around the world. If we claim to care about producing freedom and justice around the world, which is often the expressed basis for American foreign policy, then we must remain morally consistent. Palestine cannot be an exception.

In the chapters that follow, we examine Israel's escalating authoritarianism and how U.S. policy has enabled it, and we demonstrate how it is anathema to universal liberal values. We look at the effects of occupation, the siege of Gaza, and of diminishing U.S. funding for Palestinian relief needs, and how they belie the liberal values many Americans, particularly progressives, hold dear. We show how legitimate opposition to the Israeli occupation has been delegitimized, both by denying the right of an occupied people to resist and through attempts to stigmatize and criminalize nonviolent civil society efforts to pressure Israel into changing its policies. We challenge the notion that Jewish self-determination must necessarily mean Palestinian dispossession, or that Palestinian freedom must threaten Jewish safety or security. We argue that security is a right for all people but that it cannot be used as a cover for depriving one group of their equal human, civil, legal, and national rights. We explain why a policy debate is long overdue, and point toward a U.S. policy that supports full and equal rights for Israeli Jews and Palestinians, as well as self-determination for both peoples.

1

The Right to Exist

"Nobody does Israel any service by proclaiming its 'right to exist.'"

Those were the words uttered by Israeli diplomat Abba Eban in a 1981 *New York Times* op-ed. Eban went on to state that "Israel's right to exist, like that of the United States, Saudi Arabia, and 152 other states, is axiomatic and unreserved."[1] By describing Israel's right to exist as "axiomatic"—both self-evident and unquestionable—Eban was arguing that it did not need to be affirmed by another entity. He believed that such recognition was not something that any nation had the power to give, nor something that Israel or any other nation should desire to receive. As one of the premier emissaries of the Jewish state, Eban found it an annoyance that only cast Israel's existence as different than that of other states.

Eban's argument emerged at a very different political moment than the current one. In 1981, no one in Israel, the United States, or Europe was seriously considering the possibility of a Palestinian state. At the time, Palestinian rights were, at best, an afterthought within Western political discourse. Serious conversations about Palestinian self-determination were even less commonplace within diplomatic circles.

Today, however, the "right to exist" discourse serves a vastly different and significantly more powerful function. It is cynically used to justify the rejection of a Palestinian state. It is strategically used to distract from criticism about the deprivation of Palestinian rights. And it is disingenuously used to frame the case for Palestinian rights as the denial of Jewish self-determination or, even worse, as a call for anti-Semitic violence.

For decades, Israel has officially and publicly demanded that Palestinians recognize its "right to exist" and, in more recent years, recognition of its "right to exist as a Jewish state." This demand has not been made of everyone, but instead is targeted toward Palestinians, as well as supporters of their cause. Moreover, the Israeli government has used the Palestinians' ostensible refusal to recognize this right as the pretext for denying the legitimacy of Palestinian organizations, refusing to fully participate in negotiations and, at times, engaging in acts of aggression.

In the current political moment, it has become a shibboleth of mainstream liberal political discourse to affirm Israel's right to exist. Such an affirmation carries with it the presumption of a double standard, an implicit suggestion that all other nations of the world have had their right to exist affirmed, leaving Israel as the lone exception. The discourse surrounding Israel's right to exist is also often presumed to be related not only to the abstract concept of the state, but to the physical status of the state's citizens. In other words, the question of whether Israel has a right to exist is often understood to be a question of whether Israelis, or even Jews more broadly, have the right to exist. Of course, our answer to this latter question is clear and unambiguous: *The right of Israelis (and Jews throughout the world) to live in peace, safety, dignity, and with self-determination is absolute and unquestionable.*

Still, the politicization of this seemingly rhetorical question about Israel's right to exist in particular demands closer examination. Is the "right to exist" a question of sovereignty? Is it a question of the structure of a Jewish state in both theory and practice? Is it a question of the legitimacy of Palestinian resistance to occupation? Is it about attacks by other countries, perhaps ones that do not recognize Israel?

The heart of the matter is whether Israel does, in fact, face particular existential risk. Today, Israel stands as arguably the most stable state in the entire Middle East, having never faced an existential internal challenge to its fundamental structure and institutions since its establishment in 1948, nor has it faced an existential military challenge since at least 1973. Israel is a regional superpower that has established itself on par with most Western liberal-capitalist nations for its economic diversity, dynamism, innovation, and competitiveness. While Israel certainly faces threats—both of the sort that all nations do, as well as threats particular to its unique circumstance—it is unquestionable that the state not only exists, but has grown increasingly stable over the past seventy years.

By contrast, there remains no independent state of Palestine at all. The conditions in the West Bank and Gaza continue to worsen. And the political will to produce a sustainable and equitable solution seems to be dwindling within both Israel and United States. Does Palestine, as a nation, also have a right to exist? Do Palestinians have a right to a state in their homeland, whether as part of a binational entity with Israelis, as an independent sovereign entity of their own, or as part of a shared single, democratic secular state? Defining the nature of these questions is an essential starting point.

The Question of Zionism

The question of Israel's right to exist is posed primarily as a survey on the ideological undergirding of the state: Zionism. Given the many definitions, iterations, and connotations of "Zionism" throughout history and across contexts, it is important to specify how we use the term here. Fundamentally, Zionism is the nationalist ideology of the Jewish people, which constructs Judaism as not only a religion but a nationality. Zionism advances the idea that Jews of all sorts—irrespective of race, ethnicity, cultural identity, or geographic location; regardless of whether they are secular, religious, or atheist—constitute a singular modern nation.

The very idea of a "nation" is a tangled one. In his seminal work on the topic, political scientist and historian Benedict Anderson framed nations as "imagined communities." Anderson was not suggesting that nations are not real, but that they are all socially constructed, constituted by communities of people who perceive themselves to share the same collective identity. "Nation, nationality, nationalism—all have proved notoriously difficult to define, let alone to analyze," Anderson wrote. "In contrast to the immense influence that nationalism has exerted on the modern world, plausible theory about it is conspicuously meager."[2] While there has been a great deal more theorizing on nations since the 1983 publication of *Imagined Communities*, the terminology remains loosely understood even in academia, let alone everyday discourse.

Most of the world recognizes Israel as a state. With only a few exceptions, those states that withheld formal recognition, most of them in the Muslim world, have long been dealing with Israel, even if clandestinely.[3] Although Zionism is neither universally accepted among Jews, nor is it the only form of modern nationalism that Jews have experienced, it has successfully forged a national collective from the Jewish people.[4] There is nothing unusual about the forging of a nation, and it is certainly not uncommon for nations to endeavor to create states of their own. It is also not uncommon for states to come about through the dispossession of another people. This is particularly true when the incoming nation employs a strategy of settler-colonialism—as in Australia, Canada, South Africa, and the United States—whereby an imperial power creates colonies of its own people in other territories. For critics of Israel, this strategy is central to the question of legitimacy. It is also the ultimate question that Israel's advocates raise when they ask whether one supports Israel's "right to exist."

This critical view of Zionism in relation to the formation of Israel is best articulated by scholar Noura Erakat, who writes:

> Had Jews merely wanted to live in Palestine, this would not have been a problem. In fact, Jews, Muslims and Christians had coexisted for centuries throughout the Middle East. But Zionists sought sovereignty over a land where other people lived. Their ambitions required not only the dispossession and removal of Palestinians in 1948 but also their forced exile, juridical erasure and denial that they ever existed. So, during Israel's establishment, some 750,000 Palestinians were driven from their homes to make way for a Jewish majority state. . . . This is why Palestinians have been resisting for more than seven decades: They are fighting to remain on their lands with dignity. They have valiantly resisted their colonial erasure. . . . This resistance is not about returning to the 1947 borders or some notion of the past, but about laying claim to a better future in which Palestinians and their children can live in freedom and equality, rather than being subjugated as second-class citizens or worse.[5]

Erakat's analysis speaks to the harm inflicted on Palestinians, including violations of their right and ability to exist, that accompanied the modern Zionist movement. Those who defend Israel's "right to exist" often suggest that disagreement with this position implies a similar physical threat to Jews the world over. Framing the conflict in this manner raises the anxiety level of supporters of Israel and the defensiveness of supporters of Palestinian rights.[6]

In reality, however, the question is a political one. After all, there is widespread agreement that the proper remedy for the plight of the Palestinians is neither the unthinkable annihilation, nor the also reprehensible ejection, of Israeli Jews. Ali Abunimah, a fierce anti-Zionist Palestinian, explains:

> Palestinians advocating a one-state solution [cannot] simply disregard the views of Israeli Jews. We must recognize that the opposition of Israeli Jews to any solution that threatens their power and privilege stems from at least two sources. One is irrational, racist fears of black and brown hordes (in this case, Arab Muslims) stoked by decades of colonial, racist demonization. The other source—certainly heightened by the former—are normal human concerns about personal and family dislocation, loss of socioeconomic status and community security: change is scary . . . [T]he legitimate concerns of ordinary Israeli Jews can be addressed directly in any negotiated transition to ensure that the shift to democracy is orderly, and essential redistributive policies are carried out fairly. Inevitably, decolonization will cause some pain as Israeli Jews lose power and privilege, but there are few reasons to believe it cannot be a well-managed process.[7]

Although the popular discourse often refers back to fears of a "second Holocaust," many of the fiercest defenders of Israeli policy clearly grasp the political nature of the "right to exist" question, even while employing the most incendiary language. One example is given by Yossi Kuperwasser, a member of the Jerusalem Center for Public Affairs and a reserve general who served in Israeli military intelligence. In 2019, Kuperwasser wrote, referring to the anti-Zionist movement for boycott, divestment, and sanctions (BDS) against Israel, "The aim of these demands is the total annihilation of Israel as a nation-state of the Jewish people. . . . The goal of BDS is not to change the policies of Israel's government, or force it to reform. Rather, its purpose is precisely what BDS activist Ahmad [*sic*] Moor stated: to single out the Jewish state, alone among the nations of the earth, as the one country in the world that must be destroyed."[8] Kuperwasser's use of violent words shades the conversation, but he repeatedly describes the "destruction" and the goal of "bringing down" or even the "annihilation" of the state of Israel in political terms. Kuperwasser's approach speaks to the ways that Israel's right to exist is a political question that has been mis-framed, often deliberately, as a question about the physical safety or stability of Israel rather than a question about disrupting the status quo. As Noura Erakat states bluntly, "The overwhelming majority of Palestinians have not demanded Jewish-Israelis removal . . . only a relinquishment of their desire to rule."[9]

The question of Israel's right to exist is not a legitimate inquiry into whether the basic rights of Israeli Jews should be respected. This point is already affirmatively acknowledged by debaters on all sides of the question. Further, while international humanitarian law may be an imperfect vehicle with which to navigate the larger question of Israel and Palestine, it has been regularly invoked by Palestinian leadership, activists, and supportive advocates.[10] That standard protects all noncombatants, as defined by international law, to live free of physical attack. Thus, the question "Does Israel have a right to exist?" is not a question about the physical safety of Jewish citizens. The relevant political question is: Is the dispossession and ongoing denial of rights at various levels to Palestinians justified?

For some, this is a question about the legitimacy of Zionism itself. There are those, across the ideological spectrum, who see Zionism as necessitating the total denial of Palestinian national rights to the point of denying Palestinians' very existence as a people. At the same time, some Zionists go to great lengths, even risking their personal safety, to defend the rights of Palestinians.[11] From the earliest days of Zionism, there have been those who sought a Jewish connection to the land and even Jewish immigration to Palestine without the need for a Jewish state.[12] To be sure, these were fringe movements in comparison to political Zionism. Through its drive to establish a Jewish state, political Zionism ultimately became the movement's dominant and determinative iteration. Still, for the purpose of the issues raised here, it is both clearer and more fruitful to speak of the *actions* of the Zionist political movement as opposed to its disputed, and sometimes contradictory, *ideologies*.

Stepping back into history, the words of the first Likud prime minister of Israel, Menachem Begin, offer a different take on both political Zionism and the right to exist. Presenting his government to the Knesset in June 1977, Begin said:

> I wish to declare that the Government of Israel will not ask any nation, be it near or far, mighty or small, to recognize our right to exist. The right to exist? it would not enter the mind of any Briton or Frenchman, Belgian or Dutchman, Hungarian or Bulgarian, Russian,

or American, to request for his people recognition of its right to exist. Their existence per se is their right to exist. The same holds true for Israel. We were granted our right to exist by the God of our fathers, at the glimmer of the dawn of human civilization, nearly four thousand years ago. For that right, which has been sanctified in Jewish blood from generation to generation, we have paid a price unexampled in the annals of the nations. Certainly, this fact does not diminish or enfeeble our right. On the contrary. Therefore, I re-emphasize that we do not expect anyone to request, on our behalf, that our right to exist in the land of our fathers, be recognized. It is a different recognition which is required between ourselves and our neighbors: recognition of sovereignty and of the mutual need for a life of peace and understanding. It is this mutual recognition that we look forward to: For it we shall make every possible effort.[13]

Begin saw clearly the distinction between sovereignty and a "right to exist." He went even further in claiming the concept of a Jewish ancestral homeland as being a religious and historical matter, but also one whose acknowledgment by others was of no importance. Thus, Begin brings the ancient homeland claim into the internal Jewish-Israeli sphere and removes it from matters of international politics. For Begin, it was a founding national myth of Israel, not a political matter. Instead, he insisted on the recognition of sovereignty and the protection of the international system that entitles sovereign nations to live in peace.

If the contradiction of depriving another people of those same rights bothered Begin, it clearly took a back seat—as it often did—to Jewish nationalist interests. Not until the very end of his speech did he even allude, in the most abstract terms, to the Palestinians. "We call on the young generation, in the homeland and in the diaspora, to arise, go forth and settle," he proclaimed. "Come from east and west, north and south, to build together the Land of Israel. There is room in it for millions of returnees to Zion. We do not wish to evict, nor shall we evict any Arab resident from his land. Jews and Arabs, Druze and Circassians, can live together in this land. And they must live together in peace, mutual respect, equal rights, in freedom and with social-economic progress."[14]

Even if we ignore the fact that the subsequent decades witnessed many such evictions, and very little peace, respect, equal rights, freedom, or socioeconomic progress for Palestinians, Begin was still drawing a distinction between Jews and non-Jews in Israel and the territories it controls. Presaging future events and future laws in Israel, Begin was making it clear that only Jews would have national rights. And no matter how sincere he might have been about economic progress and equal rights under the law, only the Jews "returning to Zion" would be nurtured in this vision of communal growth.[15]

It is also important to note here that the demand for recognition even of Israel's sovereignty—its "right to exist" within its defined borders—is problematic, as Israel has long refused to define its borders. In addition, in some cases when it has defined its borders, they have not been recognized. The borders with Egypt and Jordan were agreed upon and recognized by much of the international community as part of the peace treaties signed between those countries.[16] Israel's claims to the Syrian Golan Heights and to East Jerusalem, both of which it has annexed, are not recognized by most of the international community. Its occupation of the West Bank, Gaza Strip, and the Shebaa Farms area in southern Lebanon renders borders in those areas in dispute.

Having established Israel's right to exist as a political

question pertaining to the indisputably heavy weight of Israel's existence in relation to Palestinians, we can explore that question in a more rational and productive manner. It is grounded not in abstract ideology (Zionism versus anti-Zionism) but in the reality of lived experiences: the stark reality of Israeli history in relation to the Palestinians. When someone asks if one supports "Israel's right to exist," they are tacitly asking if one agrees that Israel's elevation of Jewish rights above those of Palestinians in the land they all inhabit is acceptable. The question, in fact, is whether it was legitimate—after many centuries of Palestinians of numerous faiths, including Jews, living in the land between the Mediterranean Sea and the Jordan River—for Jews from Europe (and later Jews from around the world) to emigrate there with the express purpose of creating a state in which Jewish people would be privileged above others, especially the indigenous inhabitants.

The Iron Wall

Ze'ev Jabotinsky was the founder of Israel's Revisionist movement. His views would inspire the creation of the Herut party by his protégé Menachem Begin. The Herut party would later become the core of today's Likud coalition, which would gain particular notoriety under the long second term of Benjamin Netanyahu, beginning in 2009. Jabotinsky, who died in 1940, promoted an ideology that borrowed elements of the most chauvinistic forms of nationalism and classical liberalism and melded them into his unique version of Zionism. For him, the Jewish people were a nation whose homeland was in Palestine, thus giving them the right to establish their state there. But in Jabotinsky's view, the Palestinian Arabs also had a claim to the land as a national entity and, since no nation would willingly give up such a claim, the Jews, whose claim he deemed to be superior, had no choice but to use force until the Arabs recognized that defeating the Zionists was hopeless. Once that point was reached, Jabotinsky believed an agreement could be found for the two peoples to share the land in peace.

In tone, Jabotinsky's view stood against the rhetoric of Labor Zionism, the political program that would dominate the Zionist movement from the early days of the twentieth century until the Likud finally won an election in 1977. Yet, the historian Avi Shlaim makes a convincing case that Jabotinsky's thinking was a primary ingredient in early Zionist and Israeli political thought and policy formation. "In the realm of ideas, Jabotinsky was important as the founder of Revisionist Zionism," Shlaim writes. "In the realm of politics, his impact was much greater than is commonly realized. For it was not only Revisionist Zionists who were influenced by his ideas, but the Zionist movement as a whole." Shlaim greatly expands this thesis, demonstrating how Jabotinsky's ideas directly influenced, and even guided, policies toward the Palestinians and the neighboring Arab states both before and after the creation of the state of Israel, right up to the present day.[17]

Jabotinsky's revelatory 1923 essay, "The Iron Wall," offers the most lucid outline of his thinking. In the text, he argues that an agreement with the indigenous Palestinian population would only happen if they were confronted with a metaphorical "iron wall," or the reality of a Jewish majority, polity, and immovable presence in the region. Scholar Ian Lustick describes the essay as "a forceful, honest effort to grapple with the most serious problem facing the Zionist movement and as a formal articulation of what did become, in fact, the dominant rationale for Zionist and Israeli policies and attitudes toward the Arabs of Palestine from the 1920s to the late 1980s."[18]

As we examine Jabotinsky's ideas, we must bear in mind that they have only been partially enacted. His notion was that the "iron wall" would force the Palestinians to recognize Israel (as, below, we will see the Palestine Liberation Organization [PLO] did in 1988), prompting the Jews to offer terms that the Arabs could accept with dignity. In his view, this arrangement could even allow for equality between the two nations. But, as Shlaim points out, "Jabotinsky's strategy of the iron wall was designed to force the Palestinians to despair of the prospect of driving the Jews out of Palestine and to compel them to negotiate with the Jewish state from a position of weakness . . . the Labor Party put into action the second part of this strategy and achieved a breakthrough in the relations with the Palestinians. [Benjamin] Netanyahu, on the other hand, remained fixated on the first part of his ideological mentor's strategy of the iron wall and consequently undid much of the good work of his predecessors."[19] The point here is that Jabotinsky's idea of forcing the Palestinians to accept the presence of the Israeli-Jewish people was not followed by an attempt to offer anything close to the sort of positive inducements for peace that Jabotinsky described.

Jabotinsky dispensed with the idea, always popular among Labor Zionists, that the Palestinians could be made to agree to Zionist colonization: "I suggest that they consider all the precedents with which they are acquainted, and see whether there is one solitary instance of any colonization being carried on with the consent of the native population. There is no such precedent. The native populations, civilized or uncivilized, have always stubbornly resisted the colonists."[20] Paradoxically, despite the blatantly ethnocentric and racist language and approach Jabotinsky was using, he contended, with merit, that he was granting the Palestinians far more respect than were his Labor Zionist interlocutors. "To imagine, as our Arabophiles do, that they (the Palestinians) will voluntarily consent to the realization of Zionism in return for the moral and material conveniences which the Jewish colonist brings with him, is a childish notion, which has at bottom a kind of contempt for the Arab people; it means that they despise the Arab race, which they regard as a corrupt mob that can be bought and sold, and are willing to give up their fatherland for a good railway system."[21] Laying to rest any further doubt, Jabotinsky added: "Colonization carries its own explanation, the only possible explanation, unalterable and as clear as daylight to every ordinary Jew and every ordinary Arab. Colonization can have only one aim, and Palestine Arabs cannot accept this aim. It lies in the very nature of things, and in this particular regard nature cannot be changed."[22]

Given this state of affairs, conquest was the only option for the colonizer, Jabotinsky posited. Any reading of history would have to agree, even if the modes and forms of colonization might vary over time and place. As such, Jabotinsky wasted no time debating the morality of Zionism and its concomitant colonial aspirations. "[E]ither Zionism is moral and just, or it is immoral and unjust. But that is a question that we should have settled before we became Zionists. Actually we have settled that question, and in the affirmative," he wrote. Again, he offered a clear answer: "We hold that Zionism is moral and just. And since it is moral and just, justice must be done, no matter whether Joseph or Simon or Ivan or Achmet agree with it or not."[23]

Finally, Jabotinsky laid out a conceptual framework that Shlaim and many others convincingly argue has shaped Zionist and Israeli strategy ever since, long before his ideological descendants came to dominate Israeli politics, as they have for the past twenty years.[24]

This does not mean that there cannot be any agreement with the Palestine Arabs. What is impossible is a voluntary agreement. As long as the Arabs feel that there is the least hope of getting rid of us, they will refuse to give up this hope in return for either kind words or for bread and butter, because they are not a rabble, but a living people. And when a living people yields in matters of such a vital character it is only when there is no longer any hope of getting rid of us, because they can make no breach in the iron wall. Not till then will they drop their extremist leaders whose watchword is "Never!" And the leadership will pass to the moderate groups, who will approach us with a proposal that we should both agree to mutual concessions. Then we may expect them to discuss honestly practical questions, such as a guarantee against Arab displacement, or equal rights for Arab citizens, or Arab national integrity.

And when that happens, I am convinced that we Jews will be found ready to give them satisfactory guarantees, so that both peoples can live together in peace, like good neighbours.

But the only way to obtain such an agreement, is the iron wall, which is to say a strong power in Palestine that is not amenable to any Arab pressure. In other words, the only way to reach an agreement in the future is to abandon all idea of seeking an agreement at present.[25]

One can debate the sincerity of Jabotinsky's desire to eventually find an agreement with the Palestinians where the land would be shared. But it is difficult to dispute the foundation of his reasoning, despite the racist framework in which he placed it: it was impossible to imagine that Palestinians could do anything but resist Zionism. And while Jabotinsky could take it as axiomatic that the Zionist cause was just and moral, he took it as equally axiomatic that Palestinians could not possibly agree with that claim, although this was of no consequence to him.

Today, this is what is still being demanded when defenders of Israel's actions and policies call for affirmation of its right to exist. The issue is not Jews' right to constitute a nation or even to pursue a homeland. Rather, the issue is whether their national identity and historical and cultural connection to the land that has been called Israel, Palestine, Canaan, Judea, etc. justified the dispossession of the Palestinians. Demanding that not only supporters of Palestinian rights, but also Palestinians *themselves*, affirm this point is not reasonable. Jabotinsky, for all his ethnocentrism, would have been the first to agree. In the words of Palestinian-American activist and scholar Yousef Munayyer, "To ask a Palestinian not to be anti-Zionist is to ask a Palestinian not to be."[26]

Demanding Recognition

The language of recognition first entered public diplomatic parlance in the mid-1970s, during the administration of Gerald Ford. Secretary of State Henry Kissinger included the recognition demand in the framework of conditions under which the United States would agree to talk with the representatives of the Palestinian people. In the Sinai II Agreement of September 1975—part of the ongoing "shuttle diplomacy" taken up by the U.S. State Department in the wake of the 1973 war between Israel and the forces of Egypt and Syria—Kissinger included a clause stating that "the United States will continue to adhere to its present policy with respect to the Palestine Liberation Organization, whereby it will not recognize or negotiate with the Palestine Liberation Organization so long as the Palestine Liberation Organization does not recognize Israel's right to exist and does not accept Security Council Resolutions 242 and 338."[27]

The inclusion of language demanding recognition of Israel's right to exist may have seemed redundant to many, but Kissinger could not have missed the context. UN Resolution 242 affirmed the need for peace in the Middle East, which should include "termination of all claims or states of belligerency and respect for and acknowledgment of the sovereignty, territorial integrity and political independence of every State in the area and their right to live in peace within secure and recognized boundaries free from threats or acts of force."[28] UN Resolution 338 called for a cease-fire in the 1973 war and immediate "implementation of Security Council Resolution 242 (1967) in all of its parts."[29] Israel did not accept the de facto borders within which it existed, however, which necessitated the extra acknowledgment that Kissinger provided.[30] Moreover, it was only in the previous year that the PLO had hinted in its "Ten-Point Plan" that it would be open to a two-state solution, something Israel vehemently opposed at the time.[31] The inclusion of the demand that the PLO accept Israel's "right to exist" in addition to Resolutions 242 and 338 placed a major obstacle in the Palestinians' path of pursuing such a solution, while simultaneously helping to lay the groundwork against any return of Palestinian refugees that might endanger Israel's Jewish demographic majority. In working out this memorandum of agreement, Israeli negotiators pushed hard for strong American commitments. American negotiators, including Kissinger himself, softened the language to allow the United States more diplomatic flexibility. Nevertheless, the language around the U.S. conditions for dealing with the PLO was unprecedented.[32]

Ronald Reagan was the first U.S. president to repeatedly and consistently use this language to frame his administration's approach to the Palestinians, though others had used the term rhetorically before. When Reagan came into office in January 1981, he was determined to employ a different rhetorical style in foreign policy than his predecessor Jimmy Carter, who had been willing to press Israeli prime minister Menachem Begin for major territorial concessions to Egypt for the sake of a permanent peace agreement. Yet despite a shift in tone with Reagan, the bulk of American policies did not change. The demands placed on the PLO remained the same: acceptance of 242 and 338, and recognition of Israel's right to exist. But Reagan publicly repeated these conditions more often and with an increasingly hard-line tone. Distancing himself from Carter's Middle East policy, which was unpopular among Israelis and U.S. Jews because it demanded a much higher negotiating price than Begin had wanted to pay—the return of the Sinai Peninsula, which established the precedent for "land for peace"—Reagan took a stronger stance in support of Israel's point of view than Carter, who had talked more of compromise. But again, the difference was more of tone than substance. The Reagan administration conducted secret talks with the PLO through an intermediary, offering U.S. recognition of the organization. This recognition enabled the PLO to negotiate directly with the U.S. government in exchange for Palestinian agreement to Kissinger's conditions. Israel's invasion of Lebanon in June 1982 put a stop to the talks.[33]

In 1988, Arafat appeared at the United Nations General Assembly, and publicly accepted 242 and 338, but recognized Israel only through implicit reference.[34] A clarifying statement from Arafat the following day, however, was enough to convince Reagan that the PLO had met Kissinger's standards: "In my speech also yesterday it was clear that we mean our people's right to freedom and national independence according to Resolution 181 and the right of all parties concerned in the

Middle East conflict to exist in peace and security and as I have mentioned including the state of Palestine and Israel and other neighbors according to the Resolutions 242 and 338."[35] In response, Reagan stated, "The Palestine Liberation Organization today issued a statement in which it accepted United Nations Security Council Resolutions 242 and 338, recognized Israel's right to exist, and renounced terrorism. These have long been our conditions for a substantive dialogue. They have been met."[36] He subsequently opened talks with the PLO.

A week earlier, Arafat had contended that the Palestinian declaration of independence, issued on November 15, 1988, by the Palestine National Council (PNC), accepted a Palestinian state in the West Bank, Gaza Strip, and East Jerusalem territories captured by Israel in 1967.[37] This meant, Arafat argued, that Palestine had accepted Israel's existence. After a meeting with five prominent American Jews, Arafat and his delegation issued a joint statement from all the participants. The statement articulated, in part, that the PNC's declaration "established the independent state of Palestine and accepted the existence of Israel as a state in the region." At the news conference, Arafat further clarified that "The PNC accepted two states, a Palestinian state and a Jewish state, Israel. Is that clear enough?"[38] While Arafat's question would seem rhetorical, subsequent history would suggest otherwise.

Unlike the United States, Israel had never set any conditions for talking to the PLO and was not bound by the U.S. standards. But in 1988, Prime Minister Yitzhak Shamir understood very well that Reagan's decision had profound implications for Israel. Journalist Akiva Eldar was an eyewitness to Shamir's reaction:

I remember the shouts of joy in the Prime Minister's Office in the winter of 1988 when the news came in that

Arafat hadn't provided the Americans with the declaration that was a precondition for starting a dialogue between the Reagan administration and the PLO leadership. The next day, when Shamir heard that Arafat had revised the wording of the declaration and was committing himself to ending the armed struggle against Israel, that joy gave way to overt disappointment. Shamir was afraid, and rightly so, that the dialogue between the Americans and the PLO would lead to negotiations over the future of "Judea and Samaria" [the biblical name for the West Bank], and who knew where that might lead. He was afraid, and rightly so, that Washington would not view favorably the expansion of the Jewish settlements in the West Bank at the height of such negotiations.[39]

And indeed, in only five years, the "Oslo process" would begin.

In August 1993, Israeli and Palestinian officials began secretly meeting in Oslo, Norway, to establish an agreement (based on the "Framework for Peace in the Middle East" created during the 1978 Camp David Accords) for achieving the long-standing goal of granting land to the Palestinians in exchange for peace. After considerable back and forth, these negotiations resulted in the highly celebrated and oft-criticized Oslo Accords, a set of agreements that led to the withdrawal of Israeli forces from parts of the Gaza Strip and West Bank, the establishment of the Palestinian Authority as an interim self-governing body, and started the clock on a five-year period intended to be used to negotiate a permanent peace agreement.[40]

In his letter to Israeli prime minister Yitzhak Rabin just days ahead of the formal signing of the first agreement in the Oslo Accords—the Declaration of Principles on Interim

Self-Government Arrangements (Oslo I)—the very first commitment Arafat affirmed to Rabin was that "[t]he PLO recognizes the *right of the State of Israel to exist in peace and security*" (emphasis added).[41] In exchange for this and other commitments, all Rabin had to give Arafat was a letter containing a single sentence: "In response to your letter of September 9, 1993, I wish to confirm to you that, in light of the PLO commitments included in your letter, the Government of Israel has decided to recognize the PLO as the representative of the Palestinian people and commence negotiations with the PLO within the Middle East peace process."[42] Many Palestinians and their supporters have lamented the low price Arafat extracted for the valuable commitments in his letters. But in the end, Arafat's declaration of recognition of Israel meant little, as one Israeli leader after another, and their supporters, have either ignored the recognition or claimed it was invalid, demanding more steps to ensure that the Palestinian people *really* meant it when they recognized Israel.

Although the Arafat-Rabin exchange of letters in 1993 was not the first time that the PLO had unambiguously recognized Israel's sovereignty, it was the first time Israelis acknowledged the action. To be sure, there were many doubters and detractors, from all sides of the conflict and across the political spectrum. The ultimate failure of the Oslo process has borne out some of those doubts, but one that remains hotly contested is the "sincerity" of the PLO's recognition. Many Israelis doubted that sincerity and pointed to the events of the Second Intifada from 2000 to 2005 as proof of supposed Palestinian duplicity.[43] Yet for Palestinians, their leadership had formally recognized Israel, to the very same extent as had Egypt and Jordan—the two neighboring Arab countries that struck peace treaties with Israel and established normal relations with the

Jewish state—but also to the same extent as the United States and any other Western country. Moreover, the Palestinians felt that Arafat had done this three times—with the PNC declaration of independence, his clarifying statement after the UN speech, and in the exchange of letters with Rabin.

This impasse of mistrust has only deepened over the years, while the conditions of Palestinian life under Israeli occupation have deteriorated markedly. The Gaza Strip has been under siege by Israel since 2006, and a subsequent U.S.- and Israel-backed coup by Fatah left Hamas in firm control of the area.[44] The growing humanitarian crisis in Gaza and the entrenchment of the occupation in the West Bank—both politically and physically with settlement expansion—have put even more focus on the question of recognizing Israel's "right to exist." This focus became even more intense in 2007, under Prime Minister Ehud Olmert of the center-right Kadima party, when foreign minister Tzipi Livni directly demanded something new from the Palestinians. For the first time, Palestinians were asked to recognize not only Israel's right to exist, but also its right to exist as the homeland for the Jewish people. The Palestinians objected vociferously.[45]

Does the World's Only Jewish State Have a Unique Right to Exist?

No one recognizes Iran as an Islamic Republic, Saudi Arabia as an absolute monarchy, Sweden as a constitutional monarchy, or the United States as a federal republic. Other states simply recognize the territorial integrity of those states within internationally recognized borders and acknowledge (or deny) the legitimacy of the current government. Does Israel's unique status as a Jewish state, and the unusual histories of Jews and

Zionism, constitute an exceptional case whereby Israel, alone among the nation-states of the world, has not only a right to exist but deserves to have its self-defined character recognized by another people?

It is important to note that Israel does not demand that Egypt, Jordan, Saudi Arabia, Iran, the United States, Australia, or any other country recognize it as a Jewish state. This demand is unique to the Palestinians. The legitimacy of this demand, with these conditions, is really at issue.

Perhaps the best case for such recognition was made by Israeli scholar Tal Becker in 2011. A legal adviser for the Israeli foreign ministry, Becker has held many notable positions in the Israeli government, academia, and the realm of advocacy.[46] During his time as a senior fellow at the Washington Institute for Near East Policy (WINEP), a right-of-center, pro-Israel advocacy American think tank, Becker published a lengthy policy analysis that made the case for Israel's "need" for recognition as a Jewish state by the Palestinians. He accurately and fairly describes much of the case *against* such recognition, albeit for the purpose of refuting it.[47]

Becker frames the idea of Israel's "right to exist" as one of self-determination, separate from, though entangled with, the actual territory of the state of Israel. In fact, this is one of the conditions he sets forth to reconcile the objections not only of Palestinians but of other Arab states with Israeli aspirations. He argues, "The claim should be seen as seeking recognition of the Jewish people's right to self-determination in a sovereign state, rather than recognition of Israel as a Jewish state." Becker contends that it is the very idea of a Jewish national existence that is in question. Though he does not address it, this contention comes into direct conflict with the aspirations of Zionism. Throughout its many strains, Zionism always insisted that, whatever else it might need from other nations, it did not require acknowledgment from others of its national existence, which was as axiomatic as the existence of other nations.

Becker's concept of separating the recognition of a right of self-determination for a Jewish nation from the question of Israel's "right to exist" holds some intrigue. National ideology is a matter many of us take for granted. But ultimately, a nation exists because those who are part of that nation want it to. In this sense, Zionism is one of the world's most contested nationalisms. It took decades, and the global trauma of the Holocaust, before there was a clear Jewish majority behind Zionism. And while the establishment of the state of Israel has cemented that majority, the question of Jewish nationhood remains a matter of debate among Jews around the world. And while Jews, like any other large collective, are entitled to define their own existence, they are not entitled to unilaterally decide how that identification might affect others. Like any other people, Jews can and have used their collective memory and shared culture to forge a nation, and that is a Jewish prerogative. But the land that is being contested is not uniquely the homeland of Jews.[48] While Jews' right to decide the definition of their own collective existence is axiomatic, their right to displace another people to lay claim to an historic homeland from many centuries past is not.

If Becker's claim is taken at face value, it is possible to acknowledge Jewish national identity without prejudice to the disposition of land and sovereignty in Israel-Palestine. Yet if we accept as a principle that such identification is a matter for the nation itself, then Israel is demanding an empty recognition that carries no meaning. The circumstances on the ground aggravate this further, as the Palestinians are not merely another nation, but a nation dispossessed by Israel's creation.

Becker contends that Palestinian recognition of Jewish

collective rights would help establish trust. Yet even setting aside the dismal failure of decades of "confidence-building measures" between the Israeli and Palestinian people, Becker offers no rationale as to why this recognition would build trust. After all, as we discussed earlier, the long-sought recognition of Israel's sovereignty by the PLO and Arafat was greeted with suspicion and, later, outright denial that the recognition was ever given. Becker also noted that Egypt and Jordan, in their peace agreements with Israel, did not recognize Israel's "right to exist" or its "Jewish character." While Becker was clear that he and many other Israelis wanted this, he essentially ignores the fact that, despite some serious obstacles, the peace between Israel and both of those countries has held firm for decades without any unusual diplomatic recognition of Israel as a Jewish state.

Why, then, are the Palestinians—the one group who would be supporting their own oppression with such recognition—expected to offer this unique gift to Israel? As we've seen, one of Israel's founding philosophers, Jabotinsky, made it quite clear that this was a non-starter, and an unreasonable expectation. The very demand negates the fact that the PLO's grudging acknowledgment of Israel's existence is in itself an enormous compromise.[49]

Becker also contends that recognition of Israel as a Jewish state is necessary to forestall demands of Palestinian refugees to return to their former lands and homes in Israel. It hardly seems necessary to point out this is not a convincing reason for Palestinians to accept this condition. One can, of course, understand why Israel would want to reinforce its opposition to the Palestinian right of return. Becker states it clearly:

> While recognition of a Jewish state does not necessarily dictate the exact manner in which individual Palestinian

refugee claims will be resolved, such recognition does seek to allay a central Israeli concern that the claim for refugee return is in reality an attempt to undermine Jewish self-determination. Those seeking recognition argue that Palestinians cannot, on the one hand, demand the establishment of an independent state as part of a two-state solution while, on the other, pursuing the return of refugees not only to Palestine but to Israel as well. By placing the resolution of the refugee issue in the framework of two states for two peoples—as envisaged in the Clinton Parameters—the capacity for this issue to overwhelm the two-state solution of which it is a part is effectively ruled out, even if a variety of approaches to the details of a solution are not.[50]

For Palestinians, the demand for the return of refugees is as fundamental a component of their nationalism as any. As Palestinian intellectual Ghada Karmi stated, "There is not a Palestinian living who does not thrill to the idea of return or for whom it is not imbued with special meaning. The house key, which people took with them as they fled in 1948 in the belief their flight was temporary and they would return, is iconic for Palestinians, a symbol of loss, but also hope. Return is a theme that animates the lives of Palestinians everywhere, even as it grows ever more unattainable."[51] Palestinians also rightly contend that "return" is a right enshrined in international law and basic principles of human rights.[52] Israelis contend, as Becker explained, that the mere recognition of that right, let alone its implementation, would undermine the principle of a Jewish nation-state. Becker's proposed solution puts an a priori limit on a right that Palestinians rightfully cherish. He treats it as a given that Israel's right to exist as a state that privileges Jews above others trumps the right of Palestinian refugees to return to their homeland—a right supported by international law.[53]

Of course, Israel may challenge this interpretation of international law. Such challenges are fair game, both for negotiations and adjudication under international law. But it is inappropriate to suggest that such processes can be circumvented by prior political agreement. Moreover, aside from its moral and ethical contradictions, the idea of ignoring the right of return is impractical. Palestinians consider the right of return fundamental, and any attempt by its leadership to negate that right is less likely to succeed than it is to mean the end of that leadership. The only way to address this impasse is through negotiation, not by setting pre-conditions. Also, the idea that the right of return can be mitigated or compromised in order to bolster Israeli confidence in the Palestinians' commitment to coexistence is not only impractical but condescending.

Becker next examines the objection that recognizing Israel as a Jewish state would justify a secondary status for Israel's non-Jewish citizens, most of whom are Palestinian. Contending that recognition need not necessarily lead to legal discrimination, he cites Israel's High Court of Justice:

> [T]he values of the State of Israel as a Jewish and democratic state do not, by any means, suggest that the State will discriminate between its citizens. . . . Moreover: not only do the values of the State of Israel as a Jewish state not dictate discrimination on the basis of religion and nationality, they in fact proscribe such discrimination, and demand equality between religions and nationalities. . . . There is, therefore, no contradiction between the values of the State of Israel as a Jewish and democratic state and between the absolute equality of all of its citizens. The

opposite is true: equality of rights for all people in Israel, be their religion whatever it may be and be their nationality whatever it may be, is derived from the values of the State of Israel as a Jewish and democratic state.[54]

It is important to note that Becker implicitly acknowledges that there is a risk of discrimination stemming from the recognition of the Jewish nature of Israel, but contends it is not an inevitable outcome of that recognition. In practice, there is certainly discrimination against Palestinian citizens of Israel already.[55] However, the recent controversy over Israel's "Nation-State Law" provides a framework for critically evaluating Becker's contention that Palestinian recognition of Israel as a Jewish state would not necessarily be tantamount to giving tacit approval to discrimination against Palestinian citizens of Israel.

The Nation-State Law, formally known as Basic Law: Israel as the Nation-State of the Jewish People, stirred a great deal of controversy in Israel and around the world when it was finally approved by the Knesset in July 2018. For staunch supporters of Jewish nationalism, the Nation-State Law codified with sweeping principles what they saw as Israel's long-standing self-definition:

(A.) The Land of Israel is the historic homeland of the Jewish people, in which the State of Israel was established.

(B.) The State of Israel is the nation-state of the Jewish people, in which it exercises its natural, cultural, religious and historic right to self-determination.

(C.) The exercise of the right to national self-determination in the State of Israel is exclusive to the Jewish people.[56]

Adalah, an Israel-based civil rights organization, sharply summarized its objections to the law:

[T]here is a difference between racism and racist practices and a Basic Law that requires, as a constitutional mandate, racist acts. If the Basic Law is enacted, the practice will be anchored in the constitution, which stands to pass clear messages to all the branches of government and obligates them, by law, to discriminate against the Arab population. In so doing, it transforms discrimination into a constitutional, systematic, and institutional principle, and into a basic element of the foundations of Israeli law. Unlike daily practice, where one can argue against the validity of discrimination because it is committed in violation of the principle of the rule of law, a law clearly articulates its intention for the realization of its objectives, and it turns illegitimate practices in and of themselves into an expression of the rule of law. . . . The immediate repercussions of the Nakba ["catastrophe" in Arabic, referring to the displacement of Palestinians in 1948], which are mainly related to the loss of the homeland and the destruction of the Palestinian society, with all that this entails, were realized mostly through extra-legal governmental policies. Now, the Nation-State Basic Law seeks to anchor them in a clear and explicit manner, first and foremost, by the denial of the rights of the Palestinian people to self-determination in their own homeland.[57]

The issues around the Nation-State Law, which became a Basic Law (roughly tantamount to a constitutional law in the United States), were declarative. But, as Adalah's summary pointed out, the bill serves as a legal basis for current and future discriminatory laws and official policies. Adalah's objections were echoed around the world. Saeb Erekat, secretary-general of the PLO, called it a "dangerous and racist law" that "officially legalizes apartheid and legally defines Israel as an apartheid system."[58] Palestinian activist Omar Barghouti offered: "From now on, it will not just be legal to racially discriminate against the indigenous Palestinian citizens of the state. It will be constitutionally mandated and required."[59]

But objections did not emerge only from the Palestinian side. "This is a sad and unnecessary day for Israeli democracy," said Rick Jacobs, president of the Union for Reform Judaism. "The damage that will be done by this new Nation-State law to the legitimacy of the Zionist vision and to the values of the state of Israel as a democratic—and Jewish—nation is enormous." Even the American Jewish Committee, an organization that very rarely criticizes Israel but frequently has very harsh words for the Palestinians, expressed its "disappointment" with the law. They specifically noted the downgrading of Arabic from its position as a national language and, crucially, expressed concern that the law's endorsement of Jewish settlement everywhere in the "Land of Israel" would be seen as supporting Jewish-only communities.[60]

These objections speak directly to concerns that the Nation-State Law will lay the underpinnings for discrimination against the non-Jewish minorities in Israel, a sector that consists overwhelmingly of Palestinians. Even if one contends that the Nation-State Law need not necessarily lead to discriminatory outcomes, how can one possibly argue that the Palestinians be expected to acknowledge Israel's right to such a self-characterization? When Becker composed his argument defending the idea that the Palestinians should recognize Israel as a Jewish state, there was no Nation-State legislation, although the idea had been discussed for years. But now that it is law, we find enshrined in Israel's most basic legal framework a characterization that has inspired concern across the political spectrum.

However controversial Israel's self-characterization is, no one is asking the United States, European Union, Arab League, Non-Aligned Movement states, or anyone else to acknowledge it. It is the Palestinians' seal of approval for this law, and theirs alone, that Israel demands when it calls for Palestinian recognition of Israel's "right to exist as a Jewish state." This is not a pragmatic demand, and it is certainly not one that has any connection to progressive values of any sort. On the contrary, it is a demand rooted in a "might makes right" ethos that demands the utter subjugation, even humiliation, of one's rival.

Palestinian-American activist Yousef Munayyer raised an obvious parallel:

> Can you imagine asking indigenous Americans and indigenous rights activists—fighting for the rights of a population whose languages, societies, culture and possessions were categorically decimated in the process of erecting the United States—whether the United States has a "right to exist"? . . . It is intellectually dishonest and intended, almost always, to silence critics and criticism of Israeli policies. . . . [And] anyone who doesn't answer the question about Israel's right to exist with an unequivocal "yes" risks being portrayed as an eliminationist radical worthy of labels like "anti-Semite" and otherwise marginalized. In other words, it's a set-up.[61]

The demand that the character of one state be recognized by anyone outside of that state is unprecedented. The idea that Israel should be treated uniquely in this regard because of its history does not stand up under scrutiny. And the demand being made of only one group, Palestinians, the very same group that was impacted far beyond any other by Israel's creation and policies since its birth, is ethically indefensible. More than that, it is an example of Israel denying its own founders' stated aspirations. It makes the resolution of its long conflict with the Palestinians even harder to achieve.

The Israeli journalist Anshel Pfeffer has argued that Israel's constant campaign to promote its own image is self-defeating. In his view, the state undermines its legitimacy through Israeli *hasbara* (technically translated as "propaganda" but used to represent all of Israel's public relations tactics to promote its political positions and its self-identification as a Jewish and democratic state, the "only democracy in the Middle East"). "Israel has a serious racism problem," Pfeffer writes. "There is a legal and social framework that discriminates against its non-Jewish citizens. For the last 52 years it has been occupying millions of stateless Palestinians who still have no prospect of receiving their basic rights." He continues, "Acknowledging these fundamental issues has nothing to do with the argument of whether Zionism was a practical and just solution for the historical and genocidal persecution of Jews before 1948. That's why hasbara is a waste of time. All it does is undermine Israel's legitimacy. Because real countries don't have to argue they are legitimate. Hasbara's one function is to deny Israel is a real country with real problems that need dealing with."[62]

Pfeffer's point complements the Palestinian response—which was, ironically, precisely the one that Israel's founding father, Theodor Herzl, envisioned when he expressed the desire for his longed-for Jewish state to be a state like any other—to Becker's attempt to justify the demand for Palestinian recognition of Israel as a Jewish state.[63] Surely Israel anticipated the Palestinian response, which has echoed across the Palestinian political spectrum. Yet, when the Israeli journalist Nahum

Barnea asked a U.S. official from the Obama administration about Palestinian president Mahmoud Abbas's refusal to recognize Israel as a Jewish state, he replied, "We couldn't understand why it bothered him so much. For us, the Americans, the Jewish identity of Israel is obvious. We wanted to believe that for the Palestinians this was a tactical move—they wanted to get something (in return) and that's why they were saying 'no.' . . . The Palestinians came to the conclusion that Israel was pulling a nasty trick on them. They suspected there was an effort to get from them approval of the Zionist narrative."[64]

That the American official could not understand immediately why this recognition would be problematic for the Palestinians speaks volumes about the negative role the United States has played in this milieu. That is why it is imperative for those who wish to see a political resolution to this vexing dispute to insist that Israel give up this demand that the Palestinians take steps that are demanded of *no other country*, let alone a stateless people with little diplomatic power of their own. This issue transcends formulations about parameters of negotiations and whether talks should move toward a solution based on one state or two.

Israel can, in the end, take any position it wants. But it is within the power of outsiders, both states and ordinary citizens, to change the political calculus that Israel uses to conclude that it can legitimately make this pointless and humiliating demand of the Palestinians.

As we have discussed throughout this chapter, the demand for Palestinian recognition of Israel's "right to exist" is, in fact, a demand that Palestinians legitimize their own dispossession. It is a demand that no nation could possibly acquiesce to. Progressive values, not to mention international law, require such a demand be rejected. It compromises the immediate freedom and self-determination of Palestinians, as well as the long-term stability and safety of all the people living in Israel, the West Bank, and Gaza. Rather than giving Israel a unique status among the world's nations and placing a unique burden on an already vulnerable Palestinian people, a moral, ethical, and political vision that engages and protects everyone equally should guide U.S. political engagement in the region.

A progressive stance by the United States and other nations would affirm the territorial integrity of whatever state or states exist after an agreement is made. More importantly, any lasting resolution must be based on principles of equal rights, both collective and individual, and must recognize that the imbalance of power between Israel and the Palestinians necessitates that outside actors be involved to counter the disparity in power.

It is an indisputable fact that Israel exists. It is a plain fact that the Palestinian leadership, as recognized throughout the world, has acknowledged and accepted Israel's existence. Demanding Palestinian recognition of Israel as a Jewish state is to demand Palestinian admission that their national aspirations are, at best, inferior to those of Israeli Jews, and at worst, thoroughly invalid. This immoral demand is thoroughly incompatible with any possibility of resolving the ongoing struggle over the denial of Palestinian rights and the prevailing sense of insecurity in Israel.

2

Criminalizing BDS

"[T]his BDS movement is something that I do not support," U.S. senator Cory Booker declared in June 2019, several months after he announced that he would be seeking the Democratic Party's nomination for the 2020 presidential election.[1] This was not the first time that the New Jersey senator had expressed his position on BDS, the international movement to boycott, divest from, and sanction Israel over its ongoing treatment of Palestinian citizens, as well as those living in Gaza and the West Bank. But as a presidential candidate, Booker was increasingly pressed to clarify and expound upon his stances on a variety of foreign and domestic policy matters. In this case, the politics of Israel and Palestine was certainly no exception.

The need for Booker to explain his position on BDS was prompted by a Senate vote in early 2019, not long after the 116th Congress was sworn in. Like the majority of his fellow 2020 contenders for the Democratic presidential nomination, Booker voted against a bill that, according to the American Civil Liberties Union, would have stifled freedom of speech by allowing the U.S. government to stigmatize and even criminalize the BDS movement.[2] Booker explained that he did not oppose anti-BDS legislation, per se. Rather, he opposed this particular bill on the grounds that it violated the First Amendment. Leaving no room for confusion about his position, Booker further explained that he was comfortable with the government moving to quash citizen boycotts, as long as such moves could be squared with the constitutional guarantee to free speech. He told the *Huffington Post*: "I think that we should do what we can to protect American companies, and other Americans, from being attacked in a way that undermines their ability to stand up for what they believe is right. That is where I stand."[3]

For Booker, a liberal Democrat, to have such a position on this matter is difficult to understand. The unambiguous purpose of anti-BDS legislation is to stigmatize and penalize U.S. citizens from taking otherwise legal, and indeed common, action in support of a cause in which they believe. By suggesting that the government should be able to hinder the speech of citizens, to protect businesses from market pressures toward specific political ends, Booker turned the state's duty to protect free speech on its head. His explanation undermines the foundation of the right to boycott, which must, by definition, be protected against government interference of any kind.[4]

Would Booker have stood against popular boycotts of Chick-fil-A, whose ownership stood up for what "they believe is right" by funding anti-LGBTQI* groups?[5] Would he have tried to squelch organized resistance to Hobby Lobby, which denied women employees access to certain forms of contraception because of "sincerely held religious values"?[6] How would he respond to popular boycotts of Walmart protesting its widely criticized labor practices? Would Booker have asked the government to shield these entities in the same way it does Israel? It is hard to imagine, as a matter of principle or realpolitik, that Booker—a progressive senator—would take such a stance on other social and political matters.

BDS is a debate rooted in the very real suffering of a great many people. Perhaps more to the point, BDS is about collective civil action directed against another country to address this suffering. If the United States correctly allows such expressions to be directed against domestic businesses, whose protection is a responsibility of the U.S. government, how can it justify barring expression and civil action against a foreign country?

Supporting or opposing BDS merits deep intellectual and political engagement. Yet federal and state governments in the United States have aimed to criminalize or at least stigmatize BDS, undermining the possibility of robust debate and informed action. Once again, why does the issue of Israel/Palestine merit such an exceptional position in the battle of ideas? What is it about BDS that leads to political contradictions and intellectual contortions from progressive voices?

The Roots of BDS

In the early years of the twenty-first century, the Second Intifada brought extraordinary levels of violence throughout the West Bank, Gaza, and Israel.[7] During this time, Palestinian civil society groups and supporters of the Palestinian cause around the world recognized the need to establish a nonviolent movement that would inspire global solidarity and action. There had been numerous Palestinian calls for economic actions over the years, and even some from Israeli peace groups who had undertaken boycotting products originating in Israel's settlements in the West Bank and Gaza Strip. But Palestinian grassroots efforts at international boycotts had been limited and scattered. There were several efforts, for example, to call for an academic boycott of Israel in the United Kingdom in 2002. While these initiatives gained some notice as expressions of solidarity, they did not inspire a wider movement.[8] During the First Intifada, starting in 1987, Palestinian leadership used boycott calls to protest Israel's ongoing occupation of Palestinian lands, along with demonstrations and strikes.[9] In 1988, for example, the Unified National Leadership of the Uprising—a coalition of leading Palestinian factions—called on Palestinians to avoid buying all products from Israeli settlements, as well as any other Israeli products for which they could find reasonable alternatives.[10] These efforts were abandoned after the end of the First Intifada and the signing of the Oslo Accords.

Some opponents of BDS have tried to trace the movement to a long-term conspiracy against Israel led by Arab states, with roots going back even before the founding of the state.[11] In truth, BDS is a modern, grassroots nonviolent movement inspired by a 2005 call from a long and diverse list of Palestinian civil society organizations. Despite being ignored by world leaders and global media, BDS has been an integral feature of the Palestinian national movement.

Starting in September of 2000, the Second Intifada devastated much of the West Bank and Gaza, and brought a level of violence not seen within Israel's borders since 1948. Durable, organized Palestinian efforts at global boycotts of Israel emerged against the backdrop of this violence. Around the same time, various groups in Israel and around the world issued scattered calls for broader boycotts against Israel.[12] Ultimately, an unambiguous and audible call from the majority of Palestinians in the occupied territories—the people who would bear the brunt of a backlash from any economic action against Israel—was needed if there was to be sustained global activism.

In October 2003, a group of Palestinian academics issued a Palestinian Call for Boycott, which was followed in 2004 by a more organized and focused call for academic and cultural boycott from the Palestinian Campaign for the Academic and Cultural Boycott of Israel (PACBI).[13] PACBI's call inspired wider organizing and led to the call for boycott, divestment, and sanctions, issued on July 9, 2005. This call came from a large and representative coalition of Palestinian civil society, encompassing over 170 groups.[14] Many of these organizations were based in the occupied territories, although Palestinian groups from all around the world were represented. Their elaboration of the case for BDS and the specific demands they made created the basis for the global movement for direct economic action. The goal of such action was to convince Israel to radically alter its policies toward the Palestinian people.

The PACBI call reflected long-held Palestinian national aspirations and contained a summary of the Palestinian narrative. While listing many contemporary grievances, the call also noted: "Fifty-seven years after the state of Israel was built mainly on land ethnically cleansed of its Palestinian owners, most Palestinians are refugees, most of whom are stateless. Moreover, Israel's entrenched system of racial discrimination against its own Arab-Palestinian citizens remains intact."[15] Raising the issues of the Palestinian refugees and Arab citizens of Israel was a deliberate indication that the call was not going to focus only on grievances rooted in Israel's occupation of the West Bank and Gaza in 1967, but would speak to the full Palestinian experience since 1948. This approach represented a sharp break from the framework of diplomacy since the 1970s, creating considerable apprehension for Israeli Jews toward the burgeoning BDS movement. For them, the new approach represented a jolting reset of the parameters of peace, one that would place greater demands on Israel. It would also increase the likelihood of an agreement making much more profound changes to Israel than had been envisioned for many years.

Palestinians did not see their demands as abstract or rooted purely in historical grievances. Rather, each demand was a concrete issue that Palestinians contend with to this very day. These specific grievances included:

- Israel's construction of the wall in the West Bank, in areas well beyond its internationally recognized border
- Continued expansion of Jewish-only settlements in the West Bank
- Israel's unilateral annexation of East Jerusalem and the Golan Heights and the deep concern over potential annexation of large parts or even all of the West Bank[16]
- The growing global Palestinian refugee population
- Israel's discrimination against its own Arab, largely Palestinian citizens.

On the basis of these grievances, this assortment of civil society groups called for BDS "until Israel meets its obligation to recognize the Palestinian people's inalienable right to self-determination and fully complies with the precepts of international law by (1) [e]nding its occupation and colonization of all Arab lands and dismantling the Wall; (2) [r]ecognizing the fundamental rights of the Arab-Palestinian citizens of Israel to full equality; and (3) [r]especting, protecting and promoting the rights of Palestinian refugees to return to their homes and properties as stipulated in UN resolution 194."[17]

For these groups, this call represented a nonviolent way to effect a change in Israel's policies toward the Palestinians. The three demands summarized most of the Palestinian people's central grievances. The call consciously invoked the history of South African opposition to apartheid as a model, although it did not draw an explicit parallel that labeled Israeli practices as apartheid.[18]

The chosen date on which the call was issued—July 9, 2005—was equally deliberate, as it marked the first anniversary of a ruling by the International Court of Justice that the wall Israel had constructed inside the West Bank was illegal under international law. The court also ruled that the UN Security Council should consider how "to bring to an end the illegal situation resulting from the construction of the wall and the associated régime, taking due account of the present Advisory Opinion."[19] This choice of date also served as a public reminder that the demands were rooted in well-established international law. As we will see below, supporters of the Israeli position would argue that the laws in question do not apply in this case for several reasons. Still, it is clear that the demands were rooted in those laws.

The context in which the BDS call was issued is key to understanding the call itself. Although most consider the Second Intifada, or Palestinian uprising, to have ended in February 2005, the devastation wrought by over four years of large-scale and small-scale Israeli military operations and Palestinian guerilla attacks was an open wound for all of Israel and Palestine. As the occupation's grip tightened, mistrust mushroomed on both sides. The number of dead and wounded—although disproportionately greater among the Palestinians—caused deep-seated anger and fear to fester throughout the land.[20] Yet for all the bloodshed, neither side gained much. And while Palestinians, with far less firepower and a much more fragile infrastructure, suffered much greater harm, Israelis experienced great loss and trauma as well.

Palestinian towns and villages were devastated, much of their infrastructure destroyed. Israelis who had once worked for peace were now convinced, in no small measure by inaccurate statements issued by former Israeli prime minister Ehud Barak and former U.S. president Bill Clinton, that the Palestinians were unwilling to compromise or negotiate and that their response to "the most generous offer ever made by an Israeli prime minister" was to launch a massive wave of terrorism.[21] The despair and hopelessness was a dark cloud over the entire region. For Palestinians, there was also the extra burden of coming to grips with the destruction of much that they had managed to build, despite the years of brutal occupation.

This was the backdrop for the call for boycott, divestment and sanctions against Israel. The oft-repeated mantra that there is "no military solution" to the conflict in Israel and Palestine logically leads to the search for alternatives to military action, especially on the part of a stateless, occupied people who could never be a true threat to their antagonist. Israel and its supporters could have been relieved, even if grudgingly, that a huge segment of Palestinian society was embarking on an explicitly nonviolent resistance tactic.[22] But this was not the case.

The Israeli Reaction

When the many Palestinian civil society groups came together to formulate the BDS call, it was under the cloud of the aforementioned despair. While the actions taken by militant groups in the Second Intifada were aimed at fighting off the Israeli occupation, many Palestinians and their supporters saw it as an explosion of frustration and rage after thirty-three years of occupation and fifty-two years of dispossession, to which the world had responded with little more than platitudes. The BDS call was a way for civil society groups to act and to restore public visibility of the nonviolent aspect of Palestinian resistance.

Yet many Israelis and supporters around the world have

reacted with just as much fear and outrage about nonviolence as they did about violence. This reaction was disappointing to many who had hoped that, even if they were unhappy about the BDS call, Israel and its supporters would at least acknowledge and respect a nonviolent Palestinian response. After all, a long-standing criticism about Palestinians has been that they do not employ nonviolent methods. Respect for less violent means of Palestinian resistance has never come to pass.

Despite claims to the contrary, nonviolent resistance has been a central and deeply rooted component of the Palestinian struggle. From the six-month general strike in April 1936 during the British Mandate that initiated the three-year Great Revolt, to the long tradition of boycotts, Palestinians have long deployed nonviolence as a vital means of achieving their political goals.[23] As Palestinian scholar Ghada Ageel notes, the commitment to nonviolence continued even after the significant territorial losses of the 1967 war, as "Palestinians repeatedly invented creative outlets for resisting violent occupation."[24] In recent times, these outlets have included weekly peaceful protests in West Bank villages like Nabi Salih and Kufr Qaddum, as well as along the Gaza border. Despite violent responses from Israeli security forces, these protests have continued every week for months, years, and, in some cases, even decades.[25]

Palestinian nonviolence is not merely about mass protests or grand gestures. Rather, it is taken up in the practices of everyday life. Palestinian-American activist Yousef Munayyer wrote:

> The truth is that there is a long, rich history of nonviolent Palestinian resistance dating back well before 1948, when the state of Israel was established atop a depopulated Palestine. It has just never captured the world's attention the way violent acts have. . . . We tend to think of nonviolent resistance as an active rather than passive concept. In

reality, even though the majority of the native inhabitants were depopulated during the Nakba, thousands of Palestinians practiced nonviolent resistance by refusing to leave their homes when threatened. Today, through its occupation, Israel continues to make life unbearable for Palestinians, but millions resist the pressure by not leaving. This is particularly notable in occupied Jerusalem, where Palestinians are being pushed out of the city. For those who have never lived in a system of violence like the Israeli occupation, it is hard to understand how simply not going anywhere constitutes resistance, but when the objective of your oppressor is to get you to leave your land, staying put is part of the daily struggle. In this sense, every Palestinian living under the Israeli occupation is a nonviolent resister.[26]

Unfortunately, strikes and demonstrations without major incident do not generate news and media coverage even locally, let alone internationally. Attacks on civilians, hijackings, suicide bombings, and other such events do. This dynamic creates the false perception that Palestinians are overwhelmingly violent, and that expressions of nonviolence are rare.

At first, BDS was largely ignored by Israel and its supporters, who portrayed it as a fringe movement unworthy of serious attention. This began to change in 2009 and 2010, as BDS started to grow at a much faster rate. Several factors contributed to the escalated growth. Israel's devastation of Gaza in December 2008 and January 2009, known as "Operation Cast Lead," appalled many around the world, including many of Israel's erstwhile supporters.[27] Groups opposing the occupation and supporting Palestinian rights—both those that advocated BDS and those that did not—saw a powerful spike in support after people saw images of Gaza under heavy Israeli fire, and being subjected to the use of white phosphorous, a burning substance which cannot be extinguished with water.[28] Compounding the effect of Cast Lead, Benjamin Netanyahu became prime minister at the end of March 2009 after a hotly contested election. Netanyahu was a hard-line leader who was less inclined than his predecessor, Ehud Olmert, to offer nods toward resolving the Israeli-Palestinian conflict. Over the years, he would come to dominate the Israeli political landscape, despite frequent scandals and often very slim governing majorities. Netanyahu paid lip service to the idea of establishing a Palestinian state, but his Likud party's platform stood against this, and most did not believe he would ever allow such a state to come into being.[29]

After Cast Lead and Netanyahu's election, an already polarized political arena became even more sharply divided and heated. Supporters of Israel, faced with mounting negative portrayals in both mainstream and social media, felt more defensive of their positions. Those feelings became even more acute after May 31, 2010, when a flotilla of ships from the Free Gaza Movement attempted to break Israel's blockade of the Gaza Strip. On the *Mavi Marmara*, one of the ships boarded by Israeli commandoes, activists resisted the Israelis, resulting in the Israeli soldiers killing ten of them.[30] The dead activists included nine Turkish citizens and one American. The flotilla was organized in conjunction with a Turkish human rights group, IHH, which had a clear track record of humanitarian work, though Israel alleged it had connections to Hamas.[31] A U.S. State Department investigation failed to substantiate anything beyond the group having had contact with Hamas. On the basis of this information, and against the wishes of the majority of the U.S. Senate, the State Department did not label the organization a terrorist group.[32] The incident further tarnished Israel's image and ruptured Israeli-Turkish relations for years after. It also succeeded in drawing renewed attention to conditions in the Gaza Strip, which, once again, brought more people into the active BDS movement.

As the BDS movement grew, so did resistance to it from Israel's supporters around the world. Even before governments like Israel, the United States, and Germany viewed BDS as a threat worthy of a legislative response, the movement had already been condemned as anti-Semitic, and often tarred as a front for the elimination of Jews in the entire Israeli-controlled area.

Why such consternation about a nonviolent movement?

The pro-Israel response to BDS has its roots in several areas, some of which stemmed from the anger and disappointment that quickly emerged in the early years of the Oslo peace process. The Interim Agreement between Israel and the Palestinians was supposed to have lasted for five years, at the end of which the difficult issues—including Jerusalem, Palestinian refugees, final borders, water rights, and the disposition of Israeli settlements, among other issues—would be resolved through U.S.-mediated negotiations. As we know, this process failed. But the effects of the process continued to be felt in ways both subtle and blatant.

One of the challenges of the peace process was what journalist Ron Kampeas called the "everybody knows" Israel settlements.[33] In Western discourse, and in common parlance in Israel, there was a general understanding that certain large settlement blocs would remain in Israeli possession in any two-state solution. Ensuring these blocks were kept would minimize the disruption to Israeli society, as it meant that the bulk of the settler population in the West Bank would not need to be uprooted. In most (though not all) formulations of these "everybody knows" settlements, the Palestinians would be compensated with land from other parts of Israel. But the "everybody knows" concept went well beyond settlements. In 2011, Mitchell Plitnick offered a critical analysis of the universal agreement on certain points, which included that: "Israel will keep (the settlements of) Ariel and Ma'ale Adumim; The Palestinians will accept a token return of refugees; Palestinians will accept a de-militarized state with Israeli rights to their airspace; Palestinians will accept some Jordanian influence over their politics as well as agree to exclude Hamas and similar groups from the political process; and Palestinians may not like these things, but they can be made to accept them."[34] These were examples of conditions that most Israelis and Americans believed were fait accompli at one time or another during the Oslo process. They saw them as basic prerequisites for a two-state solution, and the Israeli and U.S. delegations held their negotiations with the Palestinian leadership with these assumptions, perhaps unspoken, as a framework. When the Palestine Papers—a collection of some 1,700 documents that recorded talks between Israel and the Palestine Liberation Organization between 1999 and 2010—were leaked, it became clear that the Palestinian negotiators understood these assumptions. And although the negotiators wavered in their apparent commitments to them, the assumptions themselves were never really challenged on the whole. This was why the release of those papers caused a near-panic within the Palestinian Authority.[35]

As Plitnick further outlined,

The peace process has proceeded, from the very beginning, with an ever-widening disconnect from the Palestinian people. . . . Among the Palestinian people there simply hasn't been the open, public discourse that has happened in Israel. Arafat, in the years before his death, was at least much more connected to the people than his successors. . . . When a Palestinian says she or he supports a two-state solution, what does that mean? Does that person think it ok for Israel to keep Gilo, the settlement outside of Jerusalem and right near Bethlehem? Do they accept land swaps at all? Do they accept only a token return of refugees, and that the Right of Return, which is widely viewed as an individual right, be essentially forfeited? Do they accept sharing Jerusalem and a compromise on the Haram al-Sharif/Temple Mount? Does the majority of Palestinians still support a two-state solution at all? . . . I can say from personal experience that I've heard all sorts of answers to the questions above, from Palestinians in the Territories and the Diaspora, from the relatively well-to-do and the poorest refugees, from the religious and the secular, from those in relative positions of power and the common worker. . . . But some of these things that "everybody knows" have always seemed questionable to me and many others who approach this question with a more critical eye.[36]

The BDS declaration challenged what "everybody knows." The very first BDS condition—that Israel end "its occupation and colonization of all Arab lands" and take down the barrier in the West Bank—immediately shifted the context from one that sought to accommodate Israeli political needs and security demands to one that placed Palestinian independence at the heart of the matter.[37] The second—that Israel recognize the full equality of Palestinian citizens of Israel—brought an issue into the conversation that had been mostly absent. For Israelis, it identified a problem that most had not considered part of the conflict, even irrelevant to it. For Palestinians, it was also an attempt to dismantle the social and political distinctions made between those living within and outside the state of Israel, which were further reified by the Oslo process. Both demands challenged the diplomatic dynamic as well. With the United States acting as broker, and the Arab League playing only a peripheral role, the popular will of the Palestinian people had heretofore been more of a rhetorical tool in the talks than an actual factor. Even without mentioning the Palestinian refugees, the BDS demands would disrupt the sense of comfort that Israelis and Americans felt about the general direction of a two-state solution.

But if those demands disrupted the atmosphere, the call for the recognition of the refugees' right of return shattered it. For years, many of us who moved between the peace camps of Israelis, Palestinians, and Americans could see the disconnect in how the sides viewed the refugee question. Palestinians had a variety of ideas about how to deal with the question of the return of refugees. But across the spectrum of those views, it was virtually universal that the *right* of those refugees to return was sacrosanct as both a national right for the Palestinian people collectively, and for each individual Palestinian. They would not tolerate their leaders giving it away at the negotiating table.

But this was not the message getting through to most Israelis, and outsiders, including those who were actively promoting a legitimate peace that was acceptable to all. Again, the political necessity of sacrificing the right of return was just something that "everybody knows," and that Palestinians "understood" was the price of a negotiated solution.

The confusion arose from the disparate avenues for public discourse within Israeli and Palestinian society. Israel represented a modern nation-state with a vibrant media that allowed for a wide range of views to be expressed internally and distributed around the world. Palestinians, however, struggled under the anti-democratic weight of both the Israeli occupation and a Palestinian Authority that lacked accountability and proper structures to ensure democracy and human rights. In the early years of the twenty-first century, the escalated violence only widened the disconnect between Palestinian leadership and popular views among Palestinians.[38] The separation of Israelis from Palestinians, which had grown markedly since the end of the First Intifada, had the effect of cutting off the Palestinian popular voice to Israel and much of the West, where the entire question of refugees was mentioned far less frequently than any other contentious issue.

By 2005, the understanding on each side regarding the potential resolution of the Palestinian refugee crisis was almost completely divided. And into that breach came the BDS call, which demanded full recognition of the right of return. The fact that most Israelis, and many others outside the region, did not acknowledge that right was a particular point of emphasis for the Palestinians.

The right of return was not just a matter of politics, but one of identity. Since 1948, the Palestinian national consciousness has been largely shaped by the lost land, homes, and property suffered during and after the Nakba.[39] The fact that they were unable to exercise the right of return was made even more painful because Israel fundamentally denied that right's very existence, as did most of the Western world's powers that had such sway over the politics of the Middle East.

On the Israeli side, particularly among more liberal Israelis and their supporters in the United States, the demand for full right of return came as a shock for which they were unprepared. It reinforced the narrative that had emerged from the waning days of the Ehud Barak and Bill Clinton administrations: Israel made a very generous offer to the Palestinians and the Palestinians responded with an intifada. Though contradicted by the actual events at the 2000 Camp David summit and subsequent incidents, this myth held fast and remains widely accepted to this day.[40] It utterly shattered the Israeli peace movement, drowning it under the bombs and gunfire of the Second Intifada, with many supporters of the peace process believing they had been betrayed. As a result, when Israelis were confronted with the demand for the return of refugees in the BDS call, it seemed to confirm the narrative that the Palestinian goal was not peace but the disempowerment (at best) or expulsion (at worst) of Jewish Israelis. The ongoing efforts to achieve a two-state solution, and the Palestinian Authority's repeated assurances that they were completely committed to it, had combined with vague and inconsistent words from Palestinian president Mahmoud Abbas on the matter of refugees.[41] His aim was to keep the official Palestinian stance and the BDS movement separate. At this point, the BDS movement was seen not only as obstructionist, but holding a barely hidden nefarious agenda.

A movement that Palestinians saw as a nonviolent push to claim human rights and rights granted by international law thus appeared to Israelis as a cynical and cunning shift in tactics in the wake of a crushing military defeat. When the movement grew, Israel and its supporters abroad began taking more concerted measures against it. Of particular note was the work of the Reut Institute (now the Reut Group), a strategic think tank founded in 2004, in part to combat what it calls the "delegitimization" of Israel. In 2010, Reut issued a report, which it presented to the Israeli government, analyzing the growth of the BDS movement in the context of global delegitimization efforts. The authors claimed that BDS was part of a broader, global anti-Zionist movement that worked in tandem with Israel's nemeses in the region such as Hamas, Hezbollah, and Iran. The goal of this alliance, they argued, was to implement the "Implosion Strategy," a set of tactics designed to cause Israel to collapse from within.[42] They described the strategy as one that "aims to facilitate the collapse of the Zionist entity by internal forces. These include a conflagration in the tensions between Arabs and Jews, or within the Jewish community in Israel—between Ashkenazim and Sephardim, 'hawks' and 'doves,' or religious and secular communities—which would lead to a civil war such as in Lebanon. This logic, which has percolated since the 1950s, was passive in nature. It called for ending the military struggle against Israel to allow for internal factional tensions within Israeli society to erupt."[43] But by 2010, Reut contended, this strategy had transformed into active support for the occupation, in the belief that it would increase Israel's overreach, speeding up the implosion process and gradually straining Israel's political infrastructure into collapse.

For Reut, the "resistance network" of local, mostly Palestinian groups, pursued this strategy, complemented by the "delegitimization network" that operated mostly in the United States and Western Europe. Although the strategy the report's authors outlined was somewhat intricate, they contended that these networks had no central focal point. The report did not explain how this strategy evolved or could be executed without a coordination system. In any case, by outlining the "networks" in this manner, the Reut report, intentionally or not, reinforced the existing perspectives of a wide majority of Israelis and pro-Israel activists abroad. Reut concluded that Palestinians did not want a two-state solution because such a solution would stop short of their real goal: the annihilation of Israel. Thus, Palestinians did not want the occupation to end, despite their constant refrain to the contrary.

Reut reinforced an all-too-common dichotomy among Israelis, Palestinians, and their respective supporters. Where Palestinians see a struggle for their freedom and basic rights, Israelis see an attempt to rob them of their self-determination and homes. To be sure, both sides are prone to such zero-sum thinking.

To its credit, and despite its caricaturish and suspicious view of Palestinian strategies, Reut recommended that Israel pursue an end to the occupation and establish full integration of Palestinian citizens of Israel into Israeli society. A decade later, it is obvious that the Israeli government did not choose to heed this advice. A much more successful messaging effort—both with the Israeli government and with its supporters in the United States and Europe—was the framework for responding to the so-called "delegitimizers," although even there, much of the strategy was tailored for a more moderate and diplomatic government than the right-wing regimes that have become increasingly common (and extreme) under Benjamin Netanyahu.

The crux of Reut's recommendations was based on the idea that even a political resolution to the conflict would not end the efforts of the "delegitimizers," although it would significantly undermine them. Reut's idea was to use a "network to combat a network," with hubs in major cities where the BDS movement was gaining strength, including London, Paris, Toronto, Madrid, and the San Francisco Bay Area. In those areas, Reut directed Israel's representatives to engage elites in government and the community at large, rather than try to isolate the "delegitimizers." They suggested that local Jewish and pro-Israel communities take the lead and debate BDS and other pro-Palestinian advocates rather than try to suppress them with smear campaigns. The communities should work in tandem with Israel's own Foreign Affairs Ministry to "re-brand" Israel, countering what Reut saw as an effective effort by the BDS movement to portray Israel as a violent abuser of human rights and violator of international law.

Over the early years of Netanyahu's government, there were efforts to employ this strategy, though in no sector was it ever fully implemented according to Reut's designs. Much of the effort was rhetorical. Framing Palestine solidarity groups as being "anti-Israel" is a powerful tool that was employed effectively long before the BDS movement came about, and continues to be used today. Most pro-Palestinian groups see themselves as defending Palestinian human and civil rights, calling attention to the harsh conditions Palestinians endure under Israeli rule in the West Bank and Gaza Strip, and advocating for the rights of Palestinian refugees. Israelis and many of their supporters, on the other hand, often see the same activities as working against Israel. This is precisely the zero-sum logic on which Reut based its strategy recommendations.

A zero-sum approach dictates that any gains for Palestinians must mean a loss for Israelis, and vice versa. Of course, there is some truth to that view. In any situation where one group is privileged or is more powerful than another, a regime of equal rights necessarily means the loss of some power and privilege for one group and a gain of both things for the other group. But where a universalist view would suggest that such a shift in power will lead, in short order, to a more peaceful and productive future for all, the zero-sum view presumes that the newly empowered group would subjugate the relatively disempowered one. Peaceful coexistence, while not entirely ruled out, is seen as too risky a gamble.

According to that thinking, it was logical for Reut to settle on a strategy of reframing Palestinian rights as being anti-Israel, even if that is a morally problematic conclusion.[44] When the rights of Palestinians are defined only in terms of how they affect Israel, the implicit corollary is that Israeli rights are always of superior importance. This is how, for example, the thinking of Donald Trump's ambassador to Israel, David Friedman, can evolve. When journalist Christiane Amanpour asked him if the United States still supported a two-state solution to the Israel-Palestine conflict, Friedman stated matter-of-factly: "We believe in Palestinian autonomy, we believe in Palestinian self-governance. We believe that autonomy should be extended up until the point where it interferes with Israeli security."[45]

This hierarchy of rights is both the result and a perpetuator of the framing that the struggle for Palestinian rights is an attack on Israel. It also leads to a view of all supporters of Palestinian rights as being essentially of the same stripe. That same ambassador once said that the staunchly pro-Israel peace group J Street were "worse than kapos," referring to the Jews who were forced to collaborate with the Nazis in oppressing and controlling their fellow Jews during the Holocaust.[46] With a bit more subtlety, the Anti-Defamation League began assembling a list of the "Top Ten Anti-Israel Groups in America" in 2010.[47] Its top criterion for identifying an "anti-Israel" group is whether the group engages in active work to promote boycotts, divestment, and sanctions of Israel. It is noteworthy that its initial list included groups such as "If Americans Knew," a group from which other members of the ADL top 10 have distanced themselves due to its association with anti-Semitic groups and individuals. Most notably, the US Campaign for Palestinian Rights (formerly named the US Campaign to End the Israeli Occupation) and Jewish Voice for Peace declared their disassociation with If Americans Knew and its leader, Alison Weir.[48] The ADL list also mixes groups from a wide range of political ideologies and activities, some anti-Zionist and some not, many of them have quite different approaches to the politics and policies of Israel.

By throwing all the groups together under a fear-inducing headline, the ADL effectively gives the false impression (without actually making a false statement) of a widespread motivation by pro-Palestinian justice groups to harm Israel for the sake of harming Israel. By 2013, the ADL had included such groups as the Muslim Public Affairs Council and CODEPINK, which had been excluded from earlier lists. Also, it made a more explicit association between BDS and anti-Semitism. "In addition to their national impact and influence, many of the groups included in the list are known to employ rhetoric that is extremely hostile to Israel, Zionists and/or Jews," the ADL wrote in its announcement of that year's top 10 list, failing to substantiate the accusation or differentiate between those it is accusing of engaging in such behavior and those it is not.[49]

By 2015, that mind-set had taken a powerful hold, inside and outside Israel. Even center-right Israeli politician Yair Lapid—who is seen by many as a welcomed moderate alternative to right-wing Likud rule under Netanyahu—has expressed this outlook. Speaking to a New York City audience in June 2015, he asserted, without presenting any basis, that BDS "is not about policies, or about the settlements, or about the peace process, this is classic anti-Semitism in a modern disguise."[50] Lapid went on to equate supporters of BDS with al-Qaeda, ISIS, and the Bashar al-Assad regime, as well as the most violent rebel groups opposing him, stating that "we must remind the world that behind these movements are the people responsible for 9/11, for the terror attacks in Madrid and London, and for the 250,000 people already killed in Syria."

Reporting from the same conference, Israeli journalist Chemi Shalev wrote that Lapid "says that the international BDS movement 'is actually a puppet in a theater operated by Hamas and Islamic Jihad.' He describes BDS supporters in the West as 'bleeding heart, so-called intellectuals who have no idea who they really serve.' And he believes that BDS leaders are 'out and out anti-Semites.'" Shalev reported that Lapid further stated that the BDS movement "is anti-Israeli and anti-Jewish and drew a direct line between their activities and World War II Palestinian mufti Haj Amin al-Husseini's collaboration with the Nazis, including his visit with Adolf Eichmann at Auschwitz."[51]

Lapid's words were obviously strong, offensive to BDS supporters, and intended to charge his audience to renew their vigor in opposing the BDS movement. They were also reflective of the growing hysteria around BDS. In years gone by, and after the prominence of the boycott movement in support of South Africans struggling against the apartheid system, it would have been unthinkable to legislate away the rights of individual citizens to organize boycotts. But a boycott campaign against Israel offered unique opportunities that other boycotts would not. The most obvious of these is the history of anti-Semitism and the use of boycotts as a tool in that scurrilous pursuit. Most famously, the Nazis called for a national boycott of Jewish-owned businesses and of Jewish professionals. The boycott was not very successful for even the one day for which it was called, but it helped to create an atmosphere of fear for Jews and of "otherness" around German Jews in relation to other Germans. Nazi storm troopers would stand threateningly outside Jewish shops and offices, and painted Jewish stars on windows and slogans urging Germans to bypass Jews and only patronize "fellow Germans." As the online Holocaust Encyclopedia explains: "Although the national boycott operation, organized by local Nazi party chiefs, lasted only one day and was ignored by many individual Germans who continued to shop in Jewish-owned stores, it marked the beginning of a nationwide campaign by the Nazi Party against the entire German Jewish population. A week later, the government passed a law restricting employment in the civil service to 'Aryans.' Jewish government workers, including teachers in public schools and universities, were fired."[52]

The differences between the enormous atrocities against German Jews and the non-violent BDS campaign are too numerous and obvious to detail. And in most cases, even the staunchest BDS opponents make no direct comparison. Rather, they invoke the memories of the Nazi boycott to demonstrate the purported "insensitivity" of the BDS movement to the Jewish experience. Such an invocation implies that Israel and Israeli Jews cannot ever be targets of boycotts. It follows, according to that logic, that it should also be off-limits for Israel to engage in boycotts, and especially to boycott Arabs. Yet Israeli political leader Avigdor Liberman has issued several calls for boycotts of "Arab business" in Israel.[53] Liberman did not confine his calls to Palestinian citizens of Israel. He also called for a boycott of the Israeli daily newspaper *Haaretz*, for printing an op-ed he found objectionable.[54] In none of these instances was Liberman held to the same standard as those calling for BDS, despite the fact that the grievances BDS supporters are addressing carry a far more devastating human toll than those for which Liberman raised his calls.

There has also been a concerted effort to tie the BDS movement to the Arab League anti-Zionist boycott. Those boycotts began in 1945 against the Yishuv (the Jewish community in British Mandate Palestine) and then, beginning in 1948, targeted the new state of Israel. The Arab League forbade private entities from any commercial dealings with the Israeli government, and doing business with individuals or companies that were doing business with Israel. It even established an office to monitor such dealings and to maintain a blacklist of banned companies, and prohibited Arab nationals from doing business with any business that was on that blacklist. Enforcement of the boycott has waned over the years—though Israeli products are certainly not welcomed by most of the Arab public—and its economic impact has been negligible. Also, due to the increasing globalization of trade and manufacturing as well as the use of clandestine methods, Israeli firms have found a variety of ways to do business in the Arab world.

By the early twenty-first century, the Arab League anti-Zionist boycott was less a matter of the Arab states agreeing not to do business with Israel and more one of finding ways to do business without arousing the considerable popular dislike of Israel among their citizens.[55] According to a Congressional Research Service report released in 2017, "Since the boycott is sporadically applied and ambiguously enforced, its impact, measured by capital or revenue denied to Israel by companies adhering to the boycott, is difficult to measure. . . . It appears that since intra-regional trade is small, and that the secondary and tertiary boycotts are not aggressively enforced, the boycott may not currently have an extensive effect on the Israeli economy."[56] The Arab League boycott may not have had much effect on Israel's economy, but before that economy stabilized at the end of the 1980s, it was a major concern for Israel. For much of Israel's three decades, there was enormous fear of the potential effect of the boycott, which the League had never employed to its fullest potential, to threaten European and American businesses that held the hope for a stronger Israeli economy.

If the comparison between BDS and the Arab League boycott were valid, this would have severe implications, as the United States has laws on the books to shield U.S. businesses from having to comply with the Arab League boycott. In 1965, Congress passed a law requiring a report on firms complying with the Arab League boycott.[57] While this may have dampened some of the effect of the boycott, it presented no material obstacle to firms' compliance with it. In 1976, Congress passed what was known as the Ribicoff Amendment, which denied certain tax benefits to any firm complying with the boycott.[58] In 1977, Congress passed an amendment to the Export Administration Act that included a provision penalizing

American companies that cooperate with unsanctioned boycotts by foreign states. Congress expanded that provision in 1979.[59] Although the language can apply to any boycott that fits the description, in practice, it is directed at the Arab League boycott of Israel.

The Bureau of Industry and Security (BIS), a Department of Commerce agency, monitors and enforces these regulations. According to the BIS, "The antiboycott laws were adopted to encourage, and in specified cases, require U.S. firms to refuse to participate in foreign boycotts that the United States does not sanction. They have the effect of preventing U.S. firms from being used to implement *foreign policies of other nations* [emphasis added] which run counter to U.S. policy."[60] Attempts to argue that BDS would run afoul of these laws run headlong into this point, as a *Harvard Law Review* article explains: "A key feature of both federal statutes is that they apply only to boycotts organized by foreign nations against allies of the United States. . . . By contrast, BDS is led by civil society groups, not foreign sovereigns or terrorist organizations."[61]

The Congressional Research Service notes:

> The Supreme Court has found that the government generally has more leeway to regulate expressive conduct than it has to regulate pure speech. Nonetheless, there are limits on the government's ability to regulate conduct protected by the First Amendment. The government normally may not, for example, regulate conduct because of its expressive elements. The Supreme Court has generally interpreted refusals to do business, including through boycotts, as conduct that may be permissibly regulated. Boycotts aimed at gaining an economic advantage for the boycotting parties are generally considered to be within the government's power to regulate and

even to prohibit. However, boycotts aimed at achieving something other than an economic advantage, particularly when the motivation is political or social in nature, may have more of an expressive element which, according to Supreme Court precedent, could qualify for First Amendment protection.[62]

The speculative nature of this last point is precisely what those working to illegalize BDS are trying to exploit. Professor Eugene Kontorovich, one of the most prominent and outspoken advocates for legal action against BDS, wrote, "Notably, the Anti-Boycott Law applies in full to boycott participation motivated by ideological reasons. . . . [I]f states can choose to not do business with South African companies because of their politics and practices, it also means they can choose to not do business with private companies because of other discriminatory policies—like a boycott of Israel."[63]

Kontorovich's argument is emblematic of most of the more cogent anti-BDS arguments. It rests on reversing the BDS argument, which presents Israel—with widespread Western support, especially from the United States—as an oppressive force, violating the human rights of the much weaker Palestinians. In Kontorovich's argument, the BDS movement takes on the role of a state actor (apartheid South Africa, in his formulation), while Israel is the victim of discrimination. If one accepts this formulation, Kontorovich's stance that Israel merits protection from the U.S. government and that such action is consistent with the First Amendment makes perfect sense. But it falls apart completely when we try to use that argument in the real world. If one were to analogize at all, the state actor appropriately comparable to Apartheid South Africa is Israel.[64] Casting the BDS movement as a state actor is simply wrong; it depends on the false notion of a connection between the BDS movement and the state actors involved in the Arab League boycott.

The rhetorical purpose of equating BDS with the Arab League boycott fails on its face on several levels. The Arab League was a conglomeration of states issuing a boycott for the explicit purpose of attacking Israel's economy to thwart "Zionist aims." BDS is a call of conscience to supporters in civil society around the world to use economic leverage, including lobbying their governments, in order to bring about specific changes in Israeli policies that violate human rights. The dividing line for government intervention to prevent the two different kinds of boycotts could not be clearer. One can agree with or oppose the Arab League boycott, but it is nonetheless an official act of a governmental body. U.S. measures to counter it thus constitute legitimate political decisions. It is the response of one government to the policy of a conglomeration of others, and that response contravenes no international or constitutional law. Conversely, one can agree with or oppose BDS, but its very nature is a civil society dispute. In a society that holds the freedoms of expression and dissent dear, and constitutionally protected, BDS must be held immune from government intervention.

While some have argued that many of the civil society leaders of Palestine have also been involved with various resistance groups, including some labeled as terrorist groups or other groups that do not practice nonviolence, this is hardly disqualifying. Among oppressed people, particularly those fighting for democracy or independence, there is a long history of leaders working with resistance groups. Returning to the South Africa example, Nelson Mandela is an obvious example, but we need not travel that far to find a similar case. Every early Israeli leader across the political spectrum—from David Ben-Gurion to Yitzhak Rabin, from Ariel Sharon and Yigal Allon to Golda

Meir and Menachem Begin—was a fighter in 1948 and before, whether one wants to focus on their efforts to suppress the Palestinians or to chase out the British. Some of them were labeled terrorists, including two—Begin and Yitzhak Shamir—who would go on to become Israeli prime ministers.[65]

Some have pointed out that the very first group to sign the BDS call was the Council of National and Islamic Forces in Palestine. The Palestinian leadership created this group to coordinate between the various factions during the Second Intifada. But the Council had no substantive power, not even the pseudo-state power of the Palestinian Authority. As such, it was completely incapable of compelling Palestinians to comply with the boycott call, much less coercing outside entities to do so. Nor was the group a tool of either the PLO or the Palestinian Authority, as it encompassed groups apart from those bodies.

The BDS movement is distinct in every meaningful way from the Arab League boycott, and BDS is neither a product of state action and power, nor does it seek to profit monetarily in competition with Israeli firms. These two points have been the difference between boycotts that meet or fail to meet the standard for protected speech under the First Amendment. BDS support in the United States, therefore, would seem to fit the conditions for protected speech. But the legal wrangling over this question is not over yet.

As of January 2020, twenty-eight states had laws or policies that penalize businesses, organizations, or individuals for engaging in or calling for boycotts against Israel.[66] The laws usually penalize businesses or individuals for refusing to sign a document that commits them not to participate in any way in boycotts against Israel. Some of the laws have real penalties, while others are merely declarations that the state opposes BDS. While the enactment of such laws has drawn criticism and even outrage, there are limited opportunities to test the constitutionality of the laws that do carry penalties. To do so, a person or company must incur a loss because they refused to take a course of action they deem immoral and a violation of Palestinians' rights. Thus far, three states have had their laws challenged, with the challengers prevailing every time. In Kansas, Arizona, and Texas, a federal court held that the Supreme Court had made it clear that boycotts for the purpose of political expression, as opposed to monetary gain, are protected speech under the First Amendment.[67] Opponents of BDS had hoped that, since the laws were not imposing a fine or threat of imprisonment for supporting BDS, the states could successfully argue that they were simply establishing a standard of who they wanted to do business with. The courts, however, did not agree.

In February 2019, the Senate controversially passed a bill that included the "Combating BDS Act of 2019," which would have affirmed the right of states and municipalities to follow through on the very same bills that had already been deemed unconstitutional in federal courts. The debate was particularly charged as Congress had just returned from a shutdown of the federal government, and many issues had piled up during that time, particularly several that had to do with paying federal employees and contractors. A bill concerning Israel's interests seemed, even among many of Israel's staunchest supporters, to be hastily timed under such circumstances. Defending the bill he had presented, Republican senator Marco Rubio of Florida wrote, "Indeed, it does not restrict citizens or associations of citizens from engaging in political speech, including against Israel. Rather, the bill merely clarifies that entities—such as corporations, companies, business associations, partnerships or trusts—have no fundamental right to government contracts and government investment. . . . By empowering states to counter discriminatory economic warfare targeting Israel, this bill also reinforces American policy insisting that only direct Israeli-Palestinian negotiations can resolve that conflict."[68]

Once again, we find in Rubio's argument a willful reversal of roles. Israel is here the "victim of economic warfare" by virtue of a civil society boycott. Such thinking dictates that any boycott or divestment action, wherever it may be directed, is an attack, rather than a form of political pressure. This is a particularly problematic line of thought when one considers the bombast with which it is stated. A study carried out by the Israeli consulting firm Financial Immunities, which spanned the years 2010 through late 2017, found that BDS activities had only a negligible effect on Israel's economy. The chairman of Financial Immunities, Adam Reuter, stated that, "According to our calculations, based on the information we obtained from the companies, the cumulative proportion of economic damage since 2010 was 0.004%. To put it more colorfully, if the Israeli economy's yearly income were to average NIS 1 million, the damage from the sanctions would have been NIS 40—a completely negligible amount."[69]

So, what were Rubio and many Israeli leaders and supporters so worried about?

BDS is a useful boogeyman for the Israeli and American right wings, allowing them to expand their assault on democracy while advancing the narrative that "the whole world is against Israel."[70] Rubio weaponized the BDS debate in an effort to force an internal fight among Democrats, who he knew were split between those who agreed with the Republicans and those who saw it as a violation of free speech. With the House of Representatives under the control of the Democratic Party, House Speaker Nancy Pelosi never brought the companion bill to the floor, as she understood Rubio's strategy. Instead, and in response to newly elected Democratic members of Congress who publicly supported BDS—Rashida Tlaib of Michigan and Ilhan Omar of Minnesota—the House did pass a resolution declaring its opposition to BDS. However, it refrained from any concrete measures that could support either the Senate bill or the state laws.[71]

If BDS has not yet succeeded in bringing economic pressure on Israel, it has succeeded in changing the debate on the entire question of Israel and Palestine. Despite the insistence of many critics that BDS is a push for a single state to replace Israel and the occupied territories, there are many who have supported a two-state solution who also support BDS, especially among those who advocate for having the BDS campaign directly target Israel's settlement enterprise. As Yousef Munayyer, head of the US Campaign for Palestinian Rights wrote, "The truth is that BDS isn't even a movement. Boycotts, Divestment and Sanctions are a set of non-violent tactics which are used in many movements but which Palestinian civil society institutions have asked the international community to adopt as part of a nonviolent movement for Palestinian rights, to send Israel a message that it must stop denying them."[72]

BDS shifted the conversation from a question of states, of territory, and of nationalism, to a question of equal rights. And, ultimately, this is where its power lies. Agree or disagree with the views of BDS as a movement or a tactic, but the right to engage in it is indispensable, and it is completely improper for the U.S. government to try to shut down the effort to boycott, divest from, and press for sanctions against Israel.

The United States and much of the international community insist that violence is not the path to solving this dispute. (For the moment, we will leave aside the vastly unequal representation of Palestinian violence as terrorism and Israeli violence as self-defense). The U.S. has also imposed legal and diplomatic penalties on the Palestinians for going to the International

Criminal Court (ICC), or any other international body, for relief, and even imposed penalties for the Palestinians having joined the United Nations General Assembly.[73] The only route available, then, for Palestinians to seek redress for their situation is the bilateral talks with Israel under U.S. auspices that have failed so dramatically for more than a quarter century. This is an unreasonable demand to place on a people who have been disenfranchised and have lived either in exile or under Israeli occupation for generations.

The House of Representatives' statement opposing BDS, while constitutionally permissible, was morally unacceptable. It is also inappropriate for the U.S. government to make such a statement, which is a transparent effort to discourage the movement among its citizenry, since it is a legal and protected action. Even more problematic is when BDS support is framed, as it has been by Republicans to bring political pressure on Democrats, as a sign of not being "sufficiently pro-Israel."

Even groups that staunchly oppose BDS, like the moderate pro-Israel group J Street, have come to defend the right to engage in BDS.[74] The opponents of BDS, whether they are Israelis like Benjamin Netanyahu and Yair Lapid or Americans like Marco Rubio, demonstrate that they cannot win a battle of ideas when they work so hard to shut down a collective protest action. They are worried that BDS—in concert with the world seeing the horrifying reality of Gaza and the tightening occupation in the West Bank—is raising the most uncomfortable of questions: How can we in the United States and Europe, as well as in much of Israel, comfortably enjoy our liberal privileges and democratic governments, while Palestinians are deprived of the most basic rights?

The decision to support the rights of Palestinians as equal to those of Israelis is not a complicated one. It is not necessary to engage in state-building, as it is in Somalia, or to end a civil war, as in Syria, or even to resolve a regional conflict, as is the case in Yemen. For the Palestinians, Americans and Europeans can support the simple principle of equal rights, a position that will very likely have a real political effect in time. Perhaps that is why BDS evokes such a viscerally defensive response, even from many ostensible progressives. It reminds us all too clearly that the simple support for equal rights—not in the abstract, but as the only route to a political solution in Israel-Palestine— would be easy enough for us, as citizens, to act upon.

We are not suggesting that support of BDS becomes the standard for being a progressive. Many people who support equal rights for Palestinians oppose the BDS movement for strategic, tactical, or other principled reasons. However, those who support (actively or through silent complicity) laws that stigmatize, penalize, or even criminalize BDS are absolutely out of step with liberal and progressive values. While Israel should never be unfairly isolated or targeted, it also cannot be shielded from principled and organized political pressure through boy- cotts, divestments, and sanctions. These tactics have always been critical tools for producing peace, freedom, and justice for the vulnerable. Palestine cannot be an exception.

3

Trumped-Up Policy

June 16, 2019, was a warm and breezy day in the Golan Heights. The weather provided the perfect backdrop for Prime Minister Benjamin Netanyahu, along with U.S. ambassador David Friedman, to unveil a plaque marking the birth of the latest Israeli settlement. While such announcements are always noteworthy, this one was of particular importance. *Ramat Trump*, or "Trump Heights" in English, was established to honor the U.S. president who had broken with the policies of all his predecessors and recognized Israeli sovereignty over territory the country had captured in 1967.

Though no other country recognizes Israel's sovereignty over the Golan Heights, Israel had integrated the territory so effectively that it had long since felt like a part of the country to the Jewish residents of the Golan and, indeed, to most of the country. The 1973 war saw Israel lose some parts of the Golan that it had captured in 1967. In the aftermath, a no man's land was established separating Israeli and Syrian forces. The status quo had been relatively stable.

That stability was upended on March 25, 2019, when

President Trump recognized Israel's sovereignty over the Golan Heights. Trump's proclamation read:

> The State of Israel took control of the Golan Heights in 1967 to safeguard its security from external threats. Today, aggressive acts by Iran and terrorist groups, including Hizballah, in southern Syria continue to make the Golan Heights a potential launching ground for attacks on Israel. Any potential future peace agreement in the region must account for Israel's need to protect itself from Syria and other regional threats. Based on these unique circumstances, it is therefore appropriate to recognize Israeli sovereignty over the Golan Heights.
>
> NOW, THEREFORE, I, DONALD J. TRUMP, President of the United States of America, by virtue of the authority vested in me by the Constitution and the laws of the United States, do hereby proclaim that, the United States recognizes that the Golan Heights are part of the State of Israel.[1]

With his statement, Trump undermined the most fundamental international law, which, as stated in the charter of the United Nations, forbids the acquisition of territory by force.[2] No other country joined the United States in recognizing Israel's sovereignty over the Golan, but U.S. recognition is still significant. Yet this is far from the first time that the United States has directly undermined international law for Israel's benefit. Since 1972, the U.S. has used its veto power at the UN Security Council to shield Israel from forty-four resolutions criticizing its behavior or calling on it to comply with international law and UN resolutions.[3] That is by far the highest total of vetoes of any country over that time span, and it doesn't account for resolutions that countries abandoned or withdrew because of the threat of a U.S. veto. That would be a far greater number.[4]

Trump's habit of ignoring international law when it was inconvenient wasn't unusual for the United States, although the consistent and open hostility toward all international bodies, especially legal ones, was much more pronounced under Trump. In sharp contrast, his immediate predecessor, Barack Obama, favored working within the international system whenever it fit with U.S. priorities and policies, and generally strove to build coalitions and secure international support for U.S. actions. While George W. Bush was less inclined to compromise in order to get international support, neither Republican nor Democratic administrations before Trump ever demonstrated the disdain for any involvement in the international system of diplomacy or collaboration with allies that Trump did.[5]

The recognition of the Golan was a dramatic break with decades of U.S. policy. On several occasions during the administrations of Presidents Bill Clinton and George W. Bush, the United States attempted to broker a deal between Israel and Syria for a comprehensive peace agreement in exchange for Israel returning the Golan to Syria. Although these attempts failed, the U.S. position on the Golan was consistent: it did not recognize Israel's annexation of the territory, but also did not push the Israelis very hard to give it back to Syria. The United States hoped to eventually use the Golan as a bargaining chip to help bring a comprehensive peace to the region. No administration since 1967 had ever seriously considered recognition of Israeli sovereignty over the Golan, outside of an agreement between Syria and Israel.

Hopes for such an agreement had gone into a deep freeze when the Syrian civil war broke out in 2011. Attempts at bringing the two sides together the previous year had broken down after Turkey—which had been acting as a go-between for Israel and Syria—saw its relationship with Israel shattered by the *Mavi Marmara* incident, where Israeli troops boarded a Turkish ship trying to deliver humanitarian supplies to Gaza and killed ten activists.[6] Obama had been focused on trying to salvage the Israel-Palestine peace process during his first term in office, and the outbreak of the Syrian civil war only meant that the question of the Golan was even farther down his list of priorities. This state of affairs persisted past Obama's term in office and made Trump's decision oddly precipitous, as there was absolutely no urgency for that decision to be made when it was. With Syria being torn asunder by a war that had long since attracted many outside actors, exacerbating an already horrifying situation, not even Syrian president Bashar al-Assad was thinking about Israel returning the Golan to Syria. It was, for the foreseeable future, a non-issue.

But like his predecessors, Trump knew that recognizing the Golan as Israeli territory, as with the decision to move the U.S. embassy from Tel Aviv to Jerusalem, was broadly popular among Israelis. Still, in this instance, the fact that giving up the Golan was not on any international agenda lessened the urgency. The Jewish and Christian right wings in the United States also supported Israel keeping the Golan, but the issue was not on the top of their lobbying agenda until a few members of Congress decided to use it to please their ideological-religious bases. Trump expected to win praise with his decision, and indeed he did, with the groundbreaking of the Ramat Trump settlement in June 2019 being the physical manifestation of that praise. But while the move pleased the Israeli government and most Israelis, it accomplished nothing else. The situation on the ground in the Golan was unchanged. Israelis there still had to worry about spillover from the Syrian civil war; on the Syrian side, Druze who were separated from their families since 1967 faced the same issues that they had for decades. The recognition of sovereignty did not improve security conditions for anyone. All it did was give away a potential bargaining chip that future U.S. administrations might have been able to use to leverage an agreement between Syria and Israel when conditions allowed for it. This was a key factor in why no previous president had considered unilateral recognition of Israeli sovereignty over the Golan.

When previous administrations had approached the Golan issue as a potential bargaining chip for a land-for-peace deal, the hope was that such an agreement would mirror the one that Israel struck with Egypt to return the Sinai Peninsula, also captured in 1967, in exchange for a durable peace agreement. Indeed, until 2018, there was virtually no effort to change U.S. policy toward the Golan. That year, Rep. Ron DeSantis, a Republican from Florida, brought forth a bill to encourage the president to recognize Israeli sovereignty over the Golan, but it was swiftly voted down even in the Republican-led body. Later in the year, Republican senators Tom Cotton of Arkansas and Ted Cruz of Texas also failed to pass legislation with the same purpose. But Cotton was a trusted foreign policy adviser for Trump, and his effort undoubtedly had some influence on Trump's later actions.[7]

Many saw the Golan decision as just another example of Trump going his own way, ignoring the old Washington rules and roadmaps. And, certainly, Trump's approach to Israel and Palestine has been quite different in tone from his predecessors. There was none of Barack Obama's rhetorical flourish when he spoke eloquently about the rights and aspirations of Palestinians.[8] There was no support for a Palestinian state, which George W. Bush was the first to proclaim as official United States policy.[9] Instead, there was a relentless series of presidential decisions that pleased Israelis and infuriated Palestinians. While his decision on the Golan did not directly involve the Palestinians per se, as the non-Jewish people of the Golan are Syrian, not Palestinian, the principle of unilateral recognition without any Israeli concessions set a precedent for what may eventually happen on the West Bank.

While many saw the Golan decision as emblematic of a consistent pattern of departing from long-standing policy orthodoxies with regard to Israel and Palestine, Trump's decision regarding the Golan Heights was the exception to his usual pattern, not the norm.

Despite this sharp break with prior policy, the bulk of Trump's actions were consistent with overall U.S. policy in recent decades. Instead of radically altering the status quo, what Trump often did was to merely remove all caution and rush headlong into policy decisions that would bolster Israel's rightwing government. These decisions would also further weaken the already dismally impotent Palestinian bargaining position and torpedo any potential for diplomacy, replacing that possibility with increased pressure on the already oppressed people of the West Bank and Gaza Strip. These were not departures from long-standing U.S. policy, but rather policies that the United States had long pursued, in one way or another—only now they were being executed on steroids.

Two of Trump's most significant policies starkly illustrate this dynamic: moving the U.S. embassy from Tel Aviv to Jerusalem, and cutting aid to the United Nations Relief and Works Agency (UNRWA), which provides crucial food, education, health, and other services to Palestinian refugees in Gaza, the West Bank, Lebanon, Jordan, and Syria. In both cases, unlike the Golan decision, his actions were built on years, even decades, of bipartisan support in Washington. Prior presidents recognized that acting on these policies would severely hamper their ability to work with the Palestinian negotiators, so they used their authority to push the implementation of these policies back—never did they reverse legislation or the policy discourse that called for them.

Moving the U.S. Embassy

In 1967, when Israel captured East Jerusalem, there was a palpable sense that something had shifted. Jerusalem was not just another bit of territory known for its history and religious significance. According to the Bible, King David captured Jerusalem and made it the capital of his kingdom. Later, it was also the home of Solomon's Temple and would go on to be the cultural and commercial center of Palestine for many centuries. It houses the Wailing Wall, the remains of the Second Temple, a uniquely holy site in Judaism that Jews around the world have symbolically turned to for centuries thrice a day to pray. It is the site of the Haram al-Sharif and the Dome of the Rock, and is the place where, as recounted in the Quran, Muhammad ascended to heaven. It holds the Church of the Holy Sepulcher and is the site of much of the narrative of both the Tanakh (sometimes called the Hebrew Bible) and the Gospels. In short, it is a city that, more than any other in the world, holds a massive nationalistic and religious significance for a wide variety of people, religious and secular.

The sensitivity of the issue of Jerusalem was not lost on the United Nations in 1947. Its plan to partition Palestine, enshrined in UN General Assembly Resolution 181, included making Jerusalem a *corpus separatum*, an international entity that would belong neither to the Jewish nor Arab state envisioned by the resolution.[10] When the war that Israel celebrates as its war of independence and Palestinians mourn as the Nakba (which means "catastrophe") ended with an armistice in 1949, Israel held West Jerusalem and Transjordan had East Jerusalem. In 1950, Israel claimed Jerusalem as its capital while Transjordan annexed the eastern part of the city. The international community recognized neither claim, apart from the United Kingdom and Pakistan recognizing Transjordan's annexation of East Jerusalem, and the rest of the West Bank. After Israel captured the eastern part of the city in 1967, it dissolved the boundary between the two parts and extended Israeli law over it, effectively creating one city and de facto annexing the eastern part. In 1980, Israel passed a new Basic Law, whose first clause stated that "Jerusalem, complete and united, is the capital of Israel."[11] Under Israeli law, Jerusalem was now the united capital of the state. But this changed nothing, and Israel's claim remained unrecognized by any other country. The UN Security Council censured Israel over the annexation, declared it null and void, and ordered its reversal, although Israel defied this order.[12] The UN did call for all countries to remove their diplomatic missions to Israel from the city, and until the Trump administration, there were no foreign embassies in Jerusalem.

Over the years, especially after Israel and the Palestinians entered the ill-fated Oslo Accords, an expectation arose that Jerusalem would eventually be either divided between Israel and an imagined Palestinian state or shared between the two. But the official status of Jerusalem did not change. The official U.S. position, like that of the rest of the world, evolved from the internationalization of Jerusalem, leaving its ultimate disposition to negotiations between Israel and the Palestinians.[13] The United States never officially recognized Israeli sovereignty over any part of Jerusalem. The city would remain entirely internationalized so that both Israel and the Palestinians had a stake in good faith negotiations over its final disposition, in a resolution where the city is shared or divided in a manner acceptable to both. In fact, three subsequent Security Council resolutions—one during the administration of

George H.W. Bush, one during Bill Clinton's, and one during Barack Obama's—passed without a United States veto, thus reaffirming U.S. policy.[14]

Despite these developments, the change in policy that seemed to be Trump's doing actually happened incrementally over many years. From the Lyndon B. Johnson administration through that of Jimmy Carter, U.S. policy supported the return of the land Israel had captured in 1967 in exchange for a permanent peace agreement with its neighbors. Indeed, in 1978, the Legal Adviser to the State Department, Herbert J. Hansell, reaffirmed the United States' legal position that all of that territory was held under belligerent occupation, with no exception made for East Jerusalem.[15] Vagaries of day-to-day politics aside, U.S. policy holding that Jerusalem's legal status was unchanged and its permanent status could only be resolved through negotiations based on relevant UN resolutions remained quite steady until 1981.[16] That year, Ronald Reagan, in his eagerness to capitalize on the unprecedented support he had received from the Jewish community in the 1980 election, gave the first hint of a potential shift in U.S. attitudes.

Reagan had stated during the 1980 campaign that Jerusalem should remain under Israeli control. He was the first to campaign with this pledge. It put him in good stead with a Jewish community angry at Jimmy Carter for having pressured Israeli prime minister Menachem Begin during the Camp David negotiations with Egyptian president Anwar Sadat. At a meeting with the Conference of Presidents of Major Jewish Organizations (COPJ) in November 1981, Reagan confirmed that he still held the view he had espoused during the campaign regarding Jerusalem, sending the White House and State Department into a scramble to walk back and redefine Reagan's words. They said his statement did not "represent a change in the United States' policy," and that "American policy toward

Jerusalem is that it should remain undivided, with free access to the holy sites. The future status of Jerusalem is to be determined through negotiations."[17]

But Reagan had already caused concern that he intended to fundamentally alter U.S. policy toward Israel's occupation. On February 2, 1981, Reagan had told a group of reporters, "As to the West Bank, I believe the settlements there—I disagreed when the previous Administration referred to them as illegal, they're not illegal. Not under the U.N. resolution that leaves the West Bank open to all people—Arab and Israeli alike, Christian alike." The question he was responding to did not refer to the illegality of settlements, but simply asked about Israel's apparent acceleration in settlement construction.[18] This statement, unlike his later one, was not walked back, despite the clear implication that the president was unfamiliar with the basis of the settlements' illegality.[19] The question of where the United States stood regarding policy on Israel's occupation of the West Bank, including East Jerusalem, was thrown into flux under Reagan for the first time since the end of the 1967 war. Although no formal change in policy was evident, the question was opened and was now fair game. Reagan's successor, George H.W. Bush, did not take steps to move the needle on Jerusalem policy, but the next president, Bill Clinton, did. In fact, the liberal Democrat campaigned on just such a promise.

A 2017 report in the Israeli daily *Haaretz* relayed the recollection of Martin Indyk, who served as Clinton's ambassador to Israel from 1995 to 1997: "Bill Clinton declared in February 1992, at the height of the Democratic primaries, that he supported recognizing Jerusalem as Israel's capital, a step that would alter U.S. policy. Later, during the general election campaign, Clinton attacked President George H.W. Bush for having 'repeatedly challenged Israel's sovereignty over a united Jerusalem.' He promised that he and running mate Al Gore would 'support Jerusalem as the capital of the State of Israel.'"[20] Once in office, however, he did not act on this promise. Clinton later said he was considering moving the embassy to Jerusalem, effectively recognizing the city as Israel's capital, as he was leaving office in 2000, but did not do so.[21]

Clinton's words on the campaign trail, however, left a lasting imprint on U.S. policy, establishing not only that Jerusalem was fair game for political theater, but also that Republicans like Reagan did not have a monopoly on one-sided pro-Israel policy. Clinton also shifted policy by separating Jerusalem from the rest of the West Bank. As historian Charles D. Smith explains, "Whereas former U.S. administrations had characterized 'East Jerusalem' as part of the occupied territories, meaning that it was considered West Bank land subject to negotiation, Clinton started calling it 'disputed territory' even before the 1993 (Oslo) accord, the status of which would be resolved in final talks. Administration spokespersons argued that extension of Israeli settlements around Jerusalem, which now included significant portions of the West Bank, did not violate American criteria for loans. . . . Jerusalem's status had been deferred to permanent status talks."[22]

But the most lasting impact of the Clinton years came not from the president but from Congress. On October 23, 1995, Congress passed the Jerusalem Embassy Act, which required the United States to move its embassy from Tel Aviv to Jerusalem by May 31, 1999. Clinton did not sign the bill into law, but did not veto it either. As a result, it became law on November 8, 1995, without a presidential signature. The act included a presidential waiver, allowing the president to delay the move for six months if he could report to Congress that vital American interests were at stake in doing so. The waiver was renewable, and every president renewed it until 2018.[23]

As former adviser to the Israeli government Daniel Levy explained, the Republican Congress, which had swept into office in 1994, pushed the initiative to harm Clinton and Israeli prime minister Yitzhak Rabin:

> At a particularly sensitive moment in the peace negotiations and with the 1996 presidential and congressional elections approaching, a number of AIPAC [American Israel Public Affairs Committee] and Republican leaders moved to throw a wrench in the works—the Jerusalem Embassy Act of 1995. The act required the U.S. Embassy in Israel to move from Tel Aviv to Jerusalem in a given time frame. It inflamed Arab opinion and cornered both the Clinton and Rabin governments. . . . Israel cannot publicly oppose it but has never prioritized it. Republican presidential candidate Bob Dole announced the initiative at the 1995 AIPAC Annual Conference. The Likud cheered, using it to attack Rabin precisely as the incitement that ultimately led to his assassination was reaching its peak. Itamar Rabinovich, then the Israeli ambassador in Washington, has called it the "The Jerusalem Hijack," writing about "how embarrassing it was."[24]

Despite the discomfort that the act caused Democrats, the bill passed both houses of Congress with huge bipartisan majorities. In the Senate, the vote was 93–5, while in the House, the bill passed by a tally of 374–37.[25] Much of this bipartisanship was simply due to the fact that many Democrats, knowing the act was going to pass, went along with it rather than risk being unfairly portrayed as anti-Israel in the next election. But, as Itamar Rabinovich pointed out, this was not the only reason:

The Republican Party invested an open effort in winning a considerable slice of the Jewish vote (beyond the 18 percent it won in 1992) and the aspiring presidential candidate, Bob Dole, was also courting Jewish backers and voters. [Speaker of the House, Newt] Gingrich and the conservative Republicans in Congress were among the supporters of Israel for both ideological and political reasons, but in (conscious) contrast to the Clinton-Rabin axis, Gingrich was linked to the Jewish and Israeli right. However, the importance of the American party political split on this issue should not be exaggerated, as the Democratic senator from New York, Patrick Daniel Moynihan [sic], played a key role in initiating the 1995 legislation, as he had done a decade earlier without success.[26]

The presidential waiver included in the Jerusalem Embassy Act seemed also to be a sufficient safeguard for many against turning what was an obvious political stunt at the time—and one aimed at harming the burgeoning peace process in which Rabin and Clinton were invested—into a diplomatic bomb. Obviously, Clinton would use the waiver and, public pronouncements to the contrary notwithstanding, there was reason to believe that Dole would have done so as well were he to win the election in 1996. Even George W. Bush, who was very close to the Israeli right and whose administration was heavily influenced by neoconservative figures who were closely allied with Likud leader Benjamin Netanyahu and his highly ideological approach to diplomacy, deployed the waiver consistently.[27] Despite fiery rhetoric about Jerusalem being the "eternal and undivided capital of Israel," it was understood across party lines and ideological borders that recognition of Jerusalem as Israel's capital outside of a permanent peace agreement was extremely unwise.

The bipartisan consensus on Israel has been a force for a very long time, but that consensus is not always absolute. As noted, Clinton criticized George H.W. Bush's policy toward Israel, and specifically Bush's failure to recognize Jerusalem as Israel's capital, during his campaign. But once he was in office, Clinton maintained the bipartisan consensus, which strongly supported Israel but also supported maintaining the international consensus on Jerusalem. Whatever the intentions of those who pushed the Jerusalem Embassy Act of 1995, even most of Congress saw it more as political theater than an action that would produce change on the ground in Jerusalem.

The younger Bush, George W., also pledged to move the embassy during his campaign, telling an audience at the annual AIPAC policy conference in May 2000 that "as soon as I take office I will begin the process of moving the U.S. ambassador to the city Israel has chosen as its capital."[28] But as soon as he took office, Bush made it clear that he was not moving the embassy any time soon.[29] Even Barack Obama touched on the issue, and while he did not promise to move the embassy, he did take a stand that was different from long-held U.S. policy, telling the AIPAC conference in 2008, "Jerusalem will remain the capital of Israel, and it must remain undivided."[30]

When Trump announced the recognition of Jerusalem as Israel's capital and, later, allowed the waiver to expire, he was not so much departing from long-standing U.S. policy as he was disregarding good sense in the execution of that policy. He first announced the recognition and the move of the embassy on December 6, 2017, but he signed the waiver again just hours later, allowing for a delay in the move for at least another six months.[31] That meant the embassy would be opened in Jerusalem on the seventieth anniversary of Israel's independence, "Nakba Day" for the Palestinians. In fact, the opening ceremony was held the day before, on May 14, and was marred by enormous violence and protests. At least 60 Palestinians were killed and over 2,700 wounded.[32]

The Palestinian Authority declared that the United States could no longer function as a mediator of the conflict, and diplomacy, already barely existent, went completely dark.[33] The Arab League condemned the move, the European Union called on all countries to keep their embassies out of Jerusalem, and numerous militant groups called for acts of violence, mostly aimed at Israel.[34] The United States vetoed an otherwise unanimous resolution at the UN Security Council condemning the move and calling for its reversal.[35] The General Assembly easily passed a motion condemning the U.S. decision. Not one of America's NATO allies voted against the resolution, which passed by a vote of 128–9.[36]

Trump treated the sensitive issue of Jerusalem with all the care of a bull in a china shop. While the consequences were not as dire as some had feared in the near term, this was seen by some as fool's gold. Just before Trump's announcement in December 2017, Mitchell Plitnick observed:

> If the immediate reaction is no big deal, that leads to much greater problems for the Palestinians. . . . [T]here's also a distinct possibility that after a week or two of protests, and even some violence, by the beginning of 2018, US recognition of Jerusalem as Israel's capital has become the new normal. If it does turn out that way, the Palestinians . . . will have been told that all the norms on which they have based their commitment to negotiations are nothing but smoke. They will have been told that the United States is their enemy. . . . They will have been told that the international community is either unable or unwilling to do anything to materially assist them when

the chips are down. They will have been told that their only hope is to create such pain for Israelis and unrest throughout the region that their needs will have to be addressed.

In short, the United States will have sent the message that Hamas and other armed groups have been right all along about the need to rely on armed struggle. If anything, the message would be that such efforts need to be dramatically increased. That's not the only message the Trump declaration would send. It would also tell Israel, in no uncertain terms, that its view that its national and territorial desires completely trump Palestinian rights is correct.[37]

Yet for all that, Trump's actions did not amount to overturning U.S. policy. He acted to fulfill legislation that had already been enshrined in law with enormous bipartisan support. He also capitalized on the actions of successive U.S. presidents to chip away at U.S. policy that held Jerusalem as an international city until its final disposition is settled in a hypothetical peace agreement. Qualifying his stance a bit, Trump stressed that he was still committed to the status quo regarding the holy sites in the city,[38] and that the United States was "not taking a position of any final status issues including the specific boundaries of the Israeli sovereignty in Jerusalem or the resolution of contested borders. Those questions are up to the parties involved."[39]

Of course, in practical terms, even with these qualifications, Trump had substantially changed things. He made no secret of this, proclaiming he "took Jerusalem off the table."[40] While that may have been one of his typical overstatements, Trump did dramatically shift the diplomatic playing field regarding

Jerusalem. Yet again, he was not breaking new ground, but simply accelerating a project that long preceded him. George W. Bush, in his 2004 letter to Ariel Sharon, stated that the United States expected that final borders between Israel and a hoped-for Palestinian state would be drawn in light "of new realities on the ground, including already existing major Israeli populations [sic] centers," which meant that the U.S. was backing the permanent existence of at least some Israeli settlements. Bush also promised that there would be no return of Palestinian refugees to Israel.[41]

Both of these points were—like Israel's capital being eventually recognized as the western part of Jerusalem—widely understood as being the U.S. view of what the final agreement would look like, and tacitly agreed upon by much of the international community. But, by stating these positions outright, the United States, in its role as mediator between Israel and the Palestinians, took away chips from the Palestinians that they could have used to try to press for concessions from Israel. Given the overwhelming advantages Israel has in negotiations already, when Bush, and later Trump, unilaterally declared a vision that simply gave Israel at least some of what it wanted with no balancing concession to the Palestinians, it left the Palestinians in an even weaker and more desperate position than before.

Trump's decision to move the U.S. embassy from Tel Aviv to Jerusalem was reckless and ill-considered, and he made it with no strategic goal in mind. Ironically, if Trump was seeking to ingratiate himself with American Jews, the move was less than successful as opinion about the move in that group split evenly, 46 percent in favor, 47 percent opposed, and Trump remained unpopular among the bulk of the American Jewish community.[42] It was simply Trump applying his own style to U.S. policy as it was handed down to him, no less than Barack Obama had applied his more diplomatic and realist approach to preexisting foreign policy, or George W. Bush applying his neoconservative-style, interventionist, democracy-promotion ideology.

Trump's actions look like more of a departure because his predecessors, however bold or conservative they might have been, based their tactics on the political and diplomatic conditions they found themselves in. By contrast, Trump was heavily influenced by the views of his closest advisers, all of whom were closely aligned with the far right in Israel and were part of the related segment of the American Jewish community.[43] He took a fused approach in which he both drew on that influence and characteristically acted on his own impulses. That is the Trump trademark, and it colored how he approached a U.S. policy that was shaped by presidents and Congresses decades before him. Rather than change the policy, he threw all caution to the wind and acted on it.

Cutting Off Aid to UNRWA

On August 31, 2018, the Trump administration announced it would be discontinuing all financial support to UNRWA. The United States had been, by far, the biggest donor to UNRWA, contributing about one-third of the agency's annual budget. The loss of those funds was crippling, even though some other countries did step up to make up for some of the loss in U.S. support.

UNRWA was created in 1949 to serve the specific needs of refugees resulting from the 1948 war. It was a frequent target for criticism from many quarters, but Israel, for all its bluster, had a long-term policy of supporting UNRWA's existence. After Israel captured the West Bank and Gaza, where a large percentage of refugees from both the 1948 and then the 1967 wars were situated, an exchange of letters between an Israeli official and the commissioner-general of UNRWA confirmed Israel's agreement that UNRWA should continue to operate in the newly occupied territories.[44] That policy, not coincidentally, held until it was suddenly abandoned just as Trump was deciding to eliminate U.S. funding of UNRWA.[45] It held through years where Israeli leaders and members of Congress were consistently attacking UNRWA.[46] Yet Israel was also concerned about defunding UNRWA, fearing that would mean having to assume responsibility for the refugees, particularly in Gaza, or face a humanitarian crisis that could turn world opinion sharply against the country.[47]

Trump's decision to defund UNRWA followed a shift in Benjamin Netanyahu's own position on the UN aid agency. Although Netanyahu had consistently criticized UNRWA, often harshly, for many years, he was much less consistent about calling for its demise. In June of 2017, he called for the disbanding of UNRWA, saying "I regret that UNRWA, to a large degree, by its very existence, perpetuates—and does not solve—the Palestinian refugee problem. Therefore, the time has come to disband UNRWA and integrate it into the UNHCR."[48] Netanyahu's last point—that UNRWA should be folded into the UN High Commission for Refugees (UNHCR)—is notable. UNHCR has a specific mandate to integrate refugees into host countries where possible, something UNRWA is not mandated to do because substantial portions of both the Palestinian refugees and the neighboring countries passionately oppose it.[49] This is a major point of contention for supporters of Israel who are frustrated by the fact that, as they see it, Palestinian refugees are treated differently from other refugees. Many use this as an example of Israel being treated differently than all other countries and even as evidence of anti-Semitic motivation to undermine Israel's very existence.[50]

But Netanyahu reversed his position in January 2018 and reverted to Israel's traditional position of disgruntled tolerance of UNRWA.[51] This brought him back in line with the Israeli security establishment, which opposed cutting funds to UNRWA.[52] But as time went on, Netanyahu changed his mind again. By March 2018, it was becoming clear that there was some intention to change the status quo on UNRWA, and Netanyahu was seeking alternatives. He brought up not only the idea of folding UNRWA into UNHCR, but also that the Jordanian government, which is home to some three million Palestinian refugees, get direct funding to support the refugees.[53]

By the end of the summer of 2018, Netanyahu supported eliminating funding for UNRWA. Some reports had him pressing Trump to do it,[54] others portrayed it as Israeli support for a Trump administration decision.[55] In either case, it was clear that Netanyahu had made the decision with little if any regard for the views of his security advisers.

Trump's strong inclination toward Netanyahu's policies over those of the Israeli defense and intelligence brain trust stood in sharp contrast with Barack Obama's preference for the latter's approach, a view that often put him at odds with Netanyahu. This was clearly exemplified by the Iran nuclear deal, which was supported by many in the Israeli defense establishment, and continued to be supported even after Trump decided to unilaterally withdraw from the deal.[56] Consistent with Trump's pattern from his very first day in office, he was working to reverse all that he could of Obama's policies. When he defunded UNRWA, Trump echoed another pattern—that of attempting to unilaterally alter the terms of the diplomatic debate. As with Jerusalem, Trump's move to defund UNRWA was aimed at taking the issue of Palestinian refugees off the diplomatic table, again mimicking the efforts of George W. Bush and his 2004 letter to Ariel Sharon. In this case, the *Washington Post* reported, "[T]he White House is seeking to take the right of return off the table, as Trump has said he eliminated the future of the contested city of Jerusalem from negotiations late last year when he recognized it as the capital of Israel."[57] Trump and his team believed that by crippling UNRWA, they could eliminate it, and that move would, in turn, redefine Palestinian refugees according to the terms the United States and Israel preferred. Specifically, the definition that UNRWA works under, whereby the descendants of refugees are also granted refugee status until the people are repatriated or resettled elsewhere, would become moot and only those made refugees directly by war would be counted. Under that definition, the refugee population is far smaller than the more than five million refugees who are currently registered with UNRWA. By the end of 1951, UNRWA had some 860,000 confirmed and registered Palestinian refugees, most of whom would have passed away by now. Even adding the surviving refugees created in 1967, the number would be exceedingly small compared with the number currently granted refugee status.[58]

Beyond the massive ethical questions that such an action raises, the basic assumptions are terribly flawed. As former State Department official Hady Amr explained:

> Underlying the Trump administration's cuts to UNRWA is the false premise that Palestinian refugees derive their refugee status from UNRWA. They don't. They derive it from international law. UNRWA's role is simply to provide social services to these stateless refugees—not determine who is and who isn't a refugee under international law.
>
> Also underlying Trump's attack on UNRWA is the false premise that other refugee populations don't transfer their refugee status to their children. Wrong again. International law conveys refugee status to children of

other refugee populations until permanent homes can be found. People from Afghanistan, Bhutan, Burma, and Somalia are but a number of the populations where refugee status has been conveyed to descendants.[59]

As we noted, UNRWA differs from UNHCR in that UNRWA was initially created without a mandate for resettlement, although its mandate has been expanded in some cases to allow it to make such efforts. Still, UNRWA's primary job is to provide basic services to the Palestinian refugees in the territories in which the agency works, not to resettle the refugees. It is also not UNRWA's role to establish or enforce a legal definition of Palestinian refugees. As Amr pointed out, that is defined by international law. UNRWA has developed a working definition of Palestinian refugees to facilitate its own functioning and to properly allocate its scarce resources.[60] But this is not a legally binding definition. The real point of contention, of course, is the transference of refugee status across the generations.

The legal and political arguments notwithstanding, it is crucial to examine the ethical dimensions of pulling U.S. support from UNRWA, or tying support to a discriminatory definition of refugee status. In general, laws and practices governing the treatment of refugees assume that refugee status is temporary, and of a relatively short duration. UNHCR defines a protracted refugee situation as one in which "a refugee population of 25,000 persons or more . . . have been living in exile for five years or longer."[61] The Palestinian refugee crisis is, by this definition, simply off the scale. Indeed, one thing both advocates for the Israeli position and those for the Palestinian position agree on is the unusual nature of this refugee issue, and both argue it causes an intolerable burden on their side.

Israelis are frustrated that resettlement of Palestinian

refugees has not been seriously pursued in the over seven decades of this crisis. One reason for that lack of pursuit is that Palestinians are not seeking resettlement, but repatriation to the land that was taken from their families in 1948 and 1967. Even Palestinians who have established secure lives for themselves in other countries can be, and often are, barred from visiting Israel and the West Bank and Gaza and generally have no hope of moving back to the land of their ancestors. This certainly contributes to the reluctance of refugees still living in camps to accept resettlement, although it is not the biggest reason for it.

On the other side, Palestinians reasonably argue that if the right of return cannot be passed down the generations, then a statute of limitations on driving all or most of a population from their homeland is de facto in place. In this specific instance, all Israel ever had to do was wait out the Palestinians, which by now, they would, under those rules, have successfully done. This hardly seems like an action we would want the law to sanction. And, in fact, it does not. According to former UNRWA spokesperson Chris Gunness, "The UNHCR Global Appeal for 2010 and 2011, Finding Durable Solutions estimated that about 1.2 million UNHCR refugees would return to their homes, during that period. These figures attest to the fact that voluntary repatriation is the 'preferred choice' for refugees."[62] But this is an option that Israel will not consider. Nor will Lebanon or Syria consider citizenship for Palestinian refugees. (These are two countries for whom demography is vital to the government's stability—or was, in the case of Syria, which is obviously in no position to resettle refugees after its civil war.) Jordan has already granted citizenship to most of the Palestinian refugees there, but the resource-poor country has a tough time in accommodating its current population, so 18 percent of the refugees there still live in refugee camps.[63]

In Trump's thinking, and in that of many who make the arguments against UNRWA, it is simply a matter of deciding who is or is not a refugee. If you are not, you no longer have a claim against Israel. As ethically troubling as the idea is of a statute of limitations on the need to address the loss of home and sustenance of refugees, the idea that a simple reclassification can leave no recourse to a person, or a family that is stateless and dispossessed, is much worse. Giving such a course of action a legal imprimatur would have to be challenged. Fortunately, this is not what the law says. As Amr pointed out, the Palestinian claim to the right of return is not based on the UNRWA definition, nor on that of the UNHCR.[64] Rather, it is based on several sources in international law. First of these is Article 13(2) of the Universal Declaration of Human Rights, which states, "Everyone has the right to leave any country, including his own, and to return to his country." This principle was strengthened for Palestinians specifically by UN General Assembly Resolution 194, which stated that "the refugees wishing to return to their homes and live at peace with their neighbors should be permitted to do so at the earliest practicable date, and that compensation should be paid for the property of those choosing not to return and for loss of or damage to property which, under principles of international law or in equity, should be made good by the Governments or authorities responsible."[65]

Nonetheless, Trump's effort to invalidate the status of millions of Palestinian refugees does not mark a sharp break with U.S. policy. On the surface, it may appear that this moves the United States out of a place of ambiguity and into a position unabashedly supportive of a hard-line Israeli view of the refugee issue. In fact, it is very much in line with how the U.S. has treated the refugee issue for many years.

Israel's position has been consistent from the start: the

plight of Palestinian refugees must be resolved in the context of a broader peace deal, and primarily through resettlement and compensation. In fact, the Israeli diplomat Abba Eban presented the Israeli case way back in 1949 and made it plain that this was the Israeli position; it is one that the United States had supported since at least the Lyndon Johnson administration, and refused to take any action in opposition to it from the very first UN meeting involving Israel.[66]

The 2004 letter from Bush to Sharon only clarified that the United States had no expectation that Israel would allow any return of refugees within Israel's internationally recognized borders. Trump had, in terms of broad policy, done no more than take Bush's policy to its logical conclusion. Yes, he did it in a way that was heartless and reckless, but is it any more so than the way successive U.S. administrations have allowed Palestinian refugees to live in squalor in order to accommodate Israel's perceived security, or its political needs of the moment?

Continuation, Not Deviation

Donald Trump has been, without question, an anomalous figure in many ways as a U.S. president. He possesses a dangerous combination of ignorance of the issues he was faced with and complete indifference to that ignorance. This combination allowed him to dispense with the cautionary considerations that led other presidents to reject certain actions. Trump rarely seemed to take action according to a plan of any kind, but rather on the basis of what would win him approval in the moment. Trump's policies have been an exercise in self-gratification by playing with human lives.

Trump's anomalous behavior makes it all too easy to also consider his policies anomalous. But as we have outlined, his approach to Israel and the Palestinians has more in common with long-standing U.S. policy than appearances suggest. George W. Bush's actions in 2004 raised alarm bells for some, but almost all observers understood that he really wasn't breaking new ground, just ending the theater and, as a result, reducing even further the small amount of negotiating leverage the Palestinians had. Anyone who was in any way involved in the "peace process" knew that the U.S. approach was to try to minimize the number of Israeli settlers that would be moved, come to an accommodation on Jerusalem, and find a formula to settle the refugee issue in a manner that, first and foremost, protected the existence of an overwhelming Jewish majority in Israel. Bush's letter, foolhardy though it might have been, didn't change that.

Trump's actions did not change these matters either. His move of the embassy to Jerusalem takes away a Palestinian negotiating chip, but the options for sharing or dividing Jerusalem remain open. No one accepts the attempt to redefine who is or is not a Palestinian refugee except the United States and Israel. All Trump has done is make the issue of Jerusalem more intractable and explosive, and greatly increase the suffering of Palestinian refugees and the burden those refugees place on the countries, most of whom are U.S. allies, that must now enhance their support. These actions will have lasting results. Trump's successors will find a more difficult playing field than ever, and, given the trenchant politics in Washington around this issue, it will not be easy for them to reverse what Trump has done. But these are the results of his tactics, not actual shifts in policy.

Recognition of the Golan Heights as Israeli sovereign territory was the exception that proves the rule. The Syrian civil war did mean there was no pressure on Israel—not from the United States, Europe, the United Nations, or even the Arab states—to return the Golan to Syria, nor would there be any in the foreseeable future. That made Trump's decision unnecessary, but it also made it far less impactful than it would have been in previous years. Syria obviously had other concerns and could not afford to expend the diplomatic energy to engage in sustained action over Trump's decision on the world stage, much less take any sort of military action against Israel in response.

This move did shut the door on long-standing U.S. policy supporting the return of the Golan for peace between Israel and Syria. It also marked a profound shift in how the United States views the territories captured by Israel in 1967. The argument that the West Bank and Gaza, the Palestinian territories occupied in 1967, were not really occupied because they were not legitimately the sovereign lands of Jordan and Egypt, always held significant sway in the United States. The corollary, that the Golan Heights and the Sinai, which were indisputably Syrian and Egyptian territory, should be returned in exchange for peace was solid U.S. policy until Trump. Trump's recognition of Israel's claim to the Golan overturned that, with profound implications for the international standard that considers acquisition of land by force to be anathema.

But the Jerusalem and UNRWA actions are more emblematic of what Trump has done, which is not to write a whole new act in the play that is the U.S. role in the Israeli-Palestinian conflict, but to strip the mask off the United States. These actions made it clear precisely why it is so problematic to have the same country that strongly identifies as Israel's closest ally and benefactor be the sole legitimate mediator between Israel and the Palestinians. For many years, Yasser Arafat and then Mahmoud Abbas gambled on the hope that the close relationship between Israel and the United States meant that America could convince Israel to compromise. They lost that bet, and Trump made that abundantly clear not by changing U.S. policy, but by shifting it into overdrive for all the world to see.

In addition to the policies explored in this chapter, other developments during the Trump administration are similarly built upon years of bipartisan U.S. policy and rhetoric. These included repeated cuts in aid to the Palestinian Authority, the closure of the Palestine Liberation Organization offices in Washington, a specific declaration by the State Department that settlements were legal, and the passage of a law forbidding aid until the Palestinians ended a fund that paid families of Palestinians imprisoned for acts of resistance, including violent ones, against Israel.[67] None of these ideas originated with Trump or his administration. Trump's decisions merely did away with even the flimsy pretense of American even-handedness.

For self-identified progressives, it is tempting to frame President Trump as a deviation from the political status quo. With regard to the Middle East, such a framing allows us to remain unaccountable for decades of giving left-wing support for—or at best tepid opposition to—policies that have undermined the possibility of freedom, dignity, safety, and self-determination for the Palestinian people. By painting Trump as an exceptional figure, political solutions are understood to begin and end with his administration, rather than as a commitment to resolving some of our most entrenched and dangerous progressive contradictions. To truly produce justice in the region, progressives must absolutely challenge Donald Trump's policies. But we must also acknowledge that Trump was merely a dangerous extension, not the source, of deeply rooted and thoroughly bipartisan policies that have harmed the Palestinian people—and positioned Palestine as an exception to which core liberal American values are not applied.

4

The Crisis in Gaza

On September 4, 1992, Yitzhak Rabin was in an especially candid mood. While speaking to a delegation from the Washington Institute for Near East Policy, a center-right, pro-Israel think tank, the Israeli prime minister showed none of the diplomatic finesse for which Western nations often applauded him. When the subject turned to Gaza, Rabin bluntly stated that he wished "Gaza would sink into the sea." He continued: "But since that is not going to happen a solution must be found to the problem of the Gaza Strip."[1]

As expected, Rabin's remark offended many. For example, Palestinian spokeswoman Hanan Ashrawi characterized the comment as "racist and indicative of a very alarming mind-set inconsistent with the peace process."[2] But perhaps the most insightful response came from the late Palestinian intellectual Edward Said. Paraphrasing Rabin's words, Said situated the comment within a broader political context: *"I wish Gaza would sink into the sea. It's such a millstone around our necks. It's overpopulated, a million people living under the most miserable conditions. Why should we be responsible? We'll keep the best land and we'll give Gaza to the Palestinians.* That's the basis of Oslo."[3]

Said's analysis, while sharp, is not entirely accurate. The inference that no one wants Gaza is not true. The Palestinians of Gaza don't just want their freedom; many want their freedom *in Gaza*, a place that is as much their homeland as any other part of Palestine. Scholar Helga Tawil-Souri wrote, "Gaza may force us to glimpse into the heart of darkness, but it equally reveals the heart of humanity that never gives up. Gaza is not a footnote, it is the larger than life shadow of the colonizer's fear: a people that cannot be quelled. . . . Gaza is larger than life: captivating, awesome, mythical, mesmerizing, extraordinary, impressive, monumental, unreal, burdensome, miraculous, and most of all, durable. Gaza is our obligation."[4]

If Rabin's words illustrated Israel's approach to Gaza, and Tawil-Souri casts a bright light on the Palestinian attachment to it, indifference has long characterized the view of mainstream Americans to conditions in the Strip. As journalist and pundit Mehdi Hasan observed, "[A] proud supporter of liberal interventionism will back interventions almost everywhere except the Occupied Territories. Their heart bleeds for Syrians, Libyans, Afghans, Iraqis, Rwandans, Kosovars . . . but not for Palestinians."[5] Hasan was reacting to Israel's action at a protest in Gaza on March 30, 2018, the beginnings of what was called the "Great March of Return," where Israel shot 773 people, leading to 17 fatalities.[6] He wanted to know why Democrats in Congress like Nancy Pelosi and Chuck Schumer, and former U.S. diplomats such as Samantha Power and Madeleine Albright, were silent about Israel's overwhelming and unwarranted use of firepower in the incident. He added, "Where are the righteously angry op-eds from Nicholas Kristof of the *New York Times*, or Richard Cohen of the *Washington Post*, or David

Aaronovitch of the *Times of London*, demanding concrete action against the human rights abusers of the IDF?"[7]

The silence of progressives was not absolute. In the course of the 2020 election campaign, both Senator Bernie Sanders and Senator Elizabeth Warren were mildly critical of Israel's policies toward Gaza, and toward Palestinians in general, distinguishing themselves from the overall silence of their Democratic competitors.[8] Still, the intensity of the criticism matched neither the conditions in Gaza, nor the level of American responsibility for those conditions.

Since the 1967 war, Gaza has been the hardest hit of any Palestinian territory. Egypt and Israel have maintained a blockade on the Strip, devastating an already distressed economy for nearly two decades. At the same time, periodic Israeli attacks have decimated Gaza's poor and fragile infrastructure. With only 4 percent potable water, electricity access that is limited to four hours per day, 50 percent unemployment, and the looming threat of Israeli bombs, Gaza constitutes one of the most pressing humanitarian crises in the world.

The conditions in Gaza are not happenstance, nor are they natural. Years of deprivation, limited or no access to export routes, and decades of conflict have exacerbated problems in Gaza and limited the ability of its population to take advantage of the resources it does offer. Outside forces, including the United States, have played a major role in creating Gaza's tribulations. Yet the American public hears little in the U.S. about alleviating these hardships. The relative silence from many on the right is not surprising. Their lack of desire to engage Gaza is driven by both pro-Israeli political commitments and isolationist ideologies. But many of the same liberals and progressives who routinely express outrage at global humanitarian crises and support interventions throughout the Global South, and more specifically the Middle East, do not extend the same political rationale, commitment, or sympathy toward Gaza.

How has Gaza become exceptional?

Shaping Modern Gaza

After the 1948 Arab-Israeli War ended, the armistice between Israel and Egypt specified where Israel's borders ended and the Egyptian-occupied Gaza Strip began. But whereas Israel immediately exercised sovereignty over all the land it controlled when the fighting ended in 1949, and Transjordan moved to annex the West Bank, Egypt had no such desire for Gaza.

Gaza was already becoming a focal point of Palestinian anger and protest. Some 200,000–250,000 refugees from the 1948 war had ended up in the small area, which had lost much of its most fertile agricultural land to Israel.[9] Freedom of movement into both Israel and Egypt was denied, and attempts to cross the border were very dangerous. Palestinians who were caught on the wrong side were often killed on sight. Unsurprisingly, Gaza became a central site of activism, and would remain so until the present day. Although the resistance that emanated from the Strip was meager at best, it did escalate.

Gaza remained largely stagnant under President Gamal Abdel Nasser's rule. Although Egypt did engage in some attempts at development in Gaza during the decade between Israel's withdrawal after the Sinai War of 1956 and its recapture of Gaza in June 1967, these efforts failed to establish a self-sufficient economy.[10] When Israel took Gaza in 1967, it inherited a territory that was already crowded and economically troubled. Gaza had spent the previous two decades becoming radicalized under authoritarian rule. Under Egyptian auspices, the "All-Palestine Government" was set up in Gaza in 1948, but it had very little authority, and was completely ineffectual long before being officially disbanded in 1959. Still, it meant that Palestinians tasted some very small degree of autonomy and self-determination, however fleeting and partial.[11] Over the years prior to Oslo, Gaza underwent what political economist Sara Roy refers to as "de-development," which she defines as a three-pronged process. The first prong is expropriation and dispossession, chiefly manifesting in the land and water resources Israel took for itself and its settlements, diminishing Gaza's capacity for economic change. The second, integration and externalization, is evident in Gaza's dependence on Israel through the incorporation of its limited economy into Israel's, and externalizing that economy toward Israel by shifting a significant part of the labor force away from agriculture in Gaza toward labor in Israel. The strain is compounded by redirecting much of Gaza's exports to Israel. The final process at play is deinstitutionalization—the undermining or restriction by regulation of Gaza's indigenous civil society and popular organizations.[12]

Egypt had stifled Gaza's growth by isolating it. When Israel took it over, its leadership was intent on ensuring that the country's grip on the small territory was secure. As Roy describes it, "The economic de-development of Gaza was neither planned nor accidental; rather, it was the outcome of official Israeli policies designed to secure military, political, and economic control over Gaza and the West Bank, and to protect Israel's national interests."[13]

For the first twenty-five years of the occupation, Gaza, like the West Bank, was open to Israelis. Palestinians could likewise cross into Israel, for work, commerce, or even social occasions, though they might face harassment or arrest by the military or police. Israel's initial plans for solidifying control over Gaza and the Palestinian population were executed through a combination of reducing the population—some

75,000 Gazans were expelled after the 1967 war; the return of 25–30,000 others was blocked and others were encouraged to relocate to the West Bank—and stimulating the economy. While harsh measures succeeded in pressing some people to leave Gaza, the basic conditions there stymied efforts at even marginal economic improvements.[14]

Additionally, between 1970 and 2001, Israel established twenty-one Jewish-only settlements in the Strip. This not only greatly aggravated the political situation, but also placed pressure on the available land and water resources, which the settlements, whose population never rose above some eight thousand Israeli Jews, used in quantities vastly disproportionate to their demographic representation.[15] This was a predictable effect of an occupying power settling its citizens in a territory that it controlled through military rule—and in the midst of some 1.1 million Palestinians.[16] It could be similarly anticipated that people living under such conditions would resist occupation, producing tension that would become more pronounced over time.

The Oslo Era

Gaza remained the same for the first quarter century of Israeli occupation, a concentrated microcosm of the post-1967 occupation, with overpopulation and underemployment becoming ever more pronounced. As we discussed in chapter 2, the entire question of Palestine and Israel underwent a radical shift in 1993 as Israel and the PLO consummated the Oslo Accords. The initial framework led to the first major part of the Accords: the Gaza-Jericho Agreement. This agreement granted limited autonomy to the Palestinians in the ancient West Bank city of Jericho and those areas of the Gaza Strip not occupied by Israeli settlements. In Gaza, around one-third of the land housed some six thousand Jewish settlers, several military bases, and a network of roads designed so that settlers avoided contact with the Palestinian residents. The remaining two-thirds of the territory, cut into cantons, was left to 1.1 million Palestinians, which translated to a population density of about 128 Israelis per square mile, compared with 11,702 Palestinians per square mile. The double standard, overcrowding for Palestinians, economic disparity, and resulting resentment and anger were entirely foreseeable.[17]

On December 8, 1987, an Israeli transport crashed into several Palestinian cars in Gaza, killing four. It was the spark that set off the First Intifada, and it spread quickly to the West Bank. That it started in Gaza was no surprise. Opposition to Israeli policies and material resistance were stronger in Gaza, where conditions had not improved since 1967. In the West Bank, while the occupation limited and often set back opportunities for economic growth, the basic economic conditions were somewhat stronger and potential for economic activity was better than in Gaza.

The rise of religious nationalist movements among the Palestinians was more rapid in Gaza, in part due to its proximity to Egypt, where the Muslim Brotherhood was particularly active in the 1980s. Israel, in fact, encouraged this growth, believing that the religious and secular nationalist movements would counter one another in a race for national leadership, thereby undermining unity.[18] The best known of these groups was Hamas (Arabic for "Islamic Resistance Movement"), an offshoot of the Muslim Brotherhood that coalesced in the early days of the Intifada.[19] Like other Islamic resistance groups that emerged at that time, Hamas found itself in agreement with the secular groups of the PLO in their analysis of the Israeli occupation and the need to combat it, even if there were disagreements on ideology and tactics. Thus, rather than taking advantage of a substantially weakened PLO to do away with the secular nationalist movement, as Israel had hoped, the Islamic groups boosted the strength of the resistance, despite incidents of tension between Hamas and the PLO at the time.[20]

Part of the reason Israel had preferred the religious nationalism of the Muslim Brotherhood was that it saw the group as less inclined to violent resistance than secular nationalist groups. For most of the twentieth century, the majority of active resistance, not only in Palestine and Israel but throughout the Arab world, had been carried out by secular groups.[21] Avraham Sela and Shaul Mishal note, "Hamas's turn to violence was a matter of necessity in view of its competition with the nationalist Palestinian groups—including the Islamic Jihad—which had led the armed struggle against Israel. By the second year of the Intifada, the scope, sophistication, and daring of Hamas's violent activity . . . had risen sharply." These operations included the kidnapping and killing of Israeli soldiers inside Israel, as well as knife attacks.[22] Despite launching Hamas and other groups employing violence into the spotlight, the Intifada was largely a nonviolent effort composed of labor strikes, demonstrations, and boycotts.[23]

One lesson that Israel took from the Intifada was that it needed to wean itself off its dependence on cheap Palestinian labor. To that end, Israel started bringing in foreign workers from other countries, particularly the Philippines and Thailand.[24] This change, which was gradual but noticeable within a few years, was not the only one. As the Oslo era dawned, so did the era of separation. Ostensibly in response to Palestinian attacks emanating from the Gaza Strip, Israel began constructing a barrier around the territory, which was completed in 1996.[25] After that time, Palestinians could leave Gaza only through the Erez crossing into Israel and the Rafah crossing into Egypt. Several other crossings were established for cargo.[26]

Gaza's encirclement, and the sharp restrictions imposed on entrance to and egress from the Strip, marked the beginning of divergent policies between that territory and the West Bank. In the wake of the Intifada and the Oslo Accords' division of the West Bank into three separate administrative areas,[27] Palestinian freedom of movement was sharply curtailed through the proliferation of checkpoints, Israeli-only bypass roads, and restricted military zones. However, the enclosure of Gaza's entire border with Israel, along with the barrier between Gaza and Egypt that was erected after Israel withdrew from the Sinai Peninsula in 1982 under the terms of the Camp David Accords, curtailed Gazan freedom of movement much more sharply.[28] The effective physical ghetto-ization of Gaza would, in later years, also provide a mechanism for its isolation and the siege of the Strip that continues to this day.[29]

As a result of its encirclement, Gaza became dramatically more reliant on Israel in fundamental ways. All its infrastructure—electricity, water, and trade—was now inextricably dependent on Israel, and there was no way for the people of Gaza to develop any alternative. The conditions inside Gaza continued to decline steadily, as overcrowding, unemployment, restricted access to the rest of the world, and the lack of resources progressively took their toll.[30] The effects of measures that were taken in the 1990s to improve economic conditions for the people of Gaza—such as the construction of an airport, and the opening of a safe passage route between Gaza and the West Bank—were blunted by the tight Israeli controls that were exercised over them. Moreover, these measures would, in the course of conflict, eventually be reversed by Israel.

While Israel may have understood that economic decline and political powerlessness were fueling political activity and widespread anger in Gaza, any efforts it made toward easing conditions were ultimately futile while a policy of the effective closure of Gaza remained in place.[31] By walling off Gaza, Israel made it much more difficult for Palestinian militants to enter the country. As a result, groups pursuing violent opposition to Israel turned first to increased attacks within the Strip and then to low-quality rockets and mortars, particularly after the beginning of the Second Intifada in late 2000.

For Palestinians, the years between the Oslo Accords and the Second Intifada were a period of declining hope. Scholar Salman Abu Sitta summed up this period: "In 1993, the Oslo Accords between Israel and the PLO were signed amid much euphoria in the hope that the 1967 Israeli occupation would be removed. However, by 2000, with outbreak of the second *intifada*, it became clear that Oslo was a hoax, intended to entrench the occupation, not to remove it."[32]

Most of the rockets fired from Gaza were Qassam rockets, which are erratic and cannot be aimed reliably. As Human Rights Watch explained, "Under international humanitarian law applicable to the fighting between Palestinian armed groups and the Israel Defense Forces (IDF), such weapons are inherently indiscriminate when directed towards densely populated areas. The absence of Israeli military forces in the areas struck by the rockets, as well as statements from the leaders of Hamas and other armed groups, indicate that many of these attacks are deliberately intended to strike Israeli civilians and civilian structures. Individuals who willfully authorize or carry out deliberate or indiscriminate attacks against civilians are committing war crimes."[33] Given this security justification for the ongoing closure of Gaza, the idea of easing that closure outside of a consummated agreement with the Palestinians was beyond consideration for Israelis.

As the Second Intifada waned, Israeli prime minister Ariel Sharon changed the course of Gaza's existence by withdrawing all of Israel's settlements, military installations, and soldiers from within the boundaries of the Strip. The "Gaza With-drawal," completed with the strong approval of the George W. Bush administration, might have seemed, superficially, to be a step toward independence for the Palestinians. But as Mitch-ell Plitnick put it in 2011, Israel's refusal to coordinate with the Palestinian Authority "would lead to increased misery for Gaza's Palestinian population, strengthen Hamas, increase at-tacks on Israeli border towns, and promote the illusion that Sharon wanted to end the occupation, when in fact the with-drawal would strengthen Israel's hold on the West Bank."[34] In fact, Sharon's strategy was colorfully described by his as-sociate Dov Weisglass as "the amount of formaldehyde that is necessary so there will not be a political process with the Palestinians."[35]

Weisglass, perhaps Sharon's closest adviser and an instru-mental figure in developing the Gaza disengagement plan, was central in negotiating the plan with the United States. The formaldehyde he referred to was the sacrifice of a few settle-ments and military outposts in the Gaza Strip that did Israel little good but would, by abandoning them, relieve pressure from the United States and Europe to give up any significant control on the much more important West Bank. He and Sha-ron were concerned by the Geneva Initiative, a plan born of efforts by some Palestinian leaders and former Israeli govern-ment officials and diplomats to fulfill the two-state aspirations of those who still supported the Oslo Accords.[36] He explained:

[I]n the fall of 2003 we understood that everything was stuck. And although by the way the Americans read the situation, the blame fell on the Palestinians, not on us, Arik [Sharon] grasped that this state of affairs could not last, that they wouldn't leave us alone, wouldn't get off our case. Time was not on our side. There was international erosion, internal erosion. Domestically, in the meantime, everything was collapsing. The economy was stagnant, and the Geneva Initiative had gained broad support.[37]

Weisglass's comments contradicted Sharon's public proclamations that the withdrawal from Gaza, along with the withdrawal from four small, isolated settlements in the northern West Bank, was intended to be the first phase in a broader plan of unilateral withdrawal.[38]

It is impossible to know whether the type of substantial pressure on Israel to compromise that Weisglass envisioned would have come about. It's true that both George W. Bush and Barack Obama made efforts to restart a diplomatic process. These efforts, however, never even reached the meager levels of the Clinton era.[39] Indeed, in 2003, with the Intifada raging, there was virtually no significant contact between Israel and the Palestinian leadership.

The Role of the United States—
Including the Democrats

Setting a new precedent that would increasingly characterize Israeli-Palestinian diplomacy going forward, Israel's only negotiating partner in deciding on its unilateral withdrawal from Gaza was the United States. This represented a sharp break with the Oslo Accords, which explicitly stated that "[n]either side shall initiate or take any step that will change the status of the West Bank and the Gaza Strip pending the outcome of the permanent status negotiations."[40] It also shattered the norm that had held since 1967, which also was expressed in the Oslo Accords: "The two sides view the West Bank and the Gaza Strip as a single territorial unit, the integrity and status of which will be preserved during the interim period."[41]

Israel argued that, while its withdrawal from Gaza was technically a unilateral change, it did not violate the spirit of the ban on such measures because it was an Israeli withdrawal, not an Israeli effort to exert more control over occupied territory. With the Intifada raging, Israel argued, it was impossible for them to negotiate such a move with the Palestinian Authority.[42] The withdrawal was publicly welcomed by the Palestinian Authority, despite complaints and discomfort about Israel's refusal to coordinate with the PA and suspicions that, as Weisglass had intimated, the withdrawal was really a cover for renewed Israeli reticence to reach a mutually agreeable end of its occupation.[43] As such, other Arab states, the European Union, Russia, and the United Nations could hardly do any less.

But the plan was inherently problematic. The Gaza withdrawal, while a positive step forward in some ways, signified the perpetuation of Israeli control over Palestinians, albeit in a different form. The residents of Gaza, already bereft of resources and with a completely shattered economy, had little hope of building their infrastructure. The unilateral nature of the withdrawal meant the Palestinian Authority was unable to prepare and coordinate its role in post-withdrawal Gaza and made it much more difficult for it to assume control and stabilize the situation there. Since it was carried out in the early months of Mahmoud Abbas's presidency, it made him look like a weak leader of a weak Palestinian Authority to the Palestinian people. Moreover, the likelihood of attacks on Israel from Gaza, as well as fighting among Palestinian factions there was likely to increase after the withdrawal because the PA was kept in the dark about Israel's plans.[44]

Arafat had died in November 2004, and Mahmoud Abbas was elected as his replacement in January 2005.[45] Although Abbas was not immediately able to halt the violence of the Intifada, his meeting with Sharon in February 2005 at Sharm el-Shaikh in Egypt is widely seen as marking the end of the uprising.[46] Arafat's death meant that Sharon's main justification for Israel's unilateral approach to the withdrawal of Israelis from Gaza was gone, as Sharon's long campaign against Arafat personally had led to an Israeli policy of isolating and refusing to negotiate with the longtime Palestinian leader. Abbas immediately called for a return to exclusively nonviolent resistance, although he was not prepared to risk his legitimacy in the eyes of the Palestinian people by trying to disarm the various militant groups, as both the United States and Israel wanted him to do.[47] Such an attempt was unlikely to succeed in any case. But Abbas pressed the Bush administration to ensure that Israel's withdrawal would produce tangible gains for the people of Gaza. If it did not, he argued, Hamas would be strengthened in Gaza, where the group was already at least as strong as Abbas's Fatah party and the Palestinian Authority (PA) that it led.

Scholar Khaled Elgindy explains, "On its face, Sharon's disengagement plan offered little improvement over the status quo. Sharon remained adamant about avoiding a negotiation of any kind. Under pressure from the [Bush] administration he agreed to coordinate the process with Abbas's PA while making it clear to the Americans and the Palestinians that he 'wanted the withdrawal defined entirely as an Israeli move made for Israeli interests.'"[48]

The Bush administration did not hold Abbas in high regard. Although Bush's foreign policy advisers believed Abbas to be more inclined against violent resistance than Arafat, they had little faith that he could follow through on commitments and command the sort of widespread authority that Arafat had. Moreover, the U.S. occupation of Iraq was going very badly, and the disposition of Gaza commanded less of Washington's attention as a result. Sharon's disengagement moved along as a mostly unilateral project, with only minimal coordination with the PA, even though he had made this grudging concession to the United States.

Howard Sumka, who was the USAID mission director for the West Bank and Gaza in 2005, said that the Bush administration was not trying to establish normal economic operations on Gaza's borders; it was just trying to "maintain a sufficient flow of goods so that you wouldn't have any humanitarian problems."[49] That level of economic activity was never going to make the people of Gaza feel that the departure of Israel's soldiers and settlers was a step toward a better life or an end to occupation.

It is also important to note that, on the whole, Bush's approach to occupation and the slowly decaying peace process at the time was supported not only by his own party, but also by Democrats. In analyzing the Democratic Party's official platform for the 2004 elections, the staunchly pro-Israel Washington Institute for Near East Policy (WINEP) stated that the platform "mirrors" basic outlines of Bush administration policy.[50] It also, according to WINEP, "reiterates the commitments that President Bush made to Israeli prime minister Ariel Sharon in their correspondence of April 14, 2004, calling for Palestinian refugees to return to the Palestinian state, not to Israel, labeling Israel a 'Jewish state,' and recognizing that 'it is unrealistic to expect that the outcome of final status negotiations will be a full and complete return to the armistice lines of 1949'—a de facto acknowledgement that Israel will retain some West Bank territory as part of a final settlement."[51]

As a practical matter, the physical separation between the West Bank and Gaza Strip was always a problem, one that was theoretically to be solved by a permanent safe passage route between them, although the practicality of this idea remains a matter of debate. But a guiding principle of the two-state idea, before and after the Oslo Accords, had always been that the two would be treated as if they were a single territorial unit. Yet the isolation of Gaza—enforced by Israel, Egypt, and the United States—on top of the long-standing difficulties of overcrowding and sparse resources in the Strip, created a very different set of conditions there.

The effects of the separation were not only felt on the macro-political scale, but on a very personal level as well. As Israeli restrictions on travel between Gaza and the West Bank tightened, families became separated. People were allowed to visit family in the other occupied territory, but sometimes not permitted to return to their homes and jobs. Amani Kamal 'Abd al-Majid Sharif, married and a mother of five, told her story in November 2016. She had grown up in Gaza and married a man in the West Bank on a trip in 2001. After the wedding, she tried several times to get a permit to visit her family in Gaza but was rejected, even missing her brother's wedding. Finally, her husband was given a permit, but she was again denied one. She went anyway, and eventually was permitted into Gaza. Amani was finally able to see her family again, but then problems arose:

> We stayed in Gaza for two months and then we all sub-
> mitted requests to go home to the West Bank, but they
> were denied. We kept submitting requests every month
> or two, and they were repeatedly rejected. This went on
> for three years. During that whole time my husband did
> not work, because he couldn't find work in Gaza due to
> the bad economic situation. My father supported us, and
> we were in a bad state emotionally. . . . In 2013, my hus-
> band received a permit to enter the West Bank, but my
> request and my daughters' were rejected again. During

the years we lived in Gaza, we had three more children: Sama, Haya, and Muhammad.

In March 2013, Amani's husband returned to their home in the West Bank. She says, "Since then I have submitted about twenty requests for permits and haven't succeeded in getting a single one. My husband and I have been separated against our will for four years, because of the permit issue. My husband is in one city and the children and I are in another. We're in contact by mobile phone and online. The children cry and want to go to their father, and I'm emotionally drained because of the distance from my husband and my home."[52]

Amani's story is far from unique. The initiation of the Oslo process, the Second Intifada that began in late 2000, Israel's removal of its settlements from Gaza and the resulting total isolation of the Strip, and each successive round of fighting in Gaza all made the situation worse, on both personal and large-scale levels. The barrier surrounding Gaza, which would soon be mimicked by one inside the West Bank, placed Gazans at the mercy of those who were keeping them within the barrier. Egypt and Israel, along with the West Bank, were the primary markets for Gazan exports and, despite the withdrawal of its settlements and soldiers, Israel maintained control over Gaza's airspace and coastline. Gaza also remained dependent on Israel for water and electricity.[53] These facts formed the basis for the widely held position that Gaza remains under Israeli occupation to this day.[54]

On January 25, 2006, the first Palestinian legislative elections since 1996 were held. This time, Hamas decided to run for seats in the Palestinian Legislative Council.[55] Elgindy writes: "Having concluded that the Oslo paradigm was dead, Hamas leaders no longer sought to replace the PLO or the PA, but would now work within the existing political structures to reorganize Palestinian politics."[56] Israel pressed for Hamas to be barred from the election until its leaders agreed to "recognize" Israel as the PLO had. But Abbas argued that keeping Hamas from running would undermine the legitimacy of the election.

At this point, the Bush administration was struggling to maintain any notion of legitimacy about the Iraq War. With the excuse of weapons of mass destruction no longer viable, the war was now being justified as an effort to spread democracy to the beleaguered Iraqi people. This logic undoubtedly informed the U.S. decision to support Abbas's position.

The Rise of Hamas

No one expected Hamas to win a majority in the PLC, but it did. While many in the United States and Israel read the victory as "a vote for terrorism," Hamas's militancy was, at best, a minuscule factor. Polls, before and after the election, showed that majorities of Palestinians continued to believe that diplomacy was preferable to armed struggle. The far greater factor was growing disdain for Fatah, amid continued issues with human rights violations, corruption, and cronyism. Fatah was also ill prepared for the election, despite having more time and a better infrastructure in place to get ready for it. With a younger faction challenging the old guard, the Fatah vote was split in many districts despite last-minute promises of a unified front. When this factor was added to the frustration that many Palestinians had with the PA, and the devastation of the Intifada on the heels of the decline of Palestinians' standard of living under Oslo, it turned out to be enough for Hamas to win a decisive majority in the Palestinian Legislative Council.[57] Abbas would still be president, but now Ismail Haniyeh, the leader of Hamas's political wing, would become prime minister.[58]

Hamas's success in the election came as a surprise to Israel and the international community, neither of which wanted to deal with the group. The victory also came as a surprise to Hamas itself, which was not set up for governance. Hamas's victory was immediately greeted with a harsh response. Acting Israeli prime minister Ehud Olmert declared that "[t]he state of Israel will not negotiate with a Palestinian administration if even part of it is an armed terrorist organization calling for the destruction of the state of Israel." Also responding was the Middle East Quartet, the largely ineffectual international body composed of the United States, Russian Federation, United Nations, and European Union—that was charged with managing the peace process. The Quartet stated, "A two-state solution to the conflict requires all participants in the democratic process to renounce violence and terror, accept Israel's right to exist, and disarm." The United States and the European Union independently echoed these calls.[59]

Israel quickly suspended payments to the PA of the customs taxes it collected on the Palestinians' behalf, a punishment it has employed frequently over the years and continues to this day.[60] UN Secretary-General Kofi Annan reiterated the Quartet's conditions for providing international aid to the PA: "the principles of non-violence, recognition of Israel and the acceptance of previous agreements and obligations."[61] But these initial reactions, while politically necessary, did not answer the question of what to do about the Hamas victory. For the United States and European Union, Hamas, as a designated terrorist organization, was a group they were legally obliged to shun.[62] On the other hand, cutting off aid and halting diplomacy with the PA would end the Oslo process and almost certainly lead to a renewal of the high level of violence that had only recently tapered off.

The stage was set for the status quo to continue. The PLO, not the PA, was and is still the only body recognized as representative of the Palestinian people, and Hamas was not part of that. Moreover, Abbas remained the head of the PA as well as the PLO, and the PA's official policy had not changed when Hamas won the election. Even so, the United States—on a bipartisan basis—remained determined to undermine the new government.

Although Hamas showed some flexibility, U.S. policy remained rigid. Even some centrist policy thinkers in Washington recognized that the argument that "the funding suspension is a deliberate, cold-hearted external veto upon the Palestinians' free exercise of their democratic rights, revealing the insincerity of U.S. democracy promotion," was gaining traction.[63] Abbas was unwilling to yield to U.S. demands that he nullify Hamas's victory on the basis of it being a terrorist group. This was a wise decision, as nullifying the victory would have unleashed a tsunami of fury from the Palestinian public, a natural reaction to their expressed will being vetoed. Yet Abbas's efforts to maintain some sort of working relationship with the United States, which included attempts to create mechanisms to deliver aid to the Palestinian people without going through the official PA channels that the U.S. now refused, caused great tension within the Palestinian territories, especially Gaza.

The U.S. boycott of the PA caused "financial and political chaos" that "severely affected Palestinians generally and resulted in fierce clashes between Hamas and Fatah groups."[64] With Abbas headquartered in the West Bank, where Fatah was strong, and Hamas prime minister Ismail Haniyeh based in Gaza, where his forces had the upper hand, the effective split between the two Palestinian territories was becoming much more impactful. These tensions reached a fever pitch in May, as "140,000 people formerly on the PA payroll were not paid."[65]

The Intifada had devastated both the West Bank and Gaza, and the subsequent economic crisis brought on by the loss of U.S. and European assistance after the election made things much worse. This was especially the case in Gaza, where the withdrawal of the physical Israeli presence from that territory meant escalated isolation and loss of employment, exacerbating an already dire situation. Yet the Bush administration would not tolerate any Hamas presence in a Palestinian government.[66]

If there was any doubt about the U.S. position on Hamas, and of its bipartisan nature, it was erased in May 2006 when Congress passed the Palestinian Anti-Terrorism Act of 2006. The act forbade any aid to the Palestinian Authority unless the president certified that "no PA ministry, agency, or instrumentality is controlled by Hamas." The only exception to this policy was under the condition that Hamas formally accepted and abided by the Quartet conditions and that "the Hamas-controlled PA has made demonstrable progress toward purging from its security services individuals with ties to terrorism, dismantling all terrorist infrastructure and cooperating with Israel's security services, halting anti-American and anti-Israel incitement, and ensuring democracy and financial transparency."[67] These conditions, in Hamas's view, were a non-starter for initial engagement, and there was no ambiguity on that point.[68]

The Palestinian Anti-Terrorism Act was co-sponsored by 294 members of the House of Representatives. When it came to a vote, only thirty-one Democrats along with six Republicans voted against the measure. The accompanying bill in the Senate was co-sponsored by ninety of the one hundred members of that body. Even opponents of the bill were less than forceful. Rep. Betty McCollum, for example, who has a well-earned reputation as one of the most principled defenders of Palestinian rights in Congress, was accused by a representative of the American Israel Public Affairs Committee of "supporting terrorism" because she voted against the bill. Yet in her scathing response to AIPAC, she stated that the "language contained in S. 2237 [the Senate version of the bill, which was somewhat milder than the House version and eventually became law] accurately reflects my position."[69]

There is no doubt that Hamas's victory in the 2006 elections presented genuine problems for U.S. policymakers. The American public viewed the Islamic group with hostility, and it would have been very difficult, on both a policy and political level, for the United States to be seen as indulging them. Yet the possibility that Hamas might have been capable of working within the Palestinian Authority without fundamentally changing its own positions was never explored. Only a few years later, a double standard centered on this very point would be exposed when Benjamin Netanyahu and his Likud party won back the Israeli leadership.[70]

Likud's platform explicitly rules out acceptance of a Palestinian state.[71] But Netanyahu, recognizing that this would cause more tension with the administration of President Barack Obama than he wanted at that point, publicly committed himself to a two-state solution, albeit without strictly defining what that entailed.[72] Though the Likud platform ran in parallel to the perceived discord between Hamas and the PA, Netanyahu's stated commitment to a two-state solution was deemed sufficient by the United States, since the policy of the Israeli government had not changed. There was no assumption that the Likud had to change its party platform simply because it was the most powerful party in the government. The government's official position—that it stood by the vision of a two-state solution—was what mattered, not the widespread view that Israel's *actions* were aimed at disrupting the possibility of a Palestinian state. The PA, however, was held to a higher standard. Although the PA did insist that any final agreement be dependent on a referendum of the Palestinian people, Hamas had made it clear that Abbas was still empowered to lead negotiations.[73]

It was possible that Hamas might have changed the PA's position on the negotiating principles, or might have made a political decision to allow Abbas to carry on under the existing terms. In any case, Hamas was not given the opportunity to do so. Nor was there much political pressure in Israel or the United States for Hamas to at least have that chance. Despite hand-wringing over the impending fate of the people of the Palestinian territories—recall this was all taking place in the wake of increased punitive measures by Israel and an effective boycott by the United States—voices calling to give the newly elected Palestinian government a chance to prove itself were few and far between.

Meanwhile, the situation in Gaza continued to deteriorate. Clashes between Fatah and Hamas continued apace, and the economic situation grew worse. Hamas, at this time, was trying to establish its authority and was working with other militant groups to try to control the firing of rockets into Israel, with only partial success. Dissatisfied, Israel escalated its shelling in response to a rocket attack that it blamed on Hamas in June 2006, and clashes escalated until Israel launched an incursion into Gaza at the end of the month. Israel seized two Palestinians accused of working for Hamas, and Hamas responded with a clandestine incursion over the border into Israel, where guerrillas killed two soldiers and kidnapped a third, Gilad Shalit. This prompted Israel, in defiance of Shalit's family's wishes, to launch a devastating attack on Gaza, severely damaging the Strip's power plant.[74]

The Bush administration was working clandestinely with Mohammed Dahlan, the Fatah strongman in Gaza, and training Fatah fighters to overthrow Hamas in Gaza and restore control of the PA. At the same time, the administration was pressuring Abbas to give Hamas a choice: either accept the Quartet principles or Abbas would declare a state of emergency, nullify the elections, and form an emergency government that excluded Hamas. Abbas was in a difficult position. He was well aware that obeying such an ultimatum could lead only to bloodshed, while defying the Americans would only worsen the situation for Palestinians. Abbas's preferred path of negotiation, working with Israel and the West, would prove futile. The decision to form a unity government was his desperate attempt to get out of this dilemma. Meanwhile, the United States had been working on its own contingency plan.

The Bush administration had promised Dahlan money and arms, at a time when Fatah security officers had not been paid in months. But Congress, unsure about getting the United States involved so directly in the Gaza conflict by sending money for arms, held up the funds, so, as journalist David Rose reported, "[a]ccording to State Department officials, beginning in the latter part of 2006, [Secretary of State Condoleezza] Rice initiated several rounds of phone calls and personal meetings with leaders of four Arab nations—Egypt, Jordan, Saudi Arabia, and the United Arab Emirates. She asked them to bolster Fatah by providing military training and by pledging funds to buy its forces lethal weapons. The money was to be paid directly into accounts controlled by President Abbas." These deals were facilitated by Deputy National Security Adviser Elliott Abrams, who had experience in facilitating covert arms deals, having been convicted of lying to Congress about his role in the Iran-Contra scandal of the mid-1980s.[75] Dahlan stepped up the clashes with Hamas on February 1, 2007, when Fatah forces stormed the Islamic University of Gaza, a Hamas bastion. Hamas retaliated the next day, attacking police stations staffed mostly by Fatah security men. These events prompted Abbas to escalate his efforts with the Saudis to consummate the unity agreement.[76]

The Bush administration drew up a plan for Abbas to take the political steps necessary to oust Hamas while the United States would back Dahlan with arms, planning, and funding. These resources, in addition to the greater numbers the administration believed Fatah could field, would make defeating Hamas easy. The plan was leaked at the end of April, however, alerting Hamas to the U.S.-backed Fatah coup attempt. The fighting escalated sharply and quickly. Dahlan was not in Gaza, having just had surgery in Germany, leaving Fatah without its military leader in the area. In June, another leak revealed that Abbas and the U.S. had asked Israel—which had established limits on the weaponry that Fatah could have, fearing it would be turned on them later—to authorize shipments of heavier weapons into Gaza from Egypt. This pushed matters past the point of no return, and Fatah and Hamas were now locked into a battle for control of the Gaza Strip.

Many of Fatah's forces stayed out of the fighting, and Hamas was better organized, and less ambiguous. Many of the Fatah fighters were not comfortable with the U.S. involvement, adding to the discomfort felt on all sides from Palestinians fighting each other. In just over a week, Hamas had won a decisive victory.[77] Abbas declared the state of emergency that the U.S. had demanded months before, and many Hamas legislators in the West Bank were arrested. An emergency government, excluding Hamas, was installed. With Hamas now in full control of Gaza, the separation of the two territories was a firm reality.

Israel soon tightened the closure of Gaza, starkly reducing the flow of goods into the territory to less than 20 percent of what it had been, and sharply tightening restrictions on Palestinians moving in and out of the Strip.[78] In September 2007, Israel declared Gaza a "hostile territory," which helped to codify the increased restrictions on the Strip.[79] In Gaza, Israel still controlled the supply of electricity, which it ostensibly decided to reduce in order to force Hamas to decide between supplying electricity "to hospitals or weapons lathes," according to one Israeli official.[80] The goal was to make it more difficult for Hamas to govern, although time has demonstrated that such punitive measures have largely caused the people to rally around their rulers, even if they are otherwise unhappy with them.[81]

For the next year, Hamas walked a fine line. It tried to establish itself as the authority in Gaza and worked to control the activities of other militant groups in the Strip. At the same time, it worked to maintain a sufficiently confrontational stance with Israel to maintain its legitimacy and identity. The result was sporadic rocket fire, which made life very unpleasant in Israeli towns bordering Gaza, especially the town of Sderot, which became known for the frequent rockets that landed there. In June 2008, Egypt brokered a truce between Hamas and Israel. The violence was reduced. Israel acknowledged that Hamas was working to maintain the cease-fire, and the number of rockets fired at Israel during this approximately five-month period was drastically lower than in the prior five months.[82] The cease-fire held during this period, despite Israel firing a number of times on civilians in Gaza, as well as engaging in multiple incidents in the West Bank that resulted in injuries and even several deaths among Palestinian noncombatants.[83]

Then, on November 4, the very day that Barack Obama was elected president of the United States, Israel launched a military operation in Gaza that killed six Hamas members. Hamas retaliated with a large barrage of rocket fire into Israel. The situation deteriorated until, on December 27, 2008,

Israel launched "Operation Cast Lead," the first of four major attacks on Gaza over the next six years. The onslaught would last until January 18, 2009, just two days before Obama was inaugurated.

Al-Haq, a Palestinian human rights organization, calculated that Israel killed 1,409 Palestinians, of whom 1,172 were civilians, including 342 children. Israel damaged or destroyed over eleven thousand Palestinian homes, and many commercial and public premises in what was termed "a deliberate and systematic assault against civilians and civilian infrastructure in the Gaza Strip."[84] Palestinian rocket fire killed three Israeli civilians, and ten Israeli soldiers were killed, reportedly by friendly fire.[85]

The devastation wrought by Israel in Cast Lead was shocking to many around the world. The United Nations Human Rights Council (UNHRC) initiated a fact-finding mission to determine whether war crimes had been committed. The mission was headed by Judge Richard Goldstone, a Jewish South African judge who had strong connections to Israel. Israel refused to cooperate with the investigation, citing bias at the UNHRC.[86] Nonetheless, the mission went forward and, in a 450-page report, concluded that Israel and Hamas and other armed Palestinian groups were guilty of "violations of international human rights and humanitarian law and possible war crimes and crimes against humanity."[87] Israel, as expected, dismissed the report as the product of bias, accusing its authors of equating the Israeli government with terrorists and of denying Israel the right to defend its citizens from attack.[88]

The administration of Barack Obama moved quickly to help Israel denounce the Goldstone Report and defend itself from its conclusions. A memo that was leaked to the public showed that the United States worked closely with Israel to counter the report, stating that "the objective was not to appease the international community, but to dilute the poisonous effects of the Goldstone Report. The [U.S.] Ambassador [to Israel, James Cunningham] stressed the importance of getting the word out employing a variety of means—perhaps YouTube or other outlets afforded the opportunity to help re-tell the story."[89]

Goldstone, as the report's lead author, was the frequent target of attacks and social pressures. At one point, he was even barred by the South African Zionist Federation from attending his grandson's bar mitzvah.[90] Although that ban was ultimately lifted, it was indicative of the shunning Goldstone experienced in his Jewish community, as well as in Israel. Eventually, he gave in and undermined some of his own report's findings with an op-ed he published in April 2011, in which he stated that, having seen information from Israel that it had not shared with him during the investigation, he no longer believed there was any Israeli strategy to harm the civilian population in Gaza.[91] As one Israeli analyst, Roi Maor, explained it, however, "I believe Goldstone's article . . . miss[es] a critical nuance. Israeli policy (unlike Hamas or Hezbollah) is not intended to maximize civilian casualties. Yet it does intentionally target civilians: it is intended to produce maximal civilian distress, while avoiding mass civilian casualties."[92]

Maor's point is important, as it reflects not only how Goldstone could tell both stories, but also the difference in approach and priorities of a much more powerful party and a weaker one. Israel's strategy has often been based on casting itself as being more concerned about avoiding casualties. But behind that distinction lies its powerful ability to degrade the conditions for civilians in places like Gaza without necessarily killing people in the numbers seen in other conflict situations.

In 2008, Israeli general Gadi Eisenkot, speaking of Israeli tactics two years prior in its clash with Hezbollah in southern Lebanon, said it was "complete nonsense" to try and hit rocket launchers, and that Israel should instead deter enemies from using them: "Every village from which they fire from Israel, we will deploy disproportional force, and cause massive damage and destruction. As far as we are concerned, these are military bases." According to Maor, Eisenkot emphasized that "this is not a recommendation, this is the plan and it has been approved."[93]

Goldstone has maintained from the beginning, quite accurately, that the chief recommendation of his report was for the parties involved to investigate these allegations themselves. He also bemoaned from the beginning that Israel refused to cooperate with the investigation and that if it had, the results may well have been different. His follow-up op-ed reiterated these very valid points, but also included some points that seem, at best, puzzling. Chief among these was his flat statement that the UN committee following up on his report "indicate[s] that civilians were not intentionally targeted as a matter of policy." In fact, the committee report said nothing of the kind.[94]

Contrary to what Goldstone said in his op-ed, the committee actually stated that it had no basis on which to decide whether Israeli policy in Gaza conformed to the principle of avoiding civilian targets.[95] Without access to the evidence, which was prevented by Israel, the committee could not come to a definitive conclusion. Yet human rights groups produced numerous reports that demonstrated a weighty case of circumstantial evidence of serious human rights violations and possible war crimes in Operation Cast Lead. These included the use of human shields by Israeli soldiers, indiscriminate bombing by drones, the use of the burning chemical white phosphorous in civilian areas, and other disturbing acts.[96]

The incoming Obama administration had been silent about Operation Cast Lead, and Congress was in strong support of Israel's position. The operation ended just as Obama took office, and his focus was on restoring the United States' diplomatic standing around the world, which had been undermined by George W. Bush's invasion of Iraq. In terms of Israel and Palestine, Obama had prioritized freezing settlement expansion in the West Bank. Since Israel had stopped the Gaza attacks just three days before Obama took office, he was spared having to intervene to stop the fighting. He raised some hopes by endorsing a UN call for the easing of border restrictions for both goods and people in and out of Gaza, but did nothing to make it happen. Unsurprisingly, it did not happen.

In March, Obama convened a donors' conference that pledged $4.5 billion in aid for Gaza, but from there, the administration's efforts on the issue of Palestine and Israel were firmly fixed on trying to reinvigorate a moribund peace process.[97] As the Obama administration pursued that quixotic effort, conditions in Gaza continued to deteriorate just as they had after so many other critical moments of conflict. Attempts by Hamas, both diplomatic and military, to challenge the ongoing siege of the territory would periodically lead to flareups with Israel. A particularly tense moment in 2014 became the largest conflagration since Cast Lead.

As was the case with Cast Lead, tallies of Palestinian casualties in the 2014 fighting, which Israel colorfully named "Operation Protective Edge," were disputed, particularly regarding the number of combatant casualties. These disputes arose largely because of the different definitions used by Israel on one hand and by international bodies and human rights groups on the other. The International Committee of the Red Cross developed a working definition, "ascribing 'participation in hostilities' not only to persons engaged in such activities at the time they were killed, but also to persons fulfilling a continuous combat function. This category includes persons who are trained to order or execute combative actions or operations. Such persons remain in this category even if they are not participating directly in such actions and even if they were not engaged in hostilities at the time of death."[98] But Israel takes this concept quite a bit further, and considers anyone who is a member of a group that engages in hostilities against it a combatant. This means that any member of Hamas or any other militant group that also has political and/or administrative functions would be counted by Israel as a legitimate target.[99] This is one of the primary reasons for the differing counts of civilian casualties.

During the fifty days of fighting that summer in 2014, 2,202 Palestinians were killed, of whom 1,371 were not taking part in hostilities. Sixty-eight Israelis, including five civilians, and one foreign national were killed.[100] While Israel insisted it was going to great lengths to avoid civilian casualties and damage to civilian infrastructure, the Palestinians were not the only ones who saw it differently.[101]

U.S. secretary of state John Kerry, in an unguarded moment in a television studio and unaware that his microphone was live, told an aide sarcastically, "It's a hell of a pinpoint operation. It's a hell of a pinpoint operation." Clearly unhappy with what he saw as Israel's excessive use of force and referring to the deaths of several Israeli soldiers in fighting the night before, Kerry said, "I hope they don't think that's an invitation to go do more. That better be the warning to them. . . . I think, John, we ought to go tonight. I think it's crazy to be sitting around. Let's go."[102] But Kerry quickly backed off these comments, and the official line from the White House was that the United States supported Israel's right to defend itself.[103] Congress was enthusiastic about its defense of Israeli actions, with strong bipartisan statements of support for Israel as well as authorization for $225 million in missile defense aid in addition to the annual aid already allotted to Israel.[104] The pro votes in Congress were, again, overwhelming.[105]

A New Protest in an "Unlivable" Area

In September 2015, the United Nations Conference on Trade and Development (UNCTAD) issued a grim report on the conditions in Gaza. UNCTAD determined that the Israeli-Egyptian blockade, which had lasted for eight years at the time, and the three major military operations Gaza had endured, had "shattered [Gaza's] ability to export and produce for the domestic market, ravaged its already debilitated infrastructure, left no time for reconstruction and economic recovery, and accelerated the de-development of the Occupied Palestinian Territory." The report detailed the devastation of Gaza's civilian infrastructure and the collapse of its economic sector, as revealed by the ballooning of its unemployment rate, to 44 percent in 2014, and the shrinking of its per capita GDP, by 30 percent since 1994. "Food insecurity affects 72 per cent of households, and the number of Palestinian refugees solely reliant on food distribution from United Nations agencies had increased from 72,000 in 2000 to 868,000 by May 2015." Ninety-five percent of the water in the coastal aquifers on which Gaza relied was not drinkable.[106]

By most standards, the conditions described in the report would already qualify as "unlivable." Yet 1.8 million people remain in Gaza. While the siege remains in place, there have been some meager steps taken to forestall the worst of the looming disaster. For example, Qatar agreed to pay for additional fuel for Gaza, and Israel agreed to allow the additional fuel in. In fact, it was the Palestinian Authority that objected, in an attempt to undermine Hamas, delaying the additional fuel for a time, before Qatar and Israel agreed to simply bypass the PA.[107] Ongoing tensions between Hamas and Fatah, which have come to include PA-imposed sanctions on Gaza in the hopes of forcing Hamas out of power, place another layer of complication on addressing the economic and humanitarian crisis in Gaza.[108] Still, the increase in fuel supply "has improved the delivery of water and sanitation services, while reducing expenditure on fuel for back-up generators for households and businesses. This increase has also reduced the need for the emergency fuel provided by the UN to avert the collapse of key service providers."[109] Although these steps have had some effect, Gaza continues to teeter on the brink of catastrophe.

Gaza Today

"For Palestinians in Gaza and beyond, the twin issues of refugees and Jerusalem form the core of the Palestinian quest for self-determination," wrote scholar and activist Jehad Abusalim in 2018. "Thus, it was the sense of an impending political disaster that spurred activists into action."[110] The election of Donald Trump brought less change to U.S. policy in Gaza than many other aspects of his policy in Israel and Palestine. His 2018 decision to cut off funds to the United Nations Relief and Works Agency, as we discussed at length in chapter 3, with no plan to offset the damage done to Palestinian refugees throughout the Levant, was one of the few ways Trump paid attention to Gaza at all. Yet this decision (later reinforced by his hubristic, erroneous declaration that the United States was changing the definition of a Palestinian refugee),[111] combined with his declaration of Jerusalem as Israel's capital (reinforced by moving the embassy from Tel Aviv to Jerusalem), struck at the very heart of Palestinian nationalism in Gaza, the place where Palestinians paid the highest price for adherence to their national cause.

Europe, some of the Arab states, the UN, and other international bodies boosted their financial support to make up for the loss of U.S. funding, but it has been a struggle. There have been a few incidents of rocket fire and Israeli bombings, but no new major flareups as of this writing. The leading characteristic of the Trump years in Gaza was the weekly protests at the fence separating Israel from Gaza, the demonstrations dubbed the "Great March of Return" (GMR).

The GMR is a grassroots Palestinian initiative to march toward the Gaza fence, with protesters demanding an end to the siege on Gaza and for the right of Palestinian refugees to return to the places from where they were forced or fled. Ahmed Abu Artema, a journalist and poet in Gaza, published a Facebook post that caught on and spurred action:

> What if 200,000 demonstrators accompanied by international media marched peacefully and breached the barbwire fence east of Gaza to enter a few kilometers of our occupied land, carrying Palestinian flags and keys of return? What if they erected tents on the inside, established a tent city there, which they called Bab al-Shams, and were then joined by thousands of Palestinians from al-dakhil, and insisted on peacefully remaining there without resorting to any form of violence?
>
> What could the occupation [Israel] bristling with arms do to a mass of human beings advancing peacefully? Kill ten, twenty, or fifty of them? And then what? What could it do in the face of an unwavering mass peacefully marching?

[We are] a people that want life and nothing more. Nothing can delay this idea but the shackles of our self-delusions. We are dying in this tiny besieged place, so why not bolt before the knife reaches our throats? Since they are plotting to kick us south [to Egypt] after slaughtering us wholesale, why don't we preempt them and begin to run north?

If there must be a price to pay, then let it be in the direction of what is right, in the direction of returning to Palestine, where we can get new land and deepen the enemy's existential impasse.

Once we implement this idea and achieve a historic breakthrough, we'll find out that we've wasted many years on hesitation and forbearance.

Revolt! You have nothing to lose, but your chains.

#Great_March_of_Return.[112]

The GMR drew thousands of people of the Strip to demonstrate near the barrier encircling Gaza, the greatest symbol of their isolation, a wall forming their giant, open-air prison.[113] Families were there, and there was shared food, dancing, and entertainment. The protests were held every Friday, and while a few people would throw stones or shoot weapons ineffectively, the overwhelming majority of attendees were peaceful, even when the response from Israeli soldiers nearby was not.

But the GMR, by its very nature, was frightening to most Israelis. The idea of Palestinians returning to the places where their recent and distant ancestors lived is as fundamentally threatening to Israelis as it is inspirational to Palestinians. The biggest single issue in the Israeli-Palestinian conflict since 1948 is not Jerusalem, settlements, borders, or even security. It is the Palestinian right of return. It is the one issue Israel would not discuss in talks and will not even consider compromising on. It is also the very basis of the Palestinian national movement since 1948. For seven decades, the Palestinian right of return has been the irresistible force meeting the immovable object of Israeli nationalism. It has been the time bomb that would explode if talks on all those other issues were ever successful.[114]

When Israelis speak, sometimes bombastically, about the destruction of their state, they don't always mean by bombs and missiles; sometimes they are referring to being outnumbered by Palestinians as citizens, with the inherent political power that would entail. While one hesitates to call that fear justified, it is certainly true that even the barest democratic structure would be strained in trying to maintain a state as an expression of a particular ethnic group if that group represents a minority of the state's citizens. Thus, even the symbolic march toward the barrier between Israel and Gaza sent shock waves throughout Israel, and very likely goes a long way in explaining Israel's response. After one year of demonstrations, 266 Palestinians had been killed and over 30,000 wounded. Medical workers and journalists were among the casualties.[115]

The power of the GMR partly rested on the fact that it was, as described by Tareq Baconi of the International Crisis Group, "a call from grassroots activists and ordinary inhabitants." Israel, however, was quick to characterize the GMR as Hamas-led, and to focus on a small percentage of protesters who acted in a violent manner. As Baconi notes, "At a time when the Palestinian national movement is particularly weak and fragmented, lifting the banner of return has offered a unifying framework that transcends political and geographic divisions, one rooted in the universal Palestinian demand for the right of return, as enshrined in UN Resolution 194, which was passed in 1948 and has since been regularly reaffirmed. For Israel, the demand for a Palestinian return en masse poses an existential threat to the state's Jewish majority." That characterization by Israel "prepared the way for Israel to use disproportionate force in response."[116]

There was no significant effort from the international community to convince Israel to end the siege on Gaza in response to the GMR. Palestinians are not likely to back off on their demand for return, but an end to the collective punishment and the siege on Gaza might well have been much more effective at countering the GMR than escalated violence by the Israeli military. In addition, the Palestinian Authority failed to seize the opportunity to heed the demonstrators' call for an end to the political schism between their tattered pseudo-government and Hamas.[117]

As the GMR continued as a weekly event, Hamas managed to co-opt it to some degree, which many in Gaza have resented. The characterization of the GMR as being driven by Hamas quickly took hold in the United States. The Anti-Defamation League strongly reinforced this perception, writing:

On Friday, March 30, Hamas launched its six-week-long "March of Return" campaign, which called on Gazans to gather near the border with Israel and to march on the border. Organizers claim the march is intended to highlight the plight of Gaza, the broader Palestinian situation, and the Right of Return for Palestinian refugees. . . . On the first day of demonstrations, on Friday, March 30, an estimated 30,000 Gazans joined the March. While there were many who protested peacefully, there were large groups of protestors who approached the border fence intending to damage or break through the demarcation line. These violent groups came to the protest with Molotov cocktails, explosives and burning tires, and some carried guns. The Israel Defense Forces (IDF) reacted to this activity close to the border, utilizing tear gas, rubber bullets and live fire, killing sixteen and injuring between 700–1000, primarily by tear gas and other riot dispersing weapons.[118]

On May 14, 2018, one of the deadliest days of the GMR occurred. As the ADL described it: "The largest and deadliest confrontation took place on May 14, the day of the US Embassy dedication in Jerusalem. An estimated 50,000 Palestinians protested on the Gaza border and by the end of the day at least 60 Gazans were dead, and thousands wounded. Some engaged in violent activities, including attempted infiltrations into Israel and the use of various weapons against IDF soldiers and outposts. IDF soldiers responded with riot dispersing methods, and, in some cases, live fire."[119] As bad as that sounds, the ADL's characterization severely downplayed the circumstances of that fateful day. The GMR had already been drawing disproportionate responses from the Israeli military, raising tensions. On top of the existing demands, the United States was now unilaterally recognizing Jerusalem as Israel's capital, contravening international law and escalating tensions.

The spectacle was stark: President Donald Trump and his family, as well as many Republican leaders and key Trump aides with deep ties to Israeli settlers, celebrating the Jerusalem move while considerable blood was being spilled in Gaza.[120] While Republicans partied, Democrats complained that they had not been invited to the ceremony. As the violence raged in Gaza, Democrats were as silent as their Republican colleagues.[121]

One need not defend Hamas to recognize that the people of Gaza are living in unacceptable squalor. Yet as we have demonstrated, the United States has not merely been indifferent to the crisis in Gaza, but played an active, significant, and thoroughly bipartisan role in degrading the conditions. The Strip is still that millstone that Edward Said warned Yitzhak Rabin wanted to drop from his neck, a place that no one wants—except the Palestinian people. Yet, as many have noted, the blockade of Gaza, now in its fourteenth year, has turned the Strip into the world's largest open-air prison.[122]

As Palestinian-American scholar Rashid Khalidi points out, the current conditions in Gaza amount to collective punishment: "It is punishment for Gaza's refusal to be a docile ghetto. It is punishment for the gall of Palestinians in unifying, and of Hamas and other factions in responding to Israel's siege and its provocations with resistance, armed or otherwise, after Israel repeatedly reacted to unarmed protest with crushing force. Despite years of cease-fires and truces, the siege of Gaza has never been lifted."[123] Such collective punishment is always self-defeating. More to the point, collective punishment is a war crime.[124] Far from convincing Gazans to blame Hamas, it makes the citizens reluctant to act against the Hamas authorities in Gaza, as many see such actions as aiding the United States and Israel in their efforts to dominate the Palestinian people.

It is undeniable that the United States has a grave responsibility to all of Israel and Palestine, and nowhere does this come into sharper relief than in Gaza. U.S. policy, including unconditional financial and diplomatic support for Israel, and American indifference have contributed greatly to the existing humanitarian crisis in Gaza. This involvement has also increased the looming possibility of this crisis devolving into a catastrophic blight, as the United Nations predicted. As we—the people of the United States—do nothing, nearly two million innocent people suffer some of the worst living conditions in the world.

Instead of trying to find a way to spare the people of Gaza, we have used them in our efforts to oust Hamas. By scapegoating Hamas, who is certainly more than worthy of intense criticism, we ignore the long history of U.S. involvement in the region by both Democratic and Republican administrations. In so doing, we lose our sense of collective responsibility for the current crisis.

The people of Gaza live in a situation much too precarious to be ignored. The end of the Gaza siege cannot be delayed until the broader question of Israeli occupation is answered. The universal values of compassion, justice, and human rights demand that the siege be ended. Decimating the Gazan economy and starving the people living there have devastated an already depressed and overcrowded area. Moreover, these actions have not improved the situation for Israelis. Americans share significantly in the blame for this situation. Our overwhelming silence is a betrayal of the noble, definitive ideals that liberals and progressives profess to hold dear.

Conclusion

Beyond the Limits

In the spring of 2016, Bernie Sanders was quickly catching up to Hillary Clinton in the Democratic presidential primaries. Viewed as a longshot by most observers at the beginning of the race, Sanders had now captured national attention with his progressive proposals and grassroots support. Suddenly, the Democratic primary was no longer a Clinton coronation, but a legitimate competition. During the presidential debate, Sanders said that Israel's actions in Gaza were "disproportionate" and insisted that the United States cannot "continue to be one-sided," arguing that "we are going to have to say that Netanyahu is not right all of the time."[1]

Making such statements unapologetically during a presidential election campaign—and in New York City of all places—had long been considered political suicide. Typically, presidential nominees avoid the subject of Israel-Palestine altogether, or they offer largely uncontroversial platitudes that signal their mainstream orthodoxy and political discipline rather than any legible position on the issue. For the first time ever, a viable mainstream candidate was offering a distinct critique of Israeli actions. Sanders managed to emerge from all of it unscathed. And while his pursuit of the Democratic nomination ultimately came up short, his stated positions on Israel were not generally among the dominant explanations for his loss—whether from the public, pundits, or politicians.[2]

Two years later, the United States Congress was preparing to welcome its first two Muslim women to the House of Representatives: Rashida Tlaib, a Palestinian-American from Michigan, and Ilhan Omar, a Somali refugee from Minnesota who came to the United States in 1995 when she was twelve years old.[3] The two had come to symbolize the next generation of Democrats. The young congresswomen were fiercely progressive and fearlessly outspoken, highlighting a split between the entrenched Democratic leadership and the grassroots movements that were a defining feature of the 2018 midterms. Both Tlaib and Omar defended the right to boycott Israel over its treatment of the Palestinians. Although their positions drew some controversy, both candidates won their races easily. While their victories can be attributed to the fact that Tlaib and Omar came from heavily Democratic districts, it is nonetheless noteworthy—and historically anomalous—that their stances on Israel-Palestine were not an important limiting factor.

That is not to say, however, that their positions have gone unchallenged.

Many centrist Democrats and liberal supporters of Israel voiced concern that Omar and Tlaib, as well as other new members of Congress, were being "too critical" of Israel. For instance, Brad Sherman, a prominent pro-Israel Democrat from California, told the *New York Times*: "I do worry that there are some on the extreme left of our party who adopt slogans [that are creating tensions]."[4] As is often the case among centrist Democrats, Sherman did not offer any explanation for his use of the terms "extreme" or even "left." Still, he was communicating quite clearly what he believed: taking substantive action to pressure Israel into changing its behavior toward the Palestinians was the view of a small, fringe minority within the Democratic Party.

But is that the case?

The University of Maryland Critical Issues Poll, released in December 2018, less than one month after the midterm elections, suggests that support for Palestinian rights is no longer a fringe position.[5] The poll asked how the United States should respond to the creation of new settlements. For more than five decades, since the War of 1967, successive Israeli governments have built new settlements in the West Bank to provide homes for Israeli Jews. These settlements are illegal under international law and, while the United States has routinely tolerated their presence in practice, official U.S. policy prior to November 2019 was that they were "inconsistent" with international law and "an obstacle to peace."[6] The poll offered the following options as a potential response to the settlements:

1) Do nothing
2) Criticize the action but do nothing more
3) Impose sanctions
4) Take more serious action

Faced with these choices, 56 percent of Democrats selected "impose sanctions" or "take more serious action," while only 39 percent preferred to "do nothing" or "criticize the action but do nothing more." This is not an isolated result. In January of 2018, the Pew Research Center released a surprising poll showing that sympathies among Democrats had shifted dramatically from siding with Israel (43 percent favoring Israel, 29 percent favoring the Palestinians) in 2016 to being just about evenly divided in sympathy between Israel and the

Palestinians (27 percent and 25 percent, respectively).[7] While more moderate Democrats have shifted sympathy toward the Palestinians as well, the most dramatic swing has come from liberal Democrats. In 2016, liberal Democrats had greater sympathy for Israel by a 33 percent to 22 percent margin. By 2018, the same group favored Palestinians by a margin of 35 percent to 19 percent. At the same time, Republicans have moved much more strongly toward support for Israel and its policies, the sharper rise among them correlating with greater conservatism.

The partisan divide on Israel is much stronger than it has been historically, but *within* the Democratic Party there is a clear, strong, and growing movement opposing the United States' one-sided and unwaveringly pro-Israel policies and actions. The available evidence suggests this is not a fringe position, although it remains a point of sharp division within the party itself—especially among elected officials. It also is not, as Sherman suggests, the result of slogans adopted by the "extreme left" of the Democratic Party. Rather, it is a sign that the current political moment is ripe for moving beyond the limits of orthodox political discourse, which has long framed any call for support of Palestinian rights as an exception to progressive values.

Although support for Palestinian rights is rising among self-identified Democrats in the United States, especially younger ones, the party continues to cling to its traditional positions. This is deeply troublesome, as the Republican Party has abandoned any pretense of interest in Palestinian rights. In recent years, the GOP has articulated an extreme vision of total Israeli victory and dominance over all the land that was once Palestine under Great Britain's mandate. In 2012, the Republican National Committee resolved to "support Israel in their natural and God-given right of self-governance and self-defense upon their own lands, recognizing that Israel is neither an attacking force nor an occupier of the lands of others; and that peace can be afforded the region only through a united Israel governed under one law for all people."[8] In 2016, the two-state solution was explicitly dropped from the Republican platform.[9] And once he took office, Donald Trump made it clear that the two-state solution was no longer a U.S. goal.[10] If all that wasn't clear enough, in November 2019, Secretary of State Mike Pompeo declared that Israel's settlements in the West Bank were legal under international law, a position shared by exceedingly few international law experts.[11]

Unfortunately, the Democratic response to this clear right-ward shift, even among otherwise progressive figures, has been weak. While the Right continues to advance its agenda of Palestinian marginalization, Democrats rarely, if ever, express the basic premise that Palestinians should have all of the same rights as Israelis. Also, rather than prioritizing the experiences, needs, and rights of Palestinians, the mainstream liberal and progressive response is often strongly focused on those of Israel. For example, some progressives will correctly argue that full equality for Palestinians, within whatever political alignments the people of Israel and Palestine ultimately choose, will benefit the vast majority of Israeli Jews. While persuasive and accurate, this argument reinforces the notion that Palestinian lives only matter to the extent that they converge with Israeli interests. Such an approach ignores the inherent value of Palestinian rights and freedom, as well as the morally urgent need to fight for them on their own terms.

To move beyond the current limits, progressives must embrace a more principled politics, one that begins by recognizing the fundamental humanity of Palestinians. From there, they can appeal to progressive values to assert that Palestinians are entitled to the same rights to freedom, justice, equality, safety, and self-determination as everyone else around the world. Only from this place can equal human, civil, individual, and national rights for both Israelis and Palestinians be achieved. This approach is not only morally and ethically sound; it is the only one that can win.

We contend, as we have demonstrated in this book, that a fundamental change needs to take place in the American political discussion. We have illustrated how the United States has been deeply complicit in creating the political crisis that exists today. But it is not the reactionary pro-Israel religious zealots in the Jewish and Christian communities, the conservative, Islamophobic ideologues, or aging cold warriors and War on Terror crusaders who make the Israel-Palestine crisis unique. After all, these groups are acting according to their views and beliefs. Instead, it is the self-titled progressives who *contradict* their beliefs by justifying or ignoring behavior by Israel that they oppose or at least treat gravely when it is at the hands of other state actors.

"Israel is in a tough neighborhood" is an excuse often made by both progressive and conservative defenders of Israel. Yet Israel's treatment of the Palestinians has severely strained hard-won peace treaties with Egypt and Jordan, and complicated efforts by Israel to establish relationships with other Arab states. As such, Israel has helped to create the very neighborhood that serves as a scapegoat to justify its repressive and isolating policies and practices. To move beyond the current limits, we must be willing to hold the Israeli government—not just right-wing extremists, religious zealots, or neighboring regimes—accountable for its actions in the region, and especially for its denial of basic rights to Palestinians.

The idea of an American "honest broker" in the Middle East has been a joke for decades. Only a real debate over U.S.

policy can change that. That debate cannot happen if liberals refuse to critically examine every aspect of U.S. policy toward Israel and Palestine to determine whether it is in step with their core political values. No longer can any position be "taken for granted," nor can any solution be viewed as a non-starter. Rather, we must be willing to critically interrogate our entire approach to the current crisis. We must be willing to embrace, or at least consider, any solution that will yield freedom, justice, safety, and self-determination for everyone. This has been a demand placed on Palestinians and their supporters for a very long time, requiring them to justify the fight for their rights against accusations of bias against Israel and even against Jews in general. In a conflict as fraught with passion and zealotry as this one is, this sort of critical approach must be demanded equally of all sides and key players involved.

Progressives rightly criticized Benjamin Netanyahu when he barred Congresswomen Tlaib and Omar from entering Israel in 2019.[12] Some rightly complain about settlement expansion, and many recognize the harsh conditions in the West Bank and Gaza. But when it comes to an actual substantive policy debate, there is no appetite for it. This needs to change if there is ever going to be a livable future for Palestinians and Israelis. Ultimately, American progressives and those we elect must be willing to engage in sincere and serious conversations about the current policy context. They must also be willing to place appropriate pressure on the Israeli government—something we do without hesitation to the Palestinians—to act in accordance with international law and basic human rights norms.

American progressives cannot wave a magic wand and solve the Israel-Palestine conflict, but we can certainly take action. We can push Israel to allow the people of Gaza the freedom to rebuild their economy. We can put real pressure on Israel to stop expanding its settlements, and to allow Palestinian towns to grow, as well as allow the free movement of Palestinians in the West Bank. We can make it clear that our democratic values demand that we support Palestinians having the same right to a national existence as Israelis do, and the same right to live in peace and security. We can press Israel to stop blocking the rights that Palestinians are just as entitled to as anyone else. In short, we can act on our principles, which maintain that oppressive conditions diminish life for all but the very few who profit from them.

With the rise of anti-Semitism in the United States, Europe, and elsewhere, Jewish people everywhere need and deserve solidarity with liberals to survive. But if that solidarity comes at the expense of another people, it is ultimately self-defeating. In the wake of a horrific attack on an ultra-orthodox Jewish community in Monsey, New York, during the festival of Hanukkah in December 2019, one member of that community wrote, "The natural friends of Orthodox Jews are other minority communities next to whom we live. A large part of the black, Latino and Muslim communities, our neighbors, look at us religious Jews as their natural allies against a world of enmity and hate."[13] Sharing that article across Twitter, Palestinian-American activist Linda Sarsour added, "After experiencing a horrific incident of hate & violence, Shimon Rolnitzky, Hasidic Jew from Monsey wrote this. It's all we need in this moment. Awe-inspiring. Moving. It's a call to action for our communities to reject the divisions."[14] That same spirit can animate a real change in Israel and Palestine. It can change U.S. policy toward this long-standing crisis. We have seen how much influence the United States can wield in creating injustice. Now is the time to see how much power we have to dismantle it.

Acknowledgments

We wish to thank Samer Abboud, Joel Beinin, Noura Erakat, Nadia Hijab, Treva B. Lindsey, R. L'Heureux-McCoy, Lincoln Shlensky, Melissa Valle, and Rebecca Vilkomerson for the valuable advice and feedback they generously offered. Their critical insights raised the quality of this book immeasurably.

Notes

Preface

1. For a review of some of the dissent against these decisions, see Elham Fakhro, Twitter, August 16, 2020, twitter.com/elhamfakhro/status/13050875 28828108800. For the UAE government's response, see "UAE Arrests Opponents of Israel Peace Deal," *Middle East Monitor*, August 17, 2020, www.mid dleeastmonitor.com/20200817-uae-arrests-opponents-of-israel-peace-deal. For the Bahraini government's response, see "Bahrain to Take 'Legal Steps' Against Critics of Deal with Israel," *Middle East Monitor*, October 14, 2020, www.middleeastmonitor.com/20201014-bahrain-to-take-legal-steps-against -critics-of-deal-with-israel. At this writing, Sudan was still grappling with how to address broad disagreement with the decision to normalize relations, balanced against the country's desperate need for economic relief. See, "'Ignition of New War:' Sudan Political Parties Reject Israel Deal," *Al Jazeera*, October 24, 2020, www.aljazeera.com/news/2020/10/24/sudans-political -parties-reject-israeli-normalisation-deal.

2. See "Arab Peace Initiative: Full Text," *The Guardian*, March 28, 2002, www.theguardian.com/world/2002/mar/28/israel7.

3. See for example, Greg Jaffe, "Biden Defends Obama's Policies at Pro-Israel Gathering," *South Florida Sun-Sentinel*, March 21, 2016, www.sun -sentinel.com/florida-jewish-journal/jj-biden-defends-obamas-policies-at -proisrael-gathering-20160321-story.html.

4. See "Joe Biden and the Jewish Community: A Record and a Plan of Friendship, Support and Action," Joebiden.com, joebiden.com/joe-biden-and-the-jewish -community-a-record-and-a-plan-of-friendship-support-and-action.

NOTES

Introduction: Palestine Cannot Be an Exception

1. Christopher Cadelago and Ted Hesson, "Why Trump Is Talking Nonstop About The Migrant Caravan," *Politico*, October 23, 2018, www.politico.com/story/2018/10/23/trump-caravan-midterm-elections-875888.

2. U.S. Department of State, "On U.S. Assistance to UNRWA," press release, August 31, 2018, state.gov/on-u-s-assistance-to-unrwa.

3. See Karen DeYoung, Ruth Eglash, and Hazem Balousha, "U.S. Ends Aid to United Nations Agency Supporting Palestinian Refugees," *Washington Post*, August 31, 2018, www.washingtonpost.com/world/middle_east/us-aid-cuts-wont-end-the-right-of-return-palestinians-say/2018/08/31/8e3f25b4-ad0c-11e8-8a0c-70b618c98d3c_story.html

4. Ben Riley-Smith, "Donald Trump Suggests US Soldiers Could Fire on Migrant Caravans If They Throw Rocks," *The Telegraph*, November 1, 2018, www.telegraph.co.uk/news/2018/11/01/donald-trump-says-migrant-caravans-will-meet-wall-people-border/.

5. TOI Staff and AFP, "Netanyahu: No Palestinian State on My Watch," *Times of Israel*, March 16, 2015, www.timesofisrael.com/netanyahu-no-palestinian-state-under-my-watch/.

6. B'Tselem, "The Jordan Valley," www.btselem.org/topic/jordan_valley.

7. Avi Shlaim, "Believe It or Not, Barack Obama Had Israel's Best Interest at Heart," *The Guardian*, January 17, 2017, www.theguardian.com/commentisfree/2017/jan/17/barack-obama-netanyahu-trump-israel.

8. The term "qualitative military edge" (QME) refers to the longstanding U.S. policy practice of ensuring that Israel possesses superior "weaponry, tactics, training, leadership, and other factors of military effectiveness to deter or defeat its numerically superior adversaries in the Middle East." See William Wunderle and Andre Briere, *US Foreign Policy and Israel's Qualitative Military Edge: The Need for a Common Vision*, The Washington Institute for Near East Policy, January 2008, www.washingtoninstitute.org/uploads/Documents/pubs/PolicyFocus80Final.pdf. In 2008, Congress passed a law that included a requirement that the president ensure Israel's QME. As a result, Obama was legally bound to account for that condition in considering aid packages to Israel. Nonetheless, the aid package he gave was very generous, far exceeding the minimum Israel would have needed to maintain its QME. For background on the legislation and its impact on U.S. decision-making, see Mitchell Plitnick, "Israeli Lobby Looks to 2008 Law to Justify Request for More U.S. Aid," Inter Press Service, August 28, 2013, www.ipsnews.net/2013/08/israeli-lobby-looks-to-2008-law-to-justify-request-for-more-u-s-aid/.

9. The most prominent of these religious-nationalist groups is Lehava, which is connected with the political party Otzma Yehudit. (The overtones

of the name, which means "Jewish Power," are quite intentional.) Netan-yahu courted Otzma Yehudit, but the party was so controversial that even right-of-center Jewish groups around the world decried him for working with them. For an in-depth look at Lehava, see Ayelett Shani, "'They're Not Like Neo-Nazis': Inside the Israeli Movement Fighting Jewish-Arab Inter-marriage," *Haaretz*, December 15, 2018, www.haaretz.com/israel-news/. premium.MAGAZINE-inside-israeli-movement-fighting-jewish-arab-inter marriage-1.6744186. For information on Otzma Yehudit, see David M. Halb-finger, "Netanyahu Sparks Outrage over Pact with Racist Party," *New York Times*, February 24, 2019, www.nytimes.com/2019/02/24/world/middleeast /benjamin-netanyahu-otzma-yehudit-jewish-power.html.

10. See Human Rights Watch, "Israel: Don't Lock Up Asylum Seekers," January 22, 2018, www.hrw.org/news/2018/01/22/israel-dont-lock-asylum -seekers.

11. See Hadas Yaron, Nurit Hashimshony-Yaffe, and John Campbell, "'Infiltrators' or Refugees? An Analysis of Israel's Policy towards African Asylum-Seekers." *International Migration*, eprints.soas.ac.uk/15955/1/Infli trators%20or%20refugees%20-%20final.pdf.

12. The most obvious example of a Jewish Israeli being killed for their stance on peace is the late prime minister Yitzhak Rabin, assassinated in 1995 by a right-wing extremist over his decision to grant limited autonomy to the Palestinians. The best-known example of an *activist* being killed is the case of Emil Grunzweig, a member of the group Peace Now who lost his life when a right-winger threw a grenade at a pro-peace demonstration in 1983. See "Thousands Attend Israeli's Funeral," *New York Times*, Febru-ary 12, 1983, www.nytimes.com/1983/02/12/world/thousands-attend-israeli-s -funeral.html.

Chapter 1: The Right to Exist

1. Abba Eban, "The Saudi Text," *New York Times*, November 18, 1981, www.nytimes.com/1981/11/18/opinion/the-saudi-text.html.

2. Benedict Anderson, *Imagined Communities: Reflections on the Origin and Spread of Nationalism*, rev. ed. (London: Verso Books, 2016), 1–2.

3. For example, long-rumored clandestine contacts between Israel and Saudi Arabia became increasingly transparent during the Trump adminis-tration. The Saudis still could not be completely open about it. See Agence France-Presse, "Saudi Crown Prince Won't Meet Netanyahu, Riyadh Says," *Times of Israel*, February 13, 2020, www.timesofisrael.com/saudi-crown -prince-wont-meet-netanyahu-riyadh-says/. But they clearly wanted to open their relationship more, see for example, Suzan Quitaz, "Saudi-Israeli

Relations: The Emergence of a New Alliance," The New Arab, August 14, 2019, www.alaraby.co.uk/english/indepth/2019/8/14/saudi-israeli-relations -the-emergence-of-a-new-alliance. Even Iran and Israel, despite their deadly enmity, communicated more over the years than many would believe. For a review of that relationship, see, among others, Trita Parsi, *Treacherous Alliance: The Secret Dealings of Israel, Iran, and the United States*, Yale University Press, 2008.

4. For an exploration of religious Jewish anti-Zionism, ranging across the religious Jewish spectrum, see Yakov Rabkin, *A Threat from Within: A Century of Jewish Opposition to Zionism* (London: Zed Books, 2006). For a collection of largely secular Jewish critiques of Zionism, see Adam Shatz, ed., *Prophets Outcast: A Century of Dissident Jewish Writing about Zionism and Israel* (New York: Nation Books, 2004).

For a full exploration of the question of Jewish nationhood, both in the modern sense and in terms of a longer historical consciousness, see, among others, Boas Evron, *Jewish State or Israeli Nation?* (Bloomington: Indiana University Press, 1995).

The best-known nationalist alternative to Zionism was the Jewish Labour Bund, which developed in Eastern Europe in the late nineteenth and early twentieth centuries. For background, see Jack Jacobs, ed., *Jewish Politics in Eastern Europe: The Bund at 100* (New York: New York University Press), 2001. For an overview of anti-Zionist movements and non-Zionist alternatives, both historical and contemporary, see Ben Lorber, "Jewish Alternatives to Zionism: A Partial History," *Jewish Voice for Peace*, January 11, 2019, jewishvoiceforpeace.org/a-partial-history-of-jewish-alternatives/.

5. Noura Erakat, "Palestinians Have No Choice but to Continue the Struggle," *Washington Post*, May 16, 2018, www.washingtonpost.com/news /global-opinions/wp/2018/05/16/palestinians-have-no-choice-but-to-continue -the-struggle/.

6. For example, see the fears expressed by former Israeli Knesset member Einat Wilf that by giving up the special status of Jews in Israel, this will inevitably lead to persecution of Jews, in a live debate, organized by Intelligence Squared, on the motion that "Anti-Zionism Is the New Anti-Semitism": Intelligence Squared U.S., February 27, 2020, www.intelligencesquaredus.org /debates/anti-zionism-new-anti-semitism?fbclid=IwAR0HmgggZx7foSDJyb GV1KvaWloLnz8zaKcW44enY7y8a_QjQY05ZTYIf50. See also the words of Israeli historian Benny Morris, predicting that "as soon as [the Palestinians] do have rights, the state will no longer be Jewish," and as a result, "[t]his place will decline like a Middle Eastern state with an Arab majority. The violence between the different populations, within the state, will increase.

The Arabs will demand the return of the refugees. The Jews will remain a small minority within a large Arab sea of Palestinians, a persecuted or slaughtered minority, as they were when they lived in Arab countries. Those among the Jews who can, will flee to America and the West." Ofer Aderet, "'Israel Will Decline, and Jews Will Be a Persecuted Minority. Those Who Can Will Flee to America,'" *Haaretz*, January 22, 2019, www.haaretz.com/us-news/.pre mium.MAGAZINE-israel-will-decline-and-jews-will-be-persecuted-those -who-can-will-flee-1.6848498.

7. For his full argument, see Ali Abunimah, "Israeli Jews and the One-State Solution," *Electronic Intifada*, November 10, 2009, electronicintifada .net/content/israeli-jews-and-one-state-solution/8528.

8. Brig.-Gen. (res.) Yossi Kuperwasser, "The 'Peaceful' Movement to Destroy Israel," Jerusalem Center for Public Affairs, May 3, 2019, https://jcpa .org/article/the-peaceful-movement-to-destroy-israel.

9. See Noura Erakat, *Justice for Some: Law and the Question of Palestine* (Stanford, CA: Stanford University Press, 2019), 238.

10. See, among others, Erakat, *Justice for Some*.

11. See, for example, Rabbi Arik Ascherman, "What I Wish for the Settler Who Attacked Me with a Knife," *Haaretz*, October 30, 2015, www.haaretz .com/opinion/.premium-what-i-wish-for-the-settler-who-attacked-me-with-a -knife-1.5415356. In fact, the Israeli peace movement is a mix of not only Jews and Palestinians, but of people with a wide variety of views and allegiances when it comes to Zionism.

12. For an exploration of the early history of Zionist thought, see, among others, Laurence J. Silberstein, *The Postzionism Debates: Knowledge and Power in Israeli Culture* (Oxon, UK: Routledge, 1999).

13. "Statement to the Knesset by Prime Minister Begin upon the Presentation of his Government—20 June 1977," State of Israel, Ministry of Foreign Affairs, Foreign Policy Historical Documents, 1977–1979, mfa.gov.il/MFA /ForeignPolicy/MFADocuments/Yearbook3/Pages/1%20Statement%20 to%20the%20Knesset%20by%20Prime%20Minister%20Begi.aspx.

14. "Statement to the Knesset."

15. Though correctly perceived as a right-wing hardliner, and though his initial claim to fame was as the leader of the right-wing militia, the Irgun Z'Vai Leumi (IZL, or Irgun), which had committed some clearly terrorist actions during the 1948 war, Begin was known as both a fervent Jewish nationalist and a strong believer in civil rights, even if the former would always take precedence over the latter. Like his mentor, Ze'ev Jabotinsky—the founder of the Revisionist movement that would later spawn the Herut party, the main party in the Likud coalition, both of which had Begin as their first leader—who

envisioned a state where the prime minister would be Jewish and the vice PM would be Arab, Begin was willing to consider the idea of offering the Palestinians under occupation the option of citizenship (see, for instance, "Memorandum of Conversation between US President Jimmy Carter and Israeli Prime Minister Menachem Begin and their Delegations," Foreign Relations of the United States, 1977–1980, Vol. VIII, Arab Israeli Dispute, Document 232, history.state.gov/historicaldocuments/frus1977-80v08/d232).

It is on the basis of Begin's reputation as both a strong nationalist and, secondarily, a believer in human rights that many observers have expressed the belief that Begin would be quite displeased with the Likud under Benjamin Netanyahu. See, for example, Daniel Gordis, A Dose of Nuance: Would Menachem Begin Recognize the Likud?," *Jerusalem Post*, December 11, 2014, www.jpost.com/Opinion/A-dose-of-nuance-Would-Menachem-Begin-rec ognize-the-Likud-384360; and Denouncing 'Unacceptable Remarks,' Rivlin Promises Equality for Israeli-Arabs," i24 News, March 11, 2019, www.i24 news.tv/en/news/israel/196859-190311-denouncing-unacceptable-remarks -rivlin-promises-equality-for-israeli-arabs.

16. See "Israel-Egypt Peace Treaty," Israeli Ministry of Foreign Affairs, March 26, 1979, mfa.gov.il/mfa/foreignpolicy/peace/guide/pages/israel-egypt %20peace%20treaty.aspx; "Treaty of Peace Between the Hashemite Kingdom of Jordan and the State of Israel," King Hussein Website, October 26, 1994, www.kinghussein.gov.jo/peacetreaty.html.

17. See, among others, Avi Shlaim, *The Iron Wall: Israel and the Arab World* (New York: W.W. Norton, 2000). For the cited passage, see p. 16.

18. See Ian Lustick, "To Build and to Be Built By: Israel and the Hidden Logic of the Iron Wall," *Israel Studies* 1, no. 1 (1996): 199.

19. Shlaim, *The Iron Wall*, 606.

20. Ze'ev Jabotinsky, "The Iron Wall," Jabotinsky Institute in Israel, April 11, 1923, en.jabotinsky.org/media/9747/the-iron-wall.pdf.

21. Jabotinsky, "The Iron Wall."

22. Jabotinsky, "The Iron Wall."

23. Jabotinsky, "The Iron Wall."

24. See, among others, Shlaim, "The Iron Wall"; Lustick, "To Build and to Be Built By"; See also Yakov Hagoel, "Ze'ev Jabotinsky, His Legacy and Importance in Zionism," *Jerusalem Post*, July 11, 2018, www.jpost.com/Opin ion/Zeev-Jabotinsky-his-legacy-and-importance-in-Zionism-562268; Jordan Chandler Hirsch, "Bibi's Political Forefather?," *Tablet Magazine*, April 20, 2012, www.tabletmag.com/jewish-news-and-politics/97334/bibis-political -forefather; among others.

25. Jabotinsky, "The Iron Wall."

26. See Munayyer's argument in the video of the IQ2US-hosted debate "Anti-Zionism Is the New Anti-Semitism."

27. "Memorandum of Agreement between the Governments of Israel and the United States, the Geneva Peace Conference," Gerald R. Ford Presidential Library and Museum, September 1, 1975, www.fordlibrarymuseum.gov /library/document/0331/1553991.pdf.

28. "Resolution 242 (1967)," United Nations Security Council, November 22, 1967, unispal.un.org/DPA/DPR/unispal.nsf/0/7D35E1F729DF491C 85256EE700686136.

29. "Resolution 338 (1973)," United Nations Security Council, October 22, 1973, unispal.un.org/UNISPAL.NSF/0/7FB7C26FCBE80A31852560C500 65F878.

30. The internationally recognized borders of Israel, then as now, are the armistice lines—often referred to as the "Green Line"—established at the end of the war for Israel's creation in 1949. Israel has never accepted those as formal borders and insists that those boundaries cannot be "secured." Therefore, while many countries have recognized Israel's existence within the Green Line, Israel itself has never defined its own borders, raising questions for Palestinians as to what exactly the contours of any recognition it might give would be and providing the basis, however questionable, for Israel to claim territory outside of the Green Line as an equal part of its territory as that which is within it.

31. The PLO's Ten-Point Plan maintained the goal of liberating all of historic Palestine but made it clear that it would accept a state on whatever land it could win. It also maintained the right to armed resistance, but clearly opened the door to other tactics. See Permanent Observer Mission of Palestine to the United Nations, "10 Point Program of the PLO (1974), Political Program Adopted at the 12th Session of the Palestine National Council, Cairo, 8 June 1974, archived at web.archive.org/web /20110805192136/www.un.int/wcm/content/site/palestine/cache/offonce /pid/12354;jsessionid=ED2AC7E70A82F5C7CCB42BC6357FCDEC.

Palestinians generally understood the plan to indicate that the PLO was willing to accept a truncated state and live side by side with Israel. See, for example, Muhammed Muslih, "Towards Coexistence: An Analysis of the Resolutions of the Palestine National Council," *Journal of Palestine Studies*, 19, no. 4 (1990), 3–29, jps.ucpress.edu/content/19/4/3. Some reacted quite negatively, forming what was known as the "Rejectionist Front," or, more formally, as the "Front of the Palestinian Forces Rejecting Solutions of Surrender." But the Ten-Point Plan also enjoyed support from a diverse array of Palestinians. Jewish reaction was mixed and largely suspicious, frequently describing the

Ten-Point plan as an attempt to destroy Israel by diplomacy. Conservative historian Efraim Kersh articulates the view well, calling the plan a part of the "phased strategy" of eliminating Israel piece by piece. See Karsh, "Arafat's Grand Strategy," Middle East Quarterly, Spring 2004, pp. 3–11, www.me forum.org/605/arafats-grand-strategy.

32. For a fuller account of the Sinai II Agreement negotiations and outcomes, see Edward Sheehan, "Step by Step in the Middle East," *Journal of Palestine Studies*, 5, no. 2 (1975/76), 3–53, or www.palestine-studies.org/jps/fulltext /38407. In that article, Kissinger's own aides describe the language of the memorandum, despite its mitigation by the Americans, as "mind-boggling" and cites the paragraph regarding conditions for talking to the PLO as an example.

33. Bernard Gwertzman, "Reagan Administration Held 9-Month Talks with P.L.O.," *New York Times*, February 19, 1984, www.nytimes.com/1984 /02/19/world/reagan-administration-held-9-month-talks-with-plo.html ?module=inline.

34. "Speech by Yasser Arafat to the United Nations, November 13, 1988," *Haaretz*, May 13, 2002, www.haaretz.com/1.5268352.

35. "419. Statement by Yasser Arafat, 14 December 1988," Israel Ministry of Foreign Affairs, Historical Documents, Volume 9–10: 1984–1988, mfa .gov.il/MFA/ForeignPolicy/MFADocuments/Yearbook7/Pages/419%20State ment%20by%20Yasser%20Arafat-%2014%20December%201988.aspx.

36. "Text of Reagan Statement," *New York Times*, December 15, 1988, www.nytimes.com/1988/12/15/world/text-of-reagan-statement.html.

37. The Palestinian Declaration of Independence, drafted by famed Palestinian poet Mahmoud Darwish, translated into English by scholar Edward Said, and proclaimed by Yasser Arafat on November 15, 1988, at the closing session of the 19th Palestinian National Convention, was a key document of Palestinian nationalism. The text called for a Palestinian state and proclaimed the PLO as the sole representative of the Palestinian people—a noteworthy gesture given the establishment of Hamas the prior year. The text also explicitly described Palestine as "the land of the three monotheistic faiths," thereby affirming the land's Jewish historical connection. See James Gelvin, *Israeli-Palestinian Conflict: One Hundred Years of War* (Cambridge: Cambridge University Press, 2004); Jamal R. Nassar, *The Palestinian Liberation Organization: From Armed Struggle to the Declaration of Independence* (New York: Praeger, 1991); Rashid Khalidi, "The Resolutions of the 19th Palestine National Council," *Journal of Palestine Studies* 19, no. 2 (1990): 29–42.

38. Josh M. Goshko, "Arafat PLO Accepts Israeli State," *Washington Post*, December 8, 1988, www.washingtonpost.com/archive/politics/1988/12/08 /arafat-plo-accepts-israeli-state/e0034b38-c5c1-4408-ac71-6a8c0efa22b9.

39. Akiva Eldar, "The Art of Intransigence, From Shamir to Netanyahu," *Haaretz*, July 3, 2012, www.haaretz.com/netanyahu-shamir-minus-the-mus tache-1.5199892.

40. See Seth Anziska, *Preventing Palestine: A Political History from Camp David to Oslo* (Princeton: Princeton University Press, 2018); Edward Said, *The End of the Peace Process: Oslo and After* (New York: Vintage, 2007). These works, among others, track the intent of the Oslo Accords, its flaws, and, ultimately, its failures.

41. "Israel-PLO Recognition Exchange of Letters Between PM Rabin and Chairman Arafat," UNISPAL, September 9, 1993, unispal.un.org/UNIS PAL.NSF/0/36917473237100E285257028006C0BC5.

42. "Israel-PLO Recognition Exchange of Letters."

43. *Intifada* in Arabic literally means "shaking off" and was used by Palestinians and, subsequently, by most others to describe the uprisings against the Israeli occupation.

44. David Rose, "The Gaza Bombshell," *Vanity Fair*, April 2008, www.van ityfair.com/news/2008/04/gaza200804.

45. This exchange was part of a meeting whose transcript was revealed in the "Palestine Papers," released by the Al Jazeera news network. See "'The Palestine Papers: Minutes from 8th Negotiation Team Meeting (In Preparation for Annapolis), Tuesday, 13th November 2007," Al Jazeera, January 2011, www .ajtransparency.com/en/projects/thepalestinepapers/2012182374023465 6.html. The Israeli government had previously demanded recognition as a Jewish state in its reservations to U.S. president George W. Bush's "Roadmap for Peace," where Prime Minister Ariel Sharon also connected that recognition with negating Palestinian claims for the return of refugees, stating that "declared references must be made to Israel's right to exist as a Jewish state and to the waiver of any right of return for Palestinian refugees to the State of Israel." See "Israel's Road Map Reservations," *Haaretz*, May 27, 2003, www .haaretz.com/1.5471994.

46. Tal Becker, biography, Shalom Hartmann Institute, hartman.org.il/per son/tal-becker/.

47. All subsequent discussion of Becker's work on this question refers to Tal Becker, *The Claim for Recognition of Israel as a Jewish State: A Reassessment*, Policy Focus #108, Washington Institute for Near East Policy, February 2011, www.washingtoninstitute.org/uploads/Documents/pubs/Policy Focus108.pdf.

48. For a comprehensive overview of the history of the land in question, and the many cultures it has been home to, see, among others, Nur Masalha, *Palestine: A Four Thousand Year History* (London: Zed Books, 2018).

49. For an explanation of the magnitude of the compromise in Palestinian eyes of recognizing Israel's existence on some 78 percent of the land that constituted Palestine before 1948, see Khalil Shikaki, "Do Palestinians Still Support the Two-State Solution? Why Israeli Settlements Are the Greatest Obstacle to Peace," *Foreign Affairs*, September 12, 2018, www.foreignaffairs.com/articles/middle-east/2018-09-12/do-palestinians-still-support-two-state-solution.

50. The Clinton Parameters were a set of basic parameters proposed by U.S. president Bill Clinton in December 2000 for resolving the struggles over Israel-Palestine. These negotiations emerged in the aftermath of the failed Camp David Summit in July 2000 between Clinton, Yasser Arafat, and Israeli prime minister Ehud Barak, as well as the outbreak of the Second Intifada that September. For an analysis of the complexities—and public misrepresentations—of the negotiations, see Clayton Swisher, *The Truth About Camp David: The Untold Story About the Collapse of the Middle East Peace Process* (New York: Nation Books, 2009).

51. Ghada Karmi, "Palestine and the Right of Return," *Irish Times*, September 6, 2016, www.irishtimes.com/culture/books/ghada-karmi-palestine-and-the-right-of-return-1.2781331.

52. See Article 13(2) of the Universal Declaration of Human Rights: "Everyone has the right to leave any country, including his own, and to return to his country" (www.un.org/en/universal-declaration-human-rights). See also Article 12 of the International Covenant on Civil and Political Rights, which Israel has signed and ratified (treaties.un.org/doc/publication/unts/volume%20999/volume-999-i-14668-english.pdf), and Article 5 of the International Convention on the Elimination of All Forms of Racial Discrimination (www.ohchr.org/en/professionalinterest/pages/cerd.aspx), which Israel has also signed and ratified. These agreements have the full force of international law and give that force to UN General Assembly Resolution 194, Article 11, which resolves that "the refugees wishing to return to their homes and live at peace with their neighbors should be permitted to do so at the earliest practicable date" (mfa.gov.il/mfa/internatlorgs/mfadocuments/pages/united%20nations%20general%20assembly%20resolution%20194%20-ii.aspx). For a summary of the case under international law for the Palestinian right of return, see Loureen Sayej, "Palestinian Refugees and the Right of Return in International Law," Oxford Human Rights Hub, May 14, 2018, ohrh.law.ox.ac.uk/palestinian-refugees-and-the-right-of-return-in-international-law/.

53. For an exploration of the legal background for the right of return, as well as its interaction with political realities, see Joseph Massad, "Palestinian Right of Return: The Legal Key to Undoing the Zionist Conquest,"

Middle East Eye, December 4, 2019, www.middleeasteye.net/opinion
/palestinian-right-return-legal-key-undoing-zionist-conquest.

54. Cited in Becker, updated link: H.C. 6698/95, Aadel Ka'adan v. Israel
Lands Administration, 54(1) P.D. 258, www.escr-net.org/sites/default/files
/Decision%20Kaadan_0.rtf.

55. For an overview of the problem of discrimination against minorities
in Israel, see, among others, the websites of Adalah: The Legal Center for
Arab Minority Rights in Israel, at www.adalah.org/en; the Association for
Civil Rights in Israel, www.english.acri.org.il/; and the Mossawa Center The
Advocacy Center for Arab Citizens in Israel, www.mossawa.org/eng. These
sites offer a comprehensive analysis of more than sixty-five Israeli laws that
directly or indirectly discriminate against non-Jewish citizens, as well as
residents of the occupied territories. The relative severity of this discrimination in comparison to racial/ethnic tensions in other states is a matter
of considerable debate, a fair examination of which is beyond the scope of
this book.

56. Taken from the full text of the bill's English translation found at "Basic
Law: Israel—The Nation-State of the Jewish People," translated by Avi Dich-
ter, a member of the Knesset and the bill's author, avidichter.co.il/wp-content
/uploads/2018/07/leom_law_en_press_18.7.18.pdf.

57. Adalah: The Legal Center for Arab Minority Rights in Israel, "Proposed Basic Law: Israel—The Nation State of the Jewish People," position
paper, July 16, 2018, www.adalah.org/uploads/uploads/Adalah%20Position
%20Paper%20-%20Basic%20Law%20Jewish%20Nation%20State%20-%20
ENGLISH%20-%2015072018%20-%20FINAL.pdf.

58. Bel Trew, "Israel Passes Jewish Nation Law Branded 'Racist' by Critics," *The Independent*, July 19, 2018, www.independent.co.uk/news/world
/middle-east/israel-jewish-nation-state-law-passed-arabs-segregation-pro
tests-benjamin-netanyahu-a8454196.html.

59. Palestinian Boycott, Sanctions and Divestment National Committee
(BNC), Adalah, Najwan Berekdar, and Omar Barghouti, "Israel Effectively
Declares Itself an Apartheid State," Palestinian BDS National Committee,
July 19, 2018, bdsmovement.net/news/israel-effectively-declares-itself-apart
heid-state.

60. Eric Cortellessa, "Reform and AJC Leaders Bitterly Criticize Israel's
Nation-State Bill," *Times of Israel*, July 19, 2018, www.timesofisrael.com/us
-jewish-group-deeply-disappointed-with-nation-state-bill/.

61. Yousef Munayyer, "'Does Israel Have a Right to Exist' Is a Trick Question," *The Forward*, January 22, 2019, forward.com/opinion/417930/does-is
rael-have-a-right-to-exist-is-a-trick-question/.

62. Anshel Pfeffer, "Stop Trying to Justify Israel," *Haaretz*, May 2, 2019, www
.haaretz.com/israel-news/.premium-stop-trying-to-justify-israel-1.7193231.

63. In his seminal work, Herzl wrote, "Let the sovereignty be granted us
over a portion of the globe large enough to satisfy the rightful requirements of
a nation; the rest we shall manage for ourselves." Theodor Herzl, *The Jewish
State* (New York: Dover, 1988), 92.

64. Nahum Barnea, "Inside the Talks' Failure: US Officials Open Up,"
Ynet, May 2, 2014, www.ynetnews.com/articles/0,7340,L-4515821,00.html.

Chapter 2: Criminalizing BDS

1. Kevin Robillard, "Watch HuffPost's Full Interview with Cory Booker,"
Huffington Post, June 5, 2019, www.huffpost.com/entry/full-interview-cory
-booker-video_n_5cf6e3e3e4b02b1bef093bd4.

2. For details on the ACLU's view of anti-BDS legislation, see Kate Ruane,
"Congress, Laws Suppressing Boycotts of Israel Are Unconstitutional. Sincerely, Three Federal Courts," ACLU, May 9, 2019, www.aclu.org/blog
/free-speech/congress-laws-suppressing-boycotts-israel-are-unconstitutional
-sincerely-three.

3. Robillard, "Full Interview with Cory Booker."

4. For a more elaborate expression of this argument, see Mitchell Plitnick,
"Congress Opposes Non-Violent Support for Palestinian Rights," *LobeLog*,
July 26, 2019, lobelog.com/congress-opposes-non-violent-support-for-pales
tinian-rights.

5. Gaby Del Valle, "Chick-fil-A's Many Controversies, Explained," Vox,
May 29, 2019, www.vox.com/the-goods/2019/5/29/18644354/chick-fil-a-anti
-gay-donations-homophobia-dan-cathy.

6. For an explanation of and background on the troubling Supreme Court
decision granting small corporations rights of religious freedom in Hobby
Lobby's lawsuit, see Sally Steenland, "Hobby Lobby's Win Is a Loss for Religious Liberty," Center for American Progress, July 16, 2014, www.american
progress.org/issues/religion/news/2014/07/16/93874/hobby-lobbys-win-is-a
-loss-for-religious-liberty/.

7. For casualty statistics, see B'Tselem: The Israeli Information for
Human Rights in the Occupied Territories, "10 Years to the Second
Intifada—Summary of Data," September 27, 2010, www.btselem.org
/press_releases/20100927. For a powerful and detailed Palestinian narra-
tive of the intifada, see Ramzy Baroud, "The Second Palestinian Intifada:
A Chronicle of a People's Struggle," Pluto Press, London, 2006. For an Is-
raeli view of the impact of the second intifada on Israelis, see, Ruchama
Marton, "The Psychological Impact of the Second Intifada on Israeli

Society," *Palestine-Israel Journal* 11, no. 1 (2004), www.pij.org/articles/18/the
-psychological-impact-of-the-second-intifada-on-israeli-society.

8. Suzanne Goldenberg and Will Woodward, "Israeli Boycott Divides Academics," *The Guardian*, July 8, 2002, www.theguardian.com/uk/2002/jul/08
/highereducation.israel.

9. The First Intifada lasted from December 1987 until the 1993 Oslo Accords, though some also point to the 1991 Madrid Conference as the point
of cessation.

10. Unified National Leadership of the Uprising, The Palestine Liberation
Organization, "Communique No. 16," archived on the website of Matzpen,
issued May 13, 1988, matzpen.org/english/1988-07-31/communiques
-of-the-uprising/.

11. The idea that the BDS movement was actually a plot to continue the Arab
League boycott of Israel by other means has been repeated often enough to
have become an article of faith for some opponents of BDS. But there is no evidence to support this theory. Rather, the various papers and articles that refer
to this idea either provide no evidence of such a historical connection or refer
to other articles that also do not substantiate the claim. See, for example, Adam
Milstein and Marc A. Greendorfer, "BDS Ain't New: The Arab League Boycott Gets a Makeover," *Huffington Post*, February 5, 2017, www.huffpost.com
/entry/bds-aint-new-the-arab-lea_b_9167542; Marc A. Greendorfer, "The BDS
Movement: That Which We Call a Foreign Boycott, by Any Other Name, Is
Still Illegal," *Roger Williams University Law Review* 22, no. 1 (2017), docs.rwu
.edu/rwu_LR/vol22/iss1/2; Alex Joffe, "Palestinians and Internationalization:
Means and Ends," BESA Perspectives, The Begin-Sadat Center for Strategic
Studies, Paper No. 656, November 26, 2017, besacenter.org/wp-content/uploads
/2017/11/656-Palestinians-and-Internationalization-Joffe-final.pdf; and "Background of BDS," Amcha Initiative, amchainitiative.org/BDS-background.

12. Rachel Giora, "Milestones in the History of the Israeli BDS Movement: A Brief Chronology," Israeli Committee Against Home Demolitions,
January 27, 2010, icahd.org/wp-content/uploads/2015/04/ChronologyofIs
raeliBDSMovement.pdf.

13. Palestinian Campaign for the Academic and Cultural Boycott of Israel
(PACBI), "Call for an Academic and Cultural Boycott of Israel," July 6, 2004,
bdsmovement.net/pacbi/pacbi-call.

14. Palestinian Civil Society, "Palestinian Civil Society Call for BDS,"
July 9, 2005, bdsmovement.net/call.

15. PACBI, "Call for an Academic and Cultural Boycott of Israel."

16. Until recently, no other country had recognized Israel's annexation
of East Jerusalem or the Golan Heights. In 2018, President Donald Trump

recognized Jerusalem as Israel's capital and moved the U.S. embassy there from Tel Aviv. The embassy is now in West Jerusalem, and the recognition stopped short of recognizing Israel's annexation of the eastern part of the city, but it was a sharp break with the international consensus that had held since 1967 that all of Jerusalem would retain the interim status of an internationalized city until the dispute over the holy city was resolved in final status negotiations between Israel and Palestine. The U.S. decision broke that consensus and was generally agreed to have severely prejudiced any future negotiations decidedly in Israel's favor. Trump seemed to support this assessment when he said he had taken Jerusalem "off the table." In 2019, Trump was far more direct in recognizing Israel's annexation of and sovereignty over the Golan Heights. While no other countries have followed Trump's example yet, several have indicated their intentions to move their embassies to Jerusalem.

17. Palestinian Civil Society, "Palestinian Civil Society Call for BDS."

18. The argument that Israel represents an apartheid state is a rhetorical and legal argument that was already controversial at the time and would become more so later on. BDS advocates argue that the differentiation of rights between Palestinians and Israelis—a differentiation that takes a variety of forms depending on the location of the Palestinians, i.e., whether they are in Gaza, the West Bank, East Jerusalem, or within Israel—represents the very definition of apartheid, which means having different laws for different people under the same ruling authority based on arbitrary characteristics, such as race or religion. Crucially, this argument was once confined to the margins and associated almost exclusively with the BDS movement, but has come to be used by other critics of Israeli policies, including some who do not advocate BDS. See, for example, Eric Alterman's struggle with the recognition of apartheid's applicability while still opposing BDS: "The BDS Campaign's Unpopular Front," *Democracy Journal*, Winter 2018, no. 47, democracyjournal.org/magazine/47/the-bds-campaigns-unpopular-front/. Defenders of Israeli policies argue that the comparison to South Africa does not fit because the territories are "disputed," rather than being part of Israel (the term "disputed" is further employed in order to deny that the territories are under occupation), so the status of the Palestinians is in limbo until an agreement is reached. They consider the accusation of apartheid, therefore, insulting. For the exposition of this argument, see, among numerous sources, "Response to Common Inaccuracy: Israel Is an Apartheid State," Anti-Defamation League, www.adl.org/resources/fact-sheets/response-to-common-inaccuracy-israel-is-an-apartheid-state. For the argument that Israel is an apartheid state, see, for example, Noura Erekat, *Justice for Some: Law and he Question of Palestine* (Stanford, CA: Stanford University Press, 2019), 213–18.

19. "International Court of Justice Finds Israeli Barrier in Palestinian Territory Is Illegal," United Nations, July 9, 2004, news.un.org/en/story/2004 /07/108912-international-court-justice-finds-israeli-barrier-palestinian -territory-illegal. The ICJ further noted that it was not convinced that the design of the wall's route was based on security concerns, as Israel contended. The Israeli human rights group B'Tselem noted, "A key factor in determining the barrier's route was the location of settlements, thereby laying the groundwork for the de facto annexation of most of the settlements and much land for their future expansion. The barrier thus became a major political instrument for furthering Israeli annexationist goals." See B'Tselem, "The Separation Barrier," November 11, 2017, www.btselem.org/separation _barrier.

20. Statistics from the beginning of the second intifada on September 29, 2000, until December 26, 2008, show 4,902 Palestinians killed and 1,062 Israelis killed, with the vast majority of fatalities during the period of the intifada. See B'Tselem, "Fatalities Before Operation 'Cast Lead,'" www.btselem .org/statistics/fatalities/before-cast-lead/by-date-of-death.

21. Though beyond the scope of this book, it is important to note that the account of Barak and, even more so Clinton, is very much in dispute. Most notably, Robert Malley, who was part of the Clinton administration team and attended the summit, and Hussein Agha, long-time adviser to the PLO who was deeply involved in negotiations at that time, wrote a detailed essay on the subject. Though critical of the way Yasser Arafat handled the Camp David II Summit in 2000, he placed the failure of the summit in the context of flawed decisions both prior to and during the confab. See Malley and Agha, "Camp David: The Tragedy of Errors," *New York Review of Books*, August 9, 2001, www.nybooks.com/articles/2001/08/09/camp-david-the-tragedy-of-errors. There are many accounts of what led to the failure of the Camp David II Summit. Some support Clinton's view that Arafat was solely to blame for the failure—a stance that Clinton had promised Arafat he would not take should the summit fail, and a pre-condition Arafat demanded for his attendance. Others—indeed, most others—offer a more nuanced view that spread the blame around. A few of the more notable ones include: Aaron David Miller, *The Much Too Promised Land: America's Elusive Search for Arab-Israeli Peace* (New York: Bantam, 2008); Clayton E. Swisher, *The Truth About Camp David: The Untold Story About the Collapse of the Middle East Peace Process* (New York: Bold Type Books, 2009); Shlomo Ben-Ami, *Scars of War, Wounds of Peace: The Israeli-Arab Tragedy* (New York: Oxford University Press, 2007). Also see Akram Hanieh, "The Camp David Papers," *Journal of Palestine Studies* 30, no. 2 (2001), 75–97, jps.ucpress.edu/content/30/2/75.

22. The BDS movement explicitly notes, "Any group that propagates or tolerates forms of expression or activities that conflict with the movement's principles of anti-racism and non-violence or undermines the Palestinian rights stated in the BDS Call cannot be part of the BDS movement and will be considered outside the BDS movement and will be asked, by the BNC, to no longer use the BDS acronym or claim any affiliation to the movement." This is an unambiguous refutation of any association with violence or antisemitism. See "Statement on Affiliation with the BDS Movement and the Use of the BDS Acronym," BDS National Committee, July 1, 2019, bdsmove ment.net/news/statement-affiliation-bds-movement-and-use-bds-acronym.

23. A good review, and an important perspective on the causes and results of the 1936 revolt, can be found in Rashid Khalidi, *The Iron Cage: The Story of the Palestinian Struggle for Statehood* (Boston: Beacon Press, 2006), particularly 105–24. For an in-depth look at the revolt, see, among others, Ghassan Kanafani, *The 1936–39 Revolt in Palestine*, published in English by Committee for a Democratic Palestine (New York, 1972) and by Tricontinental Society (London, 1980).

24. Ghada Ageel, "Where Is Palestine's Martin Luther King? Shot or Jailed by Israel," *Washington Report on Middle Eastern Affairs*, August–September 2018, www.wrmea.org/2018-august-september/where-is-palestines-martin -luther-king-shot-or-jailed-by-israel.html.

25. For background on the weekly protests in Nabi Saleh, see Jaclynn Ashly, "Nabi Saleh: 'It's a silent ethnic cleansing,'" Al Jazeera, September 4, 2017, www.aljazeera.com/indepth/features/2017/07/nabi-saleh-silent-ethnic -cleansing-170702123734851.html.

For a view of Kafr Qaddum, see "Clashes between Palestinian Youth and Israeli Forces in Kafr Qaddum," International Middle East Media Center, November 10, 2017, imemc.org/article/clashes-between-palestinian-youth -and-israeli-forces-in-kafr-qaddum/.

26. Yousef Munayyer, "Palestine's Hidden History of Nonviolence," *Foreign Policy*, May 18, 2011, foreignpolicy.com/2011/05/18/palestines-hidden -history-of-nonviolence-2.

27. The circumstances around the Israeli decision to launch a major military operation against Gaza on December 27, 2008, are a matter of some controversy. The dominant account is that Israel was responding to rocket fire from Gaza that had escalated for no apparent reason over the preceding weeks. For an example of this coverage, see Taghreed El-Khodary and Ethan Bronner, "Israelis Say Strikes Against Hamas Will Continue," *New York Times*, December 27, 2008, www.nytimes.com/2008/12/28/world/mid

dleeast/28mideast.html. Other accounts, however, place the Hamas rocket escalation in the context of months of cross-border Israeli provocations. See, for example, Mitchell Plitnick's article "Did Israel Provoke Increase in Rockets to Justify Operation Cast Lead?," ReThinking Foreign Policy, February 8, 2011, mitchellplitnick.com/2011/02/08/did-israel-provoke-increase-in-rockets-to-justify-operation-cast-lead/. See "Operation Cast Lead," IMEU, January 4, 2012, imeu.org/article/operation-cast-lead. For the Israeli view of events, see "Operation Cast Lead—Israel Defends Its Citizens," Israeli Ministry of Foreign Affairs, mfa.gov.il/MFA/ForeignPolicy/Terrorism/GazaFacts/Pages/Operation-Cast-Lead-Israel-Defends-its-Citizens.aspx.

28. See *Rain of Fire: Israel's Unlawful Use of White Phosphorus in Gaza*, Human Rights Watch, March 25, 2009, www.hrw.org/report/2009/03/25/rain-fire/israels-unlawful-use-white-phosphorus-gaza.

29. In fact, Netanyahu would, some years later, explicitly state that he would not allow a Palestinian state. See "Netanyahu: No Palestinian State on My Watch," *Times of Israel*, March 16, 2015, www.timesofisrael.com/netanyahu-no-palestinian-state-under-my-watch. This contradicted a qualified nod to the idea of a Palestinian state that Netanyahu gave in a famous 2009 speech at Bar-Ilan University. See "Full Text of Netanyahu's Foreign Policy Speech at Bar Ilan," *Haaretz*, June 14, 2009, www.haaretz.com/1.5064276.

30. The death toll was initially nine. The tenth person died after being in a coma for four years.

31. In Turkish, the name of the group is İnsan Hak ve Hürriyetleri ve İnsani Yardım Vakfı, hence the abbreviation "IHH." This translates to "Foundation for Human Rights and Freedoms and Humanitarian Relief." See www.ihh.org.tr.

32. See "State Department Briefing by Phillip J. Crowley," eNews Park Forest, June 3, 2010, www.enewspf.com/national-news/latest-national-news/state-department-briefing-by-phillip-j-crowley-june-3-2010/.

33. Ron Kampeas, "Leaked Maps Show Gaps in Israeli-Palestinian Negotiations," Jewish Telegraphic Agency, January 25, 2011, www.jta.org/2011/01/25/israel/leaked-maps-show-gaps-in-israeli-palestinian-negotiations.

34. Mitchell Plitnick, "Does Everybody Know What Everybody Knows?," ReThinking Foreign Policy, January 25, 2011, mitchellplitnick.com/2011/01/25/does-everybody-know-what-everybody-knows.

35. Al Jazeera, "The Palestine Papers," www.aljazeera.com/palestinepapers. See also Clayton E. Swisher, *The Palestine Papers: The End of the Road?* (London: Hesperus Press, 2011).

36. Plitnick, "Does Everybody Know What Everybody Knows?"

37. Palestinian Civil Society, "Palestinian Civil Society Call for BDS."
38. The problematic nature of this disconnect would only grow over the years. When, in 2011, the Palestine Papers were published, they revealed that the PLO negotiators had agreed to limit the number of refugees that could return to Israel in the event of a two-state solution to just ten thousand, out of a total that had, by then, grown to over 5 million.
39. This is not to suggest that Palestinian identity is reducible to experiences of loss or violence. To the contrary, there are a wide and rich array of cultural, intellectual, political, and religious currents that shape Palestinian national consciousness. Still, as Rashid Khalidi explains, it is important to acknowledge the ways that "a strong sense of Palestinian national identity developed in spite of, and in some cases because of, the obstacles it faced." See *Palestinian Identity: The Construction of Modern National Consciousness* (New York: Columbia University Press, 1993).
40. A great deal of scholarship has debunked this version of events, but because key actors such as Clinton, Barak, and U.S. negotiator Dennis Ross, among others, have stood by this story, it continues to persist. The narrative tends to omit key points, such as Arafat's extreme reluctance to have the conference, owing to his sense that the two sides were much farther apart than Barak and Clinton believed. He agreed to attend only on condition that he not be blamed for its failure, a condition that was clearly broken. Another key point is that the violence did not start immediately, and that tensions were raised much higher by then opposition leader Ariel Sharon's incendiary visit to the Temple Mount in September 2000 with an ostentatiously large military guard. Clarifying scholarship can be found in numerous sources—e.g., Raviv Drucker, "'There Was No Generous Offer': A History of Peace Talks," translated by Lisa Goldman, +972 *Magazine*, April 26, 2014, 972mag.com /on-palestinian-positions-israeli-pundits-are-all-spin/90137/; David Clark, "The Brilliant Offer Israel Never Made," *The Guardian*, April 10, 2002, www.theguardian.com/world/2002/apr/10/comment; and works cited above in note 11.
41. For example, in 2012, Abbas stated that he saw Palestine now as the West Bank and Gaza and that he did not want to return to his ancestral home in Safed, inside Israel. See Harriet Sherwood, "Mahmoud Abbas Outrages Palestinian Refugees by Waiving His Right to Return," *The Guardian*, November 4, 2012, www.theguardian.com/world/2012/nov/04/mahmoud-abbas -palestinian-territories. The backlash was swift and fierce, and Abbas quickly qualified the statement, saying it was one of "personal view," not policy. See "Mahmoud Abbas: Right to Return Quote Was 'Personal View,'" *The*

Independent, November 5, 2012, www.independent.co.uk/news/world/mid dle-east/mahmoud-abbas-right-to-return-quote-was-personal-view-8281374 .html.

42. For a report on Reut's presentation, see Barak Ravid, "Think Tank: Israel Faces Global Delegitimization Campaign," *Haaretz*, February 12, 2010, www.haaretz.com/1.5050227?=&ts=_1563831974329. For Reut's executive summary, see Reut Institute, *The Delegitimization Challenge: Creating a Political Firewall*, February 14, 2010, www.reut-institute.org/en/Publication .aspx?PublicationId=3769. The full report can be found at Reut Institute, *Building a Political Firewall Against Israel's Delegitimization Conceptual Framework*, March 2010, www.reut-institute.org/data/uploads/PDFVer/201 00310%20Delegitimacy%20Eng.pdf.

43. Reut Institute, *Building a Political Firewall*, 32.

44. It should be noted that the universalist view is not confined to either a pro-Zionist or anti-Zionist view, nor need it favor or preclude any formula for resolving the territorial and other disputes between Israelis and Palestinians. It does, however, dictate that any solution must be based on equal rights for all. It must also take such a form that Zionism—defined not as a Jewish/Israeli superior right to the land but rather as the recognition of a Jewish-Zionist nation—is no more or less valid than Palestinian nationalism. If equal rights are accepted as a fundamental principle in all matters between Israelis and Palestinians, any solution can be tailored to accommodate that principle. Indeed, this is the very essence of democratic thought, particularly in multi-ethnic settings.

45. Amanpour & Company, "David Friedman on the Israeli-Palestinian Conflict," PBS, July 30, 2019, www.pbs.org/wnet/amanpour-and-company /video/david-friedman-on-the-israeli-palestinian-conflict/.

46. David Friedman, "Read Peter Beinart and You'll Vote Donald Trump," Arutz Sheva, June 5, 2016, www.israelnationalnews.com/Articles/Article .aspx/18828.

47. Anti-Defamation League, "The Top Ten Anti-Israel Groups in America," 2010, www.adl.org/sites/default/files/documents/assets/pdf/israel-inter national/Top-10-Anti-Israel-Groups-in-America.pdf.

48. US Campaign to End the Israeli Occupation, "Statement on Complaint Filed Regarding Alison Weir and If Americans Knew," US Campaign for Palestinian Rights, July 16, 2015, uscpr.org/archive/article.php-id=4510 .html; Jewish Voice for Peace, "Jewish Voice for Peace Statement on Our Relationship with Alison Weir," June 15, 2015, jewishvoiceforpeace.org/jewish -voice-for-peace-statement-on-our-relationship-with-alison-weir.

49. Anti-Defamation League, "News: Ranking the Top 10 Anti-Israel Groups in 2013," October 21, 2013, www.adl.org/news/press-releases/news-ranking-the-top-10-anti-israel-groups-in-2013-adl.

50. Ironically, Lapid himself would be accused of anti-Semitism in August 2019 over a campaign ad he posted portraying the leaders of Israel's religious parties as scheming to get "all of Israel's money." He faced criticism even within his own party for the ad, although it is fair to say that both the ad and the response were rooted in election politics and cynicism. Lapid has a long history of harsh criticism of the orthodox Jewish community and the religious parties in Israel. Lapid, in his own defense, said that the video was directed at Netanyahu's willingness to over-compensate the religious parties for supporting him, saying, "I see that the Haredi activists are screaming 'anti-Semitism.' The video was a joke (at Bibi's expense, actually). Those that incite indiscriminately scream 'incitement.' Those conducting the hateful discourse yell 'hate.' It won't help them. I do not plan to accept moralizing from those who don't stop cursing and slandering." See Jonathan Lis, "Netanyahu Accuses Yair Lapid of Anti-Semitism Over Anti-Haredi Election Video," *Haaretz*, August 5, 2019, www.haaretz.com/israel-news/elections/.premium-kahol-lavan-s-yair-lapid-accused-of-anti-semitism-over-anti-haredi-election-video-1.7642502.

51. Chemi Shalev, "Yair Lapid: BDS Leaders Are 'Out and Out Anti-Semites,'" *Haaretz*, June 7, 2015, www.haaretz.com/jewish/.premium-yair-lapid-bds-leaders-are-out-and-out-anti-semites-1.5370150.

52. United States Holocaust Memorial Museum, "Boycott of Jewish Businesses," Holocaust Encyclopedia, encyclopedia.ushmm.org/content/en/article/boycott-of-jewish-businesses.

53. In 2014, Liberman called for a boycott on businesses owned by Palestinian citizens of Israel who were protesting Israel's attacks on Gaza by closing their shops for a day. See Ariel Ben Solomon, "FM Liberman Calls for Boycott of Israeli Arab Businesses Who Strike for Gaza," *Jerusalem Post*, July 21, 2014, www.jpost.com/Operation-Protective-Edge/FM-Liberman-calls-for-boycott-of-Israeli-Arab-businesses-who-strike-for-Gaza-368360. Liberman again called for a boycott, this time against residents of Wadi Ara, a mostly Palestinian town in Israel where there had been protests and stone-throwing in 2017. This was part of Liberman's larger plan to transfer largely Palestinian areas of Israel to the Palestinian Authority in exchange for Israeli sovereignty over settlements in the West Bank, making the Palestinians living in those areas citizens of the Palestinian Authority rather than of Israel. See Ben Lynfield, "Liberman Calls for Jewish Boycott of Wadi

Ara Arabs," *Jerusalem Post*, December 10, 2017, www.jpost.com/Arab-Israeli
-Conflict/Liberman-calls-for-Jewish-boycott-of-Wadi-Ara-Arabs-517627.

54. Alexander Fulbright, "Liberman: Boycott *Haaretz* for Op-ed Calling
Israel's Religious Right More Dangerous Than Hezbollah," *Times of Israel*,
April 13, 2017, www.timesofisrael.com/liberman-calls-for-haaretz-boycott
-over-hezbollah-comparison/.

55. See, for example, Associated Press, "Report: Arabs Secretly Trade
with Israel," Ynet, December 26, 2005, www.ynetnews.com/articles/0,73
40,L-3190534,00.html; Ephraim Kalman, "Is There a Secret Arab-Israeli
Trade?," *Middle East Quarterly*, June 1998, www.meforum.org/393/is-there-a
-secret-arab-israeli-trade; Jacob Atkins, "Israel's Exports to Gulf States Worth
Almost $1 Billion, Study Suggests," i24 News, August 16, 2018, www.i24
news.tv/en/news/international/middle-east/181924-180816-israel-s-exports
-to-gulf-states-worth-almost-1-billion-study-suggests; Sebastian Shehadi,
"The Open Secret of Israeli-Moroccan Business Is Growing," Middle East
Eye, November 5, 2018, www.middleeasteye.net/news/open-secret-israeli
-moroccan-business-growing; and "Assessing Israel's Trade with Its Arab
Neighbours," Tony Blair Institute for Global Change, August 14, 2018, institute
.global/insight/middle-east/assessing-israels-trade-its-arab-neighbours.

56. Martin A. Weiss, *Arab League Boycott of Israel*, Congressional Research
Service, August 25, 2017, fas.org/sgp/crs/mideast/RL33961.pdf.

57. Nancy Turck, "The Arab Boycott of Israel," *Foreign Affairs* 55, no. 3
(1977), 483–84, www.jstor.org/stable/20039682.

58. Public Law 94–455; 90 Stat. 1649, October 4, 1976, books.google.
com/books?id=nHAFPmI3IIAC&pg=PA1649&dq=Public+Law+94%E2
%80%93455;+90+Stat.+1649&hl=en&sa=X&ved=2ahUKEwjZo9Cn0f3jAh
UC2FkKHabHAmwQ6AEwAHoECAEQAg#v=onepage&q=Public%20
Law%2094%E2%80%93455%3B%2090%20Stat.%201649&f=false.

59. Public Law 96-72, September 29, 1979, www.govinfo.gov/content/pkg
/STATUTE-93/pdf/STATUTE-93-Pg503.pdf.

60. Office of Antiboycott Compliance (OAC), "Objectives," Bureau of Industry and Security, Department Of Commerce, www.bis.doc.gov/index.php
/enforcement/oac.

61. "S.C. Code Ann. 11-35-5300 (2015)," *Harvard Law Review* 129, no. 2029
(2016), https://harvardlawreview.org/2016/05/s-c-code-ann-11-35-3500-2015/.

62. Jim Zanotti, Martin A. Weiss, Kathleen Ann Ruane, and Jennifer K.
Elsea, *Israel and the Boycott, Divestment, and Sanctions (BDS) Movement*,
Congressional Research Service, June 9, 2017, fas.org/sgp/crs/mideast/R4
4281.pdf.

63. Eugene Kontorovich, "Can States Fund BDS?," *Tablet Magazine*, July 13, 2015, www.tabletmag.com/jewish-news-and-politics/192110/can-states-fund-bds.

64. We note here that there is an ongoing, often very heated debate over the use of the word "apartheid" to describe the situation in Israel, although Israel's consideration during 2020 of annexing significant parts of the West Bank made the argument much more commonplace. The situations are, of course, not perfectly comparable and some sharp differences exist between the former South African system and the division between Israel and the Palestinian areas of the West Bank and Gaza. While the point in terms of Kontorovich's argument is largely irrelevant since we are critiquing his apartheid analogy, which we consider distorted, we also would point out that, according to the legal definition of "apartheid" in international law—which need not necessarily be reflected absolutely in the South African model—Israel clearly qualifies. According to the International Convention on the Suppression and Punishment of the Crime of Apartheid, the "crime of apartheid . . . shall apply to the following inhuman acts committed for the purpose of establishing and maintaining domination by one racial group of persons over any other racial group of persons and systematically oppressing them:

    (a) Denial to a member or members of a racial group or groups of the right to life and liberty of person:

      (i) By murder of members of a racial group or groups;

      (ii) By the infliction upon the members of a racial group or groups of serious bodily or mental harm, by the infringement of their freedom or dignity, or by subjecting them to torture or to cruel, inhuman or degrading treatment or punishment;

      (iii) By arbitrary arrest and illegal imprisonment of the members of a racial group or groups;

    (b) Deliberate imposition on a racial group or groups of living conditions calculated to cause its or their physical destruction in whole or in part;

    (c) Any legislative measures and other measures calculated to prevent a racial group or groups from participation in the political, social, economic and cultural life of the country and the deliberate creation of conditions preventing the full development of such a group or groups, in particular by denying to members of a racial group or groups basic human rights and freedoms, including the right to work, the right to form recognized trade unions, the right to education, the right to leave and to return to their country, the right to a nationality, the right to freedom of movement and residence, the right to freedom of opinion and expression, and the right to freedom of peaceful assembly and association;

(d) Any measures including legislative measures, designed to divide the population along racial lines by the creation of separate reserves and ghettos for the members of a racial group or groups, the prohibition of mixed marriages among members of various racial groups, the expropriation of landed property belonging to a racial group or groups or to members thereof;

(e) Exploitation of the labour of the members of a racial group or groups, in particular by submitting them to forced labour;

(f) Persecution of organizations and persons, by depriving them of fundamental rights and freedoms, because they oppose apartheid."

See "International Convention on the Suppression and Punishment of the Crime of Apartheid," United Nations, G.A. res. 3068 (XXVIII)), 28 U.N. GAOR Supp. (No. 30) at 75, U.N. Doc. A/9030 (1974), 1015 U.N.T.S. 243, entered into force July 18, 1976. www.un.org/en/genocideprevention/doc uments/atrocity-crimes/Doc.10_International%20Convention%20on%20 the%20Suppression%20and%20Punishment%20of%20the%20Crime%20of %20Apartheid.pdf.

It seems to us an inescapable conclusion that, under this definition, Israel clearly has systems in place that qualify as apartheid in the West Bank. It is also clear that arguments can be made for applying the term within Israel and in Gaza. In the former case, the counter-argument would be that what Palestinian citizens of Israel face is more akin to segregation than apartheid, while in the latter, it would be that Palestinians there face a siege or a blockade, not apartheid. But in either case, applying the term "apartheid" is both defensible and debatable, while in the West Bank it much more closely matches the legal, international definition.

65. The U.K. barred Begin's entry in the 1950s and described him in intelligence documents at the time as "the well-known former leader of the notorious terrorist organisation Irgun Zvei Leumi." See Amir Oren, "British Documents Reveal: Begin Refused Entry to U.K. in 1950s," *Haaretz*, July 7, 2011, www.haaretz.com/1.5025439. Tellingly, when a former member of the British Palestine Police Force was asked if Shamir was a terrorist, he responded, "Yes, to the British Government. But to the Jews, the Stern Gang (or LEHI, the group to which Shamir belonged) were freedom fighters. But

that is the same as the P.L.O., who are terrorists to the Israelis and freedom fighters to the Arabs." See Joel Brinkley, "The Stubborn Strength of Yitzhak Shamir," *New York Times*, August 21, 1988, www.nytimes.com/1988/08/21 /magazine/the-stubborn-strength-of-yitzhak-shamir.html.

66. Lara Friedman, "State Anti-Boycott Bills - Explicit Conflation of Israel & Settlements," Foundation for Middle East Peace, August 6, 2019, fmep.org /wp/wp-content/uploads/BDS-laws-Israel-territories.pdf.

67. In *Koontz v. Watson*, Esther Koontz challenged the Kansas commissioner of education, Randall Watson. U.S. District Court for the District of Kansas, Case No. 17-4099-DDC-KG, filed January 30, 2018, www.aclu.org /legal-document/koontz-v-watson-opinion. In *Jordahl et al. v. Brnovich et al.*, Mikkel Jordahl and his contracting company sued the State of Arizona. U.S. District Court for the District of Arizona, Case No. CV-17-08263-PCT-DJH, filed September 27, 2018, www.acluaz.org/sites/default/files/field_docu ments/order_granting_plaintiffs_motion_for_preliminary_injunction.pdf. In *Amawi v. Pflugerville Independent School District et al.*, Bahia Amawi, joined by others, sued the school district. U.S. District Court for the Western District of Texas, Austin Division, Case 1:18-cv-01091-RP, filed April 25, 2019, www.aclutx.org/sites/default/files/4-25-19_bds_order.pdf.

68. Marco Rubio, "Marco Rubio: The Truth About B.D.S. and the Lies About My Bill," *New York Times*, February 5, 2019, www.nytimes.com/2019 /02/05/opinion/marco-rubio-bds-israel.html.

69. Adam Reuter, "BDS Has Zero Impact on Israeli Businesses," Globes, October 9, 2018, en.globes.co.il/en/article-bds-has-zero-impact-on-israeli -businesses-1001255776.

70. See Mitchell Plitnick, "Let's Take a Deep Breath on BDS," Facts on the Ground, June 17, 2015, lobelog.com/lets-take-a-deep-breath-on-bds/.

71. "H. Res. 246," Congress.gov, July 23, 2019, www.congress.gov/bill /116th-congress/house-resolution/246/text.

72. Yousef Munayyer, "Actually, Natalie Portman, You ARE Practicing BDS," *The Forward*, April 21, 2018, forward.com/opinion/399400/actually -natalie-portman-you-are-practicing-bds/.

73. The bulk of U.S. aid to the Palestinians can be suspended or cut permanently should the Palestinians initiate a case against Israel at the ICC, and aid can be withheld to any international body that admits Palestine as a member state, as it did with UNESCO. See Congressional Research Service, "U.S. Foreign Aid to the Palestinians," December 12, 2018, fas.org/sgp/crs /mideast/RS22967.pdf .

74. "J Street Opposes the Global BDS Movement and Defends Americans' Constitutional Right to Engage in Boycotts," J Street, press release, July 18,

2019, jstreet.org/press-releases/j-street-opposes-bds-defends-americans-right
-to-boycott/.

Chapter 3: Trumped-Up Policy

1. Donald Trump, "Proclamation on Recognizing the Golan Heights as
Part of the State of Israel," The White House, March 25, 2019, www.white
house.gov/presidential-actions/proclamation-recognizing-golan-heights-part
-state-israel/.

2. See Article 2.4 of the UN Charter, which reads, "All Members shall
refrain in their international relations from the threat or use of force against
the territorial integrity or political independence of any state, or in any other
manner inconsistent with the Purposes of the United Nations." "Charter of
the United Nations, Chapter 1," United Nations, www.un.org/en/sections
/un-charter/chapter-i/index.html. In testimony before the U.S. House of Representatives, Committee on Oversight Subcommittee on National Security
on July 17, 2018, legal scholar Eugene Kontorovich argued that Israel's acquisition was legal under international law because the Golan was captured in
a defensive war. (This is a matter that modern scholarship has questioned.
See, for example, Avi Shlaim, *The Iron Wall: Israel and the Arab World* [New
York: W.W. Norton, 2000], 236–50, and, among others, Tom Segev, *1967:
Israel, the War, and the Year That Transformed the Middle East* [New York:
Metropolitan Books, 2007].) Kontorovich added that even if international
law currently prohibits capturing land in a defensive war, it did not in 1967
because the provisions that are generally cited to support that ban come from
UNSC 242, the resolution drafted by the Security Council in response to the
1967 war. Although this view was accepted by the Trump administration and
its supporters, as well as many in Israel, few others agreed. Some argued that
the contention that the law didn't exist in 1967 fails because Israel annexed
the Golan in 1981, by which time such "defensive annexation" was clearly
illegal. See Eilav Lieblich, "The Golan Heights and the Perils of 'Defensive
Annexation,'" Just Security, April 4, 2019, www.justsecurity.org/63491/the
-golan-heights-and-the-perils-of-defensive-annexation. Lieblich's argument
also refutes Kontorovich's contention that Israel's security needs justified the
annexation on the basis of the events of 1967.

3. "U.N. Security Council: U.S. Vetoes of Resolutions Critical to Israel (1972–
Present)," Jewish Virtual Library, retrieved August 31, 2019, www.jewishvir
tuallibrary.org/u-s-vetoes-of-un-security-council-resolutions-critical-to-israel.

4. Since resolutions that are tabled due to the threat of a veto are not recorded in UNSC archives, there is no way to accurately gauge how many
times this happened over the years.

5. See, for example, Philip H. Gordon and Jeremy Shapiro, "How Trump Killed the Atlantic Alliance and How the Next President Can Restore It," *Foreign Affairs*, February 26, 2019, www.foreignaffairs.com/articles/2019 -02-26/how-trump-killed-atlantic-alliance Also see Susan B. Glasser, "Under Trump, 'America First' Really Is Turning Out to Be America Alone," *New Yorker*, June 8, 2018, www.newyorker.com/news/letter-from-trumps-washing ton/under-trump-america-first-really-is-turning-out-to-be-america-alone and Stewart Patrick/guest blogger, "America First Policies Leave America Alone and Disadvantaged," Council on Foreign Relations, June 19, 2018, www .cfr.org/blog/america-first-policies-leave-america-alone-and-disadvantaged among many others.

6. See chapter 2 for details about this incident.

7. Ariel Kahana, "U.S. Lawmakers Push for Recognition of Israeli Sovereignty over Golan," *Florida Sun-Sentinel*, June 5, 2018, www.sun-sentinel .com/florida-jewish-journal/fl-jjps-golan-0613-20180605-story.html.

8. For example, in 2013, speaking in the West Bank town of Ramallah, Obama said, "If given the chance, one thing that I'm very certain of is that the Palestinians have the talent, the drive, and the courage to succeed in their own state. I think of the villages that hold peaceful protests because they understand the moral force of nonviolence. I think of the importance that Palestinian families place on education. I think of the entrepreneurs determined to create something new, like the young Palestinian woman I met at the entrepreneurship summit that I hosted who wants to build recreation centers for Palestinian youth. I think of the aspirations that so many young Palestinians have for their future." See "Full Text of President Obama's Speech in Ramallah," *Haaretz*, March 22, 2013, www.haaretz.com /the-full-text-of-president-obama-s-speech-in-ramallah-1.5235192.

9. Although the idea of a two-state solution had been implicit U.S. policy for many years, Bush became the first president to explicitly endorse the idea on October 2, 2001, a few days after Israeli prime minister Ariel Sharon had stated his own support for the concept. "The idea of a Palestinian state has always been part of a vision, so long as the right of Israel to exist is respected," Bush told reporters in the Oval Office. See "US Backs State for Palestine," *The Guardian*, October 3, 2001, www.theguardian.com/world/2001/oct/03 /afghanistan.israel. Bush made a more formal declaration on June 24, 2002, when he laid out what would become a virtual mantra for the peace process, saying, "My vision is two states, living side by side in peace and security." In that speech, Bush also tied support for a Palestinians state to the removal of Palestinian president Yasser Arafat, whom he and Sharon held responsible for the intifada that was at its height at the time. See "Full Text of George Bush's

Speech," *The Guardian*, June 25, 2002, www.theguardian.com/world/2002/jun/25/israel.usa.

10. See "Resolution Adopted on the Report of the Ad Hoc Committee on the Palestinian Question, 181. Future Government of Palestine, United Nations, Part III, 'The City of Jerusalem,'" United Nations, undocs.org/pdf ?symbol=en/A/RES/181(II).

11. Israel's Basic Laws are the fundamental basis for all Israeli jurisprudence, in lieu of a constitution, which Israel does not have. On the pronouncement on Jerusalem, see "Basic Law: Jerusalem, Capital of Israel," Knesset, July 30, 1980, www.knesset.gov.il/laws/special/eng/basic10_eng.htm.

12. See "United Nations Security Council Resolution 478 (1980)," August 20, 1980, undocs.org/S/RES/478(1980).

13. It should be noted that Israel had rejected full international control over Jerusalem as far back as 1949, calling at that time only for international supervision over the holy sites and for the city itself to be divided into Jewish and Arab zones with Israel and Transjordan coming to an agreement about the administration of "common public facilities and services." See "Letter dated 31 May 1949, addressed by Mr. Walter Eytan, Head of the Delegation of Israel to the Chairman of the Committee on Jerusalem in response to the Questionnaire dated 3 May 1949 concerning an International Regime for the Jerusalem Area," United Nations Conciliation Commission for Palestine, Committee on Jerusalem, A/AC.25/ComJer/9, 1 June 1949, archive.fo/20130705171032/unispal.un.org/UNISPAL.NSF/0 /2C25E1B7AADB7CC685256AF5005F6D18#selection-91.0-97.11.

14. These were UNSC 672, which condemned the actions in 1990 of Israeli security forces at the al-Aqsa Mosque that claimed twenty Palestinian lives, and referred to Israel as the "occupying power"; UNSC 1322, which condemned the visit of Israeli opposition leader Ariel Sharon to the Haram al-Sharif/Temple Mount and again referred to Israel as the "occupying power" of that site; and UNSC 2334, which condemned Israeli settlement expansion and again specified that Jerusalem was included in the areas over which Israel was the "occupying power." See: United Nations Security Council, "Resolution 672 (1990)," October 12, 1990, undocs.org/S/RES/672(1990); United Nations Security Council, "Resolution 1322 (2000)," October 7, 2000, undocs.org/S/RES/1322(2000); United Nations Security Council, "Resolution 2334 (2016)," December 23, 2016, undocs.org/S/RES/2334(2016).

15. East Jerusalem was part of the West Bank, which Hansell specifically included among the territories his legal decision covered. Hansell wrote, in a letter to Congress explaining his ruling, "Israeli forces entered Gaza, the West Bank, Sinai, and the Golan Heights in June 1967, in the course of an

armed conflict. Those areas had not previously been part of Israel's sovereign territory, nor otherwise under its administration. By reason of such entry of its armed forces, Israel established control and began to exercise authority over these territories; and under international law, Israel thus became a belligerent occupant of these territories." Hansell, like all international juridical bodies of the day, did not distinguish legally between East Jerusalem and the rest of the West Bank, even if the politics around Jerusalem held many different aspects. Whether what Israel captured from Jordan in 1967 had, at one time, been intended to be part of an Arab state, a Jewish state, or an international *corpus separatum*, the key issue was that it had not been Israel's before the war and was under its control now. As Hansell explicitly stated, "Territory coming under the control of a belligerent occupant does not thereby become its sovereign territory." Although the ensuing years have seen major shifts in U.S. policy on this issue, there has never been an official repudiation of Hansell's legal findings. See "United States: Letter of the State Department Legal Adviser Concerning the Legality of Israeli Settlements in the Occupied Territories," *International Legal Materials* 17, no. 3 (1978), 777–79, www.jstor.org/stable/20691910.

16. This had been U.S. policy since the end of the 1967 war, and it included a stance against dividing Jerusalem again. It must be recalled that, at this time, the idea of a two-state solution was not acceptable in American discourse on the Israel-Palestine issue, as a Palestinian state was seen as a radical idea and a non-starter. Moreover, even within the PLO, people spoke in hushed tones of the idea of a Palestinian state on the territory occupied by Israel in 1967, as it was highly controversial for many Palestinians to even consider the idea of acquiescing to the loss of 78 percent of what had been Mandatory Palestine. Although Yasser Arafat had adopted the concept of the two-state solution as far back as 1974, it was not officially articulated and adopted unambiguously until the Palestinian Declaration of Independence was issued in 1988. See Rashid Khalidi, *The Iron Cage: The Story of the Palestinian Struggle for Statehood* (Boston: Beacon Press, 2006), 154–56, 193–200. Also see Naseer H. Aruri, *Dishonest Broker: The U.S. Role in Israel and Palestine* (Cambridge, MA: South End Press, 2003), 3–4 and 217–18.

17. "White House Clarifies Policy After Reagan Statement," *New York Times*, November 20, 1981, www.nytimes.com/1981/11/20/world/white-house-clarifies-policy-on-jerusalem-after-reagan-statement.html.

18. "Excerpts from Interview with President Reagan Conducted by Five Reporters," *New York Times*, February 3, 1981, www.nytimes.com/1981/02/03/world/excerpts-from-interview-with-president-reagan-conducted-by-five-reporters.html.

19. The final clause in Article 49 of the Geneva Convention reads, "The Occupying Power shall not deport or transfer parts of its own civilian population into the territory it occupies." See "Convention (IV) Relative to the Protection of Civilian Persons in Time of War. Geneva, 12 August 1949, Deportations, Transfers, Evacuations," International Committee of the Red Cross, Treaties, States Parties and Commentaries, ihl-databases.icrc.org/applic /ihl/ihl.nsf/WebART/380-600056.

20. Amir Tibon, "From Bill Clinton to Trump: The Never-Ending Story of the Jerusalem Embassy Move," *Haaretz*, February 5, 2017, www.haaretz.com /israel-news/.premium-the-never-ending-story-of-the-jerusalem-embassy -move-1.5494231.

21. Jim Geraghty, "Next Year in Jerusalem—Wait, No, They Might Really Mean It This Time!," *National Review*, December 6, 2017, www.national review.com/the-morning-jolt/jerusalem-embassy-move-no-they-might-really -mean-it-time.

22. Charles D. Smith, *Palestine and the Arab-Israeli Conflict: A History with Documents*, 9th ed. (New York: Bedford/St. Martin's Press, 2017), 440. Smith is referring here to Israel's expansion of the metropolitan area of Jerusalem, creating what has since come to be referred to as "Greater Jerusalem." The term is amorphous, and can refer to different areas, depending, in most cases, on the political expediencies of the moment. It is precisely because the United States has allowed the idea that Jerusalem is considered differently than other occupied lands in the West Bank that this sleight of hand is useful. For a fuller explanation, see Daniel Seidemann, "The Struggle for Land in Jerusalem - An Interoiew [sic]," *Palestine-Israel Journal* 4, no. 2 (1997), pij.org /articles/479.

23. "Jerusalem Embassy Act of 1995, Public Law 104–45—Nov. 8, 1995," Congress.gov, www.congress.gov/104/plaws/publ45/PLAW-104publ45.pdf.

24. Daniel Levy, "Is It Good for the Jews?," *American Prospect*, June 18, 2006, archive.is/20070810193628/www.prospect.org/cs/articles?articleId=116 47#selection-967.0-967.24.

25. For the Senate vote, see "Roll Call Vote 104th Congress—1st Session, on Passage of the Bill (S.1322 as Amended)," United States Senate, October 24, 2995, www.senate.gov/legislative/LIS/roll_call_lists/roll_call_vote_cfm .cfm?congress=104&session=1&vote=00496. It is worth noting that of the five votes against the bill, only one, plus the one "Not Voting" entry, were Democrats. For the House vote, see "Final Vote Results for Roll Call 734, On Motion to Suspend the Rules and Pass, Jerusalem Embassy Relocation Implementation Act," Clerk of the United States House of Representatives, October 24, 1995, clerk.house.gov/evs/1995/roll734.xml. In contrast to the

Senate vote, the nays in the House were overwhelmingly Democratic, with Democrats, along with Independent Rep. Bernie Sanders of Vermont, making up 31 of the 37 nay votes and 16 of the 22 who voted "present" or did not vote.

26. Itamar Rabinovich, "The Jerusalem Hijack," *Haaretz*, August 8, 2003, www.haaretz.com/1.5357765. Moynihan, it should be noted, not only had a long record of supporting militaristic Israeli policies but is often seen as an example of a "liberal hawk," and has been grouped among neoconservatives of his era such as Bill Kristol and Norman Podhoretz, among others. Moynihan's policies were difficult to classify with such broad labels, but he was unquestionably a staunch supporter of tough policies toward the Palestinians and Israel's other neighbors, and was someone who would not hesitate to work with Republicans and against fellow Democrats on that issue, as well as others.

27. Although Bush himself was a strong admirer and close ally of Israeli prime minister Ariel Sharon, many of his closest advisers, including Paul Wolfowitz, Richard Perle, Douglas Feith, and others, had close ties to Sharon's rival, Benjamin Netanyahu. These neoconservatives were the most closely aligned with Netanyahu among American foreign policy elites. For more, see, among others, James Mann, *The Rise of the Vulcans* (New York: Penguin, 2004); see also Ian Buruma, "How to Talk About Israel," *New York Times Magazine*, August 31, 2003, www.nytimes.com/2003/08/31/magazine /how-to-talk-about-israel.html; Jason Vest, "The Men from JINSA and CSP," *The Nation*, August 15, 2002, www.thenation.com/article/men-jinsa-and -csp/ and others.

28. Alison Mitchell, "Bush Says Clinton Misstepped in Israel," *New York Times*, May 23, 2000, www.nytimes.com/2000/05/23/us/bush-says-clinton -misstepped-in-israel.html.

29. Tibon, "From Bill Clinton to Trump."

30. "Transcript: Obama's Speech at AIPAC," NPR, June 4, 2008, www.npr .org/templates/story/story.php?storyId=91150432.

31. "After Jerusalem Recognition, Trump Signs Waiver Delaying Embassy Move," *Times of Israel*, December 7, 2017, www.timesofisrael.com/after-jeru salem-recognition-trump-signs-waiver-delaying-embassy-move/.

32. Matthew Weaver and Amanda Holpuch, "Gaza: Nakba Day Protests as Palestinians Bury Those Killed in Embassy Unrest—as It Happened," *The Guardian*, May 15, 2018, updated November 19, 2018, www.theguardian .com/world/live/2018/may/15/gaza-israel-nakba-day-protests-as-palestinians -bury-those-killed-in-embassy-unrest-live-updates.

33. "Arab League Condemns US Jerusalem Move," Al Jazeera News, December 10, 2017, www.aljazeera.com/news/2017/12/arab-league-condemns -move-dangerous-illegal-171209185754563.html.

34. "Arab League Condemns US Jerusalem Move"; John Irish and Robin Emmott, "Trump's Jerusalem Plan Revives Tensions in EU Diplomacy," Reuters, December 8, 2017, www.reuters.com/article/us-usa-trump-israel -france/u-s-has-excluded-itself-from-middle-east-peace-process-france-id USKBN1E2102; Mona Kanwal Sheikh, "Trump's Jerusalem Statements Open Up a New Front for Transnational Jihadists," Danish Institute for International Studies, December 12, 2017, www.diis.dk/en/node/11704.

35. Michael Schwirtz and Rick Gladstone, "U.S. Vetoes U.N. Resolution Condemning Move on Jerusalem," New York Times, December 18, 2017, www.nytimes.com/2017/12/18/world/middleeast/jerusalem-un-security -council.html.

36. "UN Jerusalem Resolution: How Each Country Voted," Al Jazeera, December 21, 2017, www.aljazeera.com/news/2017/12/jerusalem-resolution -country-voted-171221180116873.html.

37. Mitchell Plitnick, "Trump's Jerusalem Declaration Is Even Worse Than You Think," LobeLog, December 6, 2017, lobelog.com/trumps-jerusalem-dec laration-is-even-worse-than-you-think/#comments.

38. Daniel Seidemann, a leading authority on Jerusalem and director of Terrestrial Jerusalem, explains the status quo thus: "Israel has had de facto (and, under Israeli law, de jure) overall authority over the Temple Mount/ Haram al Sharif. However, from the start, Israel delegated certain authorities at the site to Jordan and the Jordanian Waqf (which operates on the Haram al Sharif/Temple Mount itself) and Israel formally recognized Jordan's special role at the site in the 1995 Jordan-Israel peace treaty. In this way, Israel has since 1967 preserved many of the pre-existing arrangements at the site, and it is these arrangements that are generally what is referred to when people talk about the Status Quo—but even these have changed and evolved over time. . . . With respect to access, since before 1967, through today, the site is open to non-Muslims and Muslims access alike for purposes of visits, and open to only Muslims for purposes of worship. With respect to entry, since 1967, Israel has been responsible for security on the perimeter of the site and the Waqf (the Islamic Authorities at the site which operates under Jordanian Authority) is in principle responsible for security on the Esplanade itself. In practice, the Waqf has been reluctant to exert its authority and Israel has maintained a symbolic presence on the site, including a police station, and has always exercised its authority to deploy its security forces on the Mount during disturbances. Such intervention has become much more common as tensions have soared. The presence of the Israeli police on the site has increased over the years also due to the need to escort, and contain, Jewish groups inside the site." "Tough Questions, Expert Answers,"

Americans for Peace Now, peacenow.org/page.php?name=tough-questions
-expert-answers.

39. "Full Video and Transcript: Trump's Speech Recognizing Jerusalem as the Capital of Israel," *New York Times*, December 6, 2017, www.nytimes.com/2017/12/06/world/middleeast/trump-israel-speech-transcript.html?module=inline.

40. See Jacob Magid, "Trump: No More Aid Unless Palestinians Talk Peace; Jerusalem Is 'Off the Table,'" *Times of Israel*, January 25, 2018, www.timesofisrael.com/trump-no-more-aid-unless-palestinians-accept-that-jerusalem-is-off-the-table/ for one of many instances when Trump said words to this effect.

41. "Letter from President Bush to Prime Minister Sharon," George W. Bush Archives, The White House, April 14, 2004, georgewbush-whitehouse.archives.gov/news/releases/2004/04/20040414-3.html.

42. "AJC 2018 Survey of American Jewish Opinion," American Jewish Committee, June 10, 2018, www.jewishdatabank.org/content/upload/bjdb/AJC-2018_Survey_of_United_States_Jewish_Opinion.pdf. Trump has never been popular among U.S. Jews. He received only 24 percent of the Jewish vote in 2016, to 71 percent for his opponent, Hillary Clinton. See "U.S. Presidential Elections: Jewish Voting Record (1916–Present)," Jewish Virtual Library, www.jewishvirtuallibrary.org/jewish-voting-record-in-u-s-presidential-elections. In the 2018 midterms, 79 percent of Jews voted for Democrats versus only 17 percent for Republicans. See Dareh Gregorian, "Trump: Jewish People Who Vote Democratic Show 'Great Disloyalty,'" NBC News, August 21, 2019, www.nbcnews.com/politics/donald-trump/trump-jewish-people-who-vote-democrat-show-great-disloyalty-n1044621. In 2019, Trump showed a much lower job approval rating among Jews, at 29 percent, much lower than the overall population's rating of 42 percent. See Frank Newport, "American Jews, Politics and Israel," Pew Research Group, Polling Matters, August 27, 2019, news.gallup.com/opinion/polling-matters/265898/american-jews-politics-israel.aspx.

43. These included his son-in-law, Jared Kushner, his ambassador to Israel, David Friedman, and his Middle East envoy, Jason Greenblatt. None of these men had any prior diplomatic experience nor any Middle East experience outside of supporting the Israeli far right as donors and activists for years.

44. "Comay-Michelmore Letters, Exchange of Letters Constituting a Provisional Agreement Concerning Assistance to Palestine Refugees," Israeli Ministry of Foreign Affairs, June 14, 1967, www.mfa.gov.il/mfa/foreignpolicy/mfadocuments/yearbook1/pages/exchange%20of%20letters%20constituting%20a%20provisional%20agreement%20concerning%20assistance%20to%20palestine%20refugees.aspx.

45. See Barak Ravid, "Scoop: Netanyahu Asked U.S. to Cut Aid for Palestinian Refugees," Axios, September 2, 2018, www.axios.com/benjamin-net anyahu-israel-policy-unrwa-palestine-aid-5a92b1ed-babd-42d9-a933-6aec 816da717.html.

46. For a summary of some recent attacks on UNRWA in Congress, see Josh Ruebner, *Shattered Hopes: Obama's Failure to Broker Israeli-Palestinian Peace* (New York: Verso Books, 2013), 200–202; also see John G. Lindsay, *Fixing UNRWA: Repairing the UN's Troubled System of Aid to Palestinian Refugees*, Policy Focus #91, Washington Institute for Near East Policy, January 2009, drive.google.com/file/d/0B__vpNpiu4cUM2QzNjI3MjctODMwMy00OD dlLTk$MWEtZmRhODZhZjcwMjhm/view?hl=en. For more specific criticisms, see, for example, Asaf Romirowsky and Alexander Joffe, "Defund the UNRWA," *Wall Street Journal*, April 1, 2011, www.wsj.com/articles/SB10001 424052748704396904576226452357028480; and Asaf Romirowsky and Jonathan Spyer, "How UNRWA Creates Dependency," Middle East Forum, December 3, 2007, www.meforum.org/1807/how-unrwa-creates-dependency.

47. Even when Trump started to move to defund UNRWA, Netanyahu initially opposed it, though he later changed course. See "Netanyahu Urging Americans Not to Cut Funding for UNRWA—TV Report," *Times of Israel*, January 4, 2018, www.timesofisrael.com/netanyahu-urging-americans-not-to -cut-funding-for-unrwa-tv-report. For a broader explanation of this phenomenon, see Mitchell Plitnick, "Cutting Aid to the Palestinians," *LobeLog*, January 26, 2018, lobelog.com/cutting-aid-to-the-palestinians.

48. Herb Keinon, "Netanyahu Calls to Disband UNRWA and to Stop Foreign-Funded NGOs," *Jerusalem Post*, June 12, 2017, www.jpost.com/Is rael-News/Politics-And-Diplomacy/Netanyahu-puts-UNRWA-and-foreign -funded-NGOs-in-his-sights-496552.

49. This claim is made despite the fact that UNRWA has, in some instances, seen its mandate expanded by the UN General Assembly such that it has integrated and settled refugees. For an in-depth look at UNRWA's activities in this regard, as well as a comparison between it and the UNHCR and policy recommendations for sustainable integration that would address the needs of Palestinian refugees, see Noura Erakat, "Palestinian Refugees and the Syrian Uprising: Filling the Protection Gap During Secondary Forced Displacement," *Oxford International Journal of Refugee Law* 26, no. 4 (2014): 518–621.

50. For an example of this argument, see Noah Lewis, "UNRWA and the Perpetuation of the World's Most Unique 'Refugee Crisis,'" *Times of Israel*, August 10, 2019, blogs.timesofisrael.com/unrwa-and-the-perpetuation-of -the-worlds-most-unique-refugee-crisis/. Lewis is a research analyst at

HonestReporting, Canada, an organization which reports on news articles, op-eds, and media pieces across the spectrum which deviate from the pro-Israeli narrative and, in the view of many observers, offers talking points and argument to counter any such deviations. The organization describes itself thus: "HonestReporting Canada is an independent grass-roots organization promoting fairness and accuracy in Canadian media coverage of Israel and the Middle East."

51. "Netanyahu Urging Americans Not to Cut Funding for UNRWA—TV Report," *Times of Israel*, January 4, 2018, www.timesofisrael.com/netanyahu-urging-americans-not-to-cut-funding-for-unrwa-tv-report/.

52. Colum Lynch, "U.S. to End All Funding to U.N. Agency That Aids Palestinian Refugees," *Foreign Policy*, August 28, 2018, foreignpolicy.com/2018/08/28/middle-east-palestinian-israel-pompeo-trump-kushner-u-s-to-end-all-funding-to-u-n-agency-that-aids-palestinian-refugees/.

53. Barak Ravid, "Netanyahu Wants to Transfer Part of UNRWA Funding to Jordan," Axios, March 8, 2018, www.axios.com/netanyahu-wants-to-transfer-part-of-unrwa-funding-to-jordan-1520536468-431459ab-afa2-4b03-87ae-19c126b76e14.html.

54. Barak Ravid, "Scoop: Netanyahu Asked U.S. to Cut Aid for Palestinian Refugees," Axios, September 2, 2018, www.axios.com/benjamin-netanyahu-israel-policy-unrwa-palestine-aid-5a92b1ed-babd-42d9-a933-6aec816da717.html.

55. "Israel Welcomes End of US Funding for UN Palestinian Refugee Agency," *Times of Israel*, September 1, 2018, www.timesofisrael.com/israel-welcomes-end-of-us-funding-for-un-palestinian-refugee-agency/.

56. "Ex-Mossad Chief Supports Iran Nuclear Deal," NPR, July 31, 2015, www.npr.org/2015/07/31/427990359/ex-mossad-chief-supports-iran-nuclear-deal; Allison Kaplan Sommer, "Top Brass vs. Netanyahu's Government: Where Israel Stands on Nixing Nuke Iran Deal," *Haaretz*, May 8, 2018, www.haaretz.com/israel-news/.premium-where-israel-s-leaders-stand-on-the-iran-nuclear-deal-1.6070237.

57. Karen DeYoung and Ruth Eglash, "Trump Administration to End U.S. Funding to U.N. Program for Palestinian Refugees," *Washington Post*, August 30, 2018, www.washingtonpost.com/world/national-security/trump-administration-to-end-us-funding-to-un-program-for-palestinian-refugees/2018/08/30/009d9bc6-ac64-11e8-b1da-ff7faa680710_story.html.

58. See UNRWA, Frequently Asked Questions, "Who Is a Palestine Refugee?," www.unrwa.org/who-we-are/frequently-asked-questions.

59. Hady Amr, "In One Move, Trump Eliminated US Funding for UNRWA and the US Role as Mideast Peacemaker," Brookings Institute, September 7,

2018, www.brookings.edu/blog/order-from-chaos/2018/09/07/in-one-move -trump-eliminated-us-funding-for-unrwa-and-the-us-role-as-mideast-peace maker/.

60. "Consolidated Eligibility and Registration Instructions (CERI)," UNRWA, www.unrwa.org/userfiles/2010011995652.pdf.

61. Maan News Agency, "Exploding the Myths: UNRWA, UNHCR and the Palestine Refugees," UNRWA, June 27, 2011, www.unrwa.org/newsroom /features/exploding-myths-unrwa-unhcr-and-palestine-refugees.

62. Maan News Agency, "Exploding the Myths."

63. "Where We Work—Jordan," UNRWA, www.unrwa.org/where-we -work/jordan.

64. UNHCR's Handbook on Procedures and Criteria for Determining Refugee Status, in paragraph 184, provides: "If the head of a family meets the criteria of the definition [for refugee status], his dependents are normally granted refugee status according to the principle of family unity.'" (*Handbook on Procedures and Criteria for Determining Refugee Status Under the 1951 Convention and the 1967 Protocol Relating to the Status of Refugees*, UNHCR, https://www.unhcr.org/4d93528a9.pdf). This is unambiguous. The difference between UNRWA and UNHCR lies not in the law, but in their mandates. For UNHCR, this issue simply doesn't come up very often because it is focused on resettlement and repatriation. Gunness quoted the minutes of the UNHCR standing committee meeting of 2008, stating that "the substantial decrease in the number of refugees in protracted situations can be attributed to a handful of major repatriation operations in recent years. In 2005 and 2006, more than 1.8 million long-term refugees returned to their country of origin, more than a million of them to Afghanistan alone. Substantial numbers were also repatriated in Africa, particularly Angola, Burundi, Liberia and Sudan." Maan News Agency, "Exploding the Myths."

65. "Universal Declaration of Human Rights," United Nations, www.un- .org/en/universal-declaration-human-rights/. The counter-argument that is sometimes offered—that there is not now and never was an independent state of Palestine, and therefore this clause does not apply to Palestinians— is blatantly disingenuous, and obviously contrary to the spirit of this clause, whose plain intent was to ensure that people who left their homeland, for whatever reason and regardless of the status of that homeland, had the right to return. General Assembly Resolution, A/RES/194 (III) 11 December 1948, United Nations, unispal.un.org/DPA/DPR/unispal.nsf/0 /C758572B78D1CD0085256BCF0077E51A. Although General Assembly resolutions, unlike those from the Security Council, are often not considered to have the force of law, this one rests on principles of long-standing

customary international law as well as having been repeatedly reinforced by the UNGA and having been endorsed in principle by UNSC Resolution 237, which clearly set out the responsibility of Israel to facilitate the return of refugees caused by the 1967 war and thus can be argued to apply in principle to the refugees from 1948 as well. See Mark LeVine, "Why Palestinians Have a Right to Return Home," Al Jazeera, September 23, 2011, www.aljazeera.com/indepth/opinion/2011/09/2011922135540203743.html. Other bases for the right in international law include the International Convention on Civil and Political Rights (ICCPR), Article 12, (https://treaties.un.org/doc/publication/unts/volume%20999/volume-999-i-14668-english.pdf) which states that "no one shall be arbitrarily deprived of their right to enter his own country," and the International Convention on the Elimination of All Forms of Racial Discriminations (CERD), which, in Article 5, (http://www.hrcr.org/docs/CERD/cerd3.html) requires State parties to "prohibit and to eliminate racial discrimination . . . and guarantee the rights of everyone . . . in particular [to] the right to leave any country, including one's own and to return to one's country." See also Loureen Sayej, "Palestinian Refugees and the Right of Return in International Law," Oxford Human Rights Hub, May 18, 2018, ohrh.law.ox.ac.uk/palestinian-refugees-and-the-right-of-return-in-international-law.

66. See "Notes of Ad Hoc Committee Application of Israel for Admission to Membership in the United Nations (A/818), Fifty-Fourth Meeting," A/AC.24/SR.45, May 5, 1949, web.archive.org/web/20120203124136/unispal.un.org/UNISPAL.NSF/85255a0a0010ae82852555340060479d/1db943e43c280a26052565fa004d8174?OpenDocument#Mr.%20EBAN%20(Israel)%20understood%20tha.

67. For background and analysis on the closure of the PLO offices, see Khaled Elgindy and Lara Friedman, "Locking Palestinians in a Flawed Peace Process," Brookings Institute, December 5, 2017, www.brookings.edu/blog/markaz/2017/12/05/locking-palestinians-in-a-flawed-peace-process/. For background on the declaration about the settlements, see Lara Jakes and David M. Halbfinger, "In Shift, U.S. Says Israeli Settlements in West Bank Do Not Violate International Law," *New York Times*, November 18, 2019, www.nytimes.com/2019/11/18/world/middleeast/trump-israel-west-bank-settlements.html. The legislation dealing with aid to Palestinians was called the Taylor Force Act. For background and analysis, see Henriette Chacar, "U.S. Law Cutting Aid to Palestinians Punishes Any and All Resistance to Israeli Occupation," *The Intercept*, May 25, 2018, theintercept.com/2018/05/25/israel-palestine-aid-taylor-force-act/. For the text of the legislation, see "H.R.1164—Taylor Force Act," 115th Congress,

2017–2018, www.congress.gov/bill/115th-congress/house-bill/1164. It was passed into law as part of H.R.1625—115th Congress (2017–2018). See Title X, Taylor Force Act, www.congress.gov/bill/115th-congress/house-bill /1625. For a general list of some of the most impactful steps taken, see Miriam Berger, "Timeline: Trump's Policies Toward the Palestinians," *Washington Post*, January 28, 2020, www.washingtonpost.com/world/2020/01 /28/timeline-trumps-policies-toward-palestinians.

Chapter 4: The Crisis in Gaza

1. "Rabin Expresses His Frustration with Palestinian Stance in Talks," Jewish Telegraphic Agency, September 4, 1992, www.jta.org/1992/09/04/ar chive/rabin-expresses-his-frustration-with-palestinian-stance-in-talks.

2. "Rabin Expresses His Frustration."

3. "David Barsamian Interviews Edward Said," *Arts and Opinion* 2, no. 3 (2003), reprinted from ZNet, www.artsandopinion.com/2003_v2_n3/said .htm.

4. Helga Tawil-Souri, "Gaza as Larger Than Life," in *Gaza as Metaphor*, eds. Helga Tawil-Souri and Dina Mattar (London: C. Hurst, 2016), 26–27.

5. Mehdi Hasan, "Israel Kills Palestinians and Western Liberals Shrug. Their Humanitarianism Is a Sham," *The Intercept*, April 2, 2018, theinter cept.com/2018/04/02/israel-killing-palestine-civilian-liberal-humanitarian/.

6. Hazem Balousha and Oliver Holmes, "Palestinians Hold Day of Mourning After 773 'Shot with Live Ammunition,'" *The Guardian*, March 31, 2018, www.theguardian.com/world/2018/mar/31/palestinians-hold-day-of-mourn ing-after-773-shot-with-live-ammunition.

7. Hasan, "Israel Kills Palestinians and Western Liberals Shrug."

8. John Bowden, "Sanders, Warren Speak Out Against Israel-Gaza Violence," *The Hill*, November 14, 2019, thehill.com/homenews/campaign /470542-sanders-warren-speak-out-against-israel-gaza-violence; Ron Kampeas and Staff, "Senators Sanders, Warren Push Resolution Decrying PM's West Bank Annexation Idea," *Times of Israel*, June 7, 2019, www.timesofisrael .com/sanders-warren-introduce-resolution-decrying-israel-annexation-plans; Amir Tibon, "Where Democratic Candidates Stand on Israel's Latest Round of Gaza Violence," *Haaretz*, November 15, 2019, www.haaretz.com/us-news /.premium-where-democratic-candidates-stand-on-israel-s-latest-round -of-gaza-violence-1.8129950.

9. Beryl Cheal, "Refugees in the Gaza Strip, December 1948–May 1950," *Journal of Palestine Studies* 18, no. 1 (1988), 138–157, available at JSTOR, www.jstor.org/stable/2537600. See also Sara Roy, *Failing Peace: Gaza and the Palestinian-Israeli Conflict* (London: Pluto Press, 2007), 54–55.

10. See Jean-Pierre Filiu, among others, *Gaza: A History* (New York: Oxford University Press, 2017), chapters 4–7, 57–122.

11. See Avi Shlaim, "The Rise and Fall of the All-Palestine Government in Gaza,"*Journal of Palestine Studies* 20, no. 1 (1990): 37–53, online.ucpress.edu/jps/article/20/1/37/2050/The-Rise-and-Fall-of-the-All-Palestine-Government.

12. See Roy, *Failing Peace*, among others, chapters 7–9, 161–287. Each chapter explains one of the three prongs of de-development in great depth.

13. Roy, *Failing Peace*, 135.

14. Roy, *Failing Peace*, 139–141.

15. For information on the Gaza settlements, see B'Tselem, *Thirsty for a Solution: The Water Crisis in the Occupied Territories and Its Resolution in the Final-Status Agreement*, July 2000, www.btselem.org/download/200007_thirsty_for_a_solution_eng.doc.

16. The figure is based on an estimate in 2000 using data from the U.S. Census Bureau. See "The West Bank and Gaza: A Population Profile," Population Reference Bureau, April 22, 2002, www.prb.org/thewestbankandgazaapopulationprofile.

17. Roy, *Failing Peace*, 239.

18. Charles D. Smith, *Palestine and the Arab-Israeli Conflict: A History with Documents*, 9th ed. (New York: Bedford/St. Martin's Press, 2017), 399–405.

19. See Jean-Pierre Filiu, *From Deep State to Islamic State: The Arab Counter-Revolution and Its Jihadi Legacy* (Oxford: Oxford University Press, 2015).

20. See, among others, Zaki Chehab, *Inside Hamas: The Untold Story of the Militant Islamic Movement* (New York: Nation Books, 2007), chap. 2, "Hamas is Born," 15–38.

21. For an exposition on both the tensions and harmonies between Islamic and secular resistance movements in the Arab world, see Sukant Chandan, "Secularism and Islamism in the Arab World," Islamic Human Rights Commission, January 4, 2009, www.ihrc.org.uk/palestine-internationalist/palint-vol4-issue1/20035-palestinians-under-occupation-living-without-human-rights-2_trashed-3/.

22. Shaul Mishal and Avraham Sela, *The Palestinian Hamas: Vision, Violence, and Coexistence* (New York: Columbia University Press, 2006), 57.

23. For a broad yet personal overview of the First Intifada, see Khalid Farraj, "The First Intifada: Hope and the Loss of Hope," *Journal of Palestine Studies* 47, no. 1 (2017): 86–97.

24. See Dan Levin, "Israel Grows Uneasy over Reliance on Migrant Labor," *New York Times*, July 4, 2010, www.nytimes.com/2010/07/05/world/middleeast/05workers.html; and David Hoffman, "Palestinian Labor a Dilemma

for Israel," *Washington Post*, April 1, 1993, www.washingtonpost.com/archive
/politics/1993/04/01/palestinian-labor-a-dilemma-for-israel/cfb5243c-778c
-4f06-bc33-d004fb7a8a29/. For a broader analysis of Israel's use of migrant
labor, see, among others, Matan Kaminer, "By the Sweat of Other Brows:
Thai Migrant Labor and the Transformation of Israeli Settler Agriculture"
(PhD diss., University of Michigan, 2019), deepblue.lib.umich.edu/bitstream
/handle/2027.42/151478/mkaminer_1.pdf.

25. Maj. Gen. (res.) Doron Almog, "Lessons of the Gaza Security Fence
for the West Bank," *Jerusalem Center for Public Affairs* 4, no. 12 (2004), www
.jcpa.org/brief/brief004-12.htm.

26. For background on crossings and other key details of Israel's control
of the Gaza Strip, see "The Gaza Cheat Sheet," Gisha: The Legal Center
for Freedom of Movement, gisha.org/reports-and-data/the-gaza-cheat-sheet.

27. The Interim Agreement, or Oslo II, established the division of the West
Bank into Area A, which was under full Palestinian administrative control
with Palestinian internal security control, although Israel retained control
of the perimeter and reserved the power to enter Area A for the purpose of
arrests; Area B, where Israel maintained full security control but the Palestinian Authority was permitted to administer the day-to-day activities; and
Area C, which remained under full Israeli control. For the full text of the
agreement, see "The Israeli-Palestinian Interim Agreement," Israeli Ministry
of Foreign Affairs, September 28, 1995, mfa.gov.il/mfa/foreignpolicy/peace
/guide/pages/the%20israeli-palestinian%20interim%20agreement.aspx. For
an explanation of the impact of the division of the West Bank in this manner,
see "Planning Policy in the West Bank," B'Tselem: The Israeli Information
Center for Human Rights In the Occupied Territories, November 11, 2017,
updated February 6, 2019, www.btselem.org/planning_and_building.

28. The barrier between Gaza and Egypt was fortified over the years, from
barbed wire fencing to a concrete wall to a steel wall, as the buffer zone,
known as the Philadelphi Corridor, widened. See Human Rights Watch, *Raz-
ing Rafah: Mass Home Demolitions in the Gaza Strip*, October 2004, www
.hrw.org/reports/2004/rafah1004/rafah1004text.pdf.

29. For frequently updated materials on the situation in Gaza, see "The
Gaza Strip," United Nations Office for the Coordination of Humanitarian
Affairs (UNOCHA), www.ochaopt.org/location/gaza-strip; Gisha: The Legal
Center for Freedom of Movement, gisha.org; Palestinian Centre for Human
Rights, particularly, among others, "Closure on the Gaza Strip," pchrgaza.org
/en/?cat=92, and "The War on the Gaza Strip," pchrgaza.org/en/?cat=87.

30. For an in-depth examination of Gaza by the time Israel abandoned its settlements there, see Trude Strand, "Tightening the Noose: The Institutionalized

Impoverishment of Gaza, 2005–2010," *Journal of Palestine Studies* 43, no. 2 (2014): 6–23.

31. See, among others, Sara Roy, *The Gaza Strip: The Political Economy of De-Development*, 3rd ed. (Washington, DC: Institute for Palestine Studies, 2016) 333–77.

32. See Salman Abu Sitta, "Gaza Strip: The Lessons of History," in Tawil -Souri and Mattar, *Gaza As Metaphor*, 110.

33. Bill Van Esveld, *Rockets from Gaza: Harm to Civilians from Palestinian Armed Groups' Rocket Attacks*, Human Rights Watch, August 6, 2009, www .hrw.org/report/2009/08/06/rockets-gaza/harm-civilians-palestinian-armed -groups-rocket-attacks. There is a crucial distinction drawn in this report that bears emphasizing. A people under belligerent military occupation is entitled to defend itself against that occupation, including by means of violence. However, this right does not extend to the targeting of civilians, and the use of violence is subject to the same laws of war that are binding on the occupying power. As Human Rights Watch indicates here, the intentional targeting or indiscriminate harm inflicted on civilians is a war crime. By the same token, as will be explored later in this chapter and elsewhere, Israel has repeatedly been credibly accused of both targeting civilians, with testimonies supporting such actions from former IDF soldiers gathered by the Israeli organization Breaking the Silence (www.breakingthesilence.org.il), among many sources. Arguments defending the targeting of civilians or the use of indiscriminate weapons have been made by defenders of both Israel and Palestinian militant groups. While this is not the space to fully explore these debates, it is important to note that one argument—that the "other side" does it, so "our side" is not bound by that restriction—is explicitly denied by common jurisprudence. This question is fully explored in David Tuck and Thomas de Saint Maurice, "International Humanitarian Law: A Legal Framework for Exceptional Circumstances," *Humanitarian Law & Policy*, International Committee of the Red Cross, November 30, 2017, blogs.icrc.org/law-and-policy/2017 /11/30/international-humanitarian-law-legal-framework-exceptional-circum stances. All of this notwithstanding, military personnel and locations are legitimate targets, although such actions by the Palestinians are often treated no differently in the media and by Israel.

34. This was a description of the reasoning for a demonstration Plitnick helped organize in 2004 with Jewish Voice for Peace. See, Mitchell Plitnick, "American Liebermans," *Souciant Magazine*, October 5, 2011, souciant.com /2011/10/american-liebermans.

35. Ari Shavit, "Top PM Aide: Gaza Plan Aims to Freeze the Peace Process," *Haaretz*, October 6, 2004, www.haaretz.com/1.4710372.

36. For general background on Sharon's plan as presented publicly, see Sharon Otterman, "Middle East: The Disengagement Plan," Council on Foreign Relations, February 7, 2005, www.cfr.org/backgrounder/middle-east-disengagement-plan. Debate carried on for years over whether Weisglass's view reflected Sharon's actual plans or his own view, though Weisglass plainly presented it as Sharon's view. Many believed that, after the Israeli public recovered from the upheaval of removing thousands of settlers, Sharon would continue on the path of withdrawal. See, for instance, Elhanan Miller, "Sharon Was About to Leave Two-Thirds of the West Bank," *Times of Israel*, February 19, 2013, www.timesofisrael.com/sharon-was-about-to-leave-two-thirds-of-the-west-bank. The fact of the matter will never be known because, on January 4, 2006, less than four months after Israel completed its withdrawal from Gaza, Sharon suffered a stroke that put him in a coma in which he would remain until his death eight years later. His successor, Ehud Olmert, tried to take up the mantle with his own "Realignment Plan," but it was widely unpopular among Israelis, and strongly opposed by the Palestinians and by most of the international community. The outbreak of fighting between Israel and Hezbollah in July 2006 sidelined the plan, and it was never revived. For its demise, see Doug Struck, "Israel Shelves Plan to Pull Out of Settlements in West Bank," *Washington Post*, August 23, 2006, www.washingtonpost.com/wp-dyn/content/article/2006/08/22/AR2006082201088_pf.html. For details of Olmert's plan, see "Convergence Plan," Reut Institute, www.reut-institute.org/Publication.aspx?PublicationId=338.

37. For the full text of the initiative, see "The Geneva Accord: A Model Israeli-Palestinian Peace Agreement, Draft Permanent Status Agreement," at www.geneva-accord.org/mainmenu/english. The agreement was drafted by a group of Israeli and Palestinian activists, some of whom were former government officials, some who still held official positions, and others who were longtime advocates and activists. All were supporters of a two-state solution. The agreement was based on the various agreements that constituted or grew out of the Oslo Accords, and, as a result, was supported by those who were, in the face of the Second Intifada, desperately trying to save the two-state solution envisioned by the Oslo process. It was opposed, for the most part, by Israelis who rejected the idea of a Palestinian state and by Palestinians who rejected the de facto sacrifice of their right of return in exchange for a state.

The following is a partial list of prior agreements that formed the basis of the Geneva Initiative: Clinton Parameters, see "Clinton Parameters," Foundation for Middle East Peace, December 23, 2000, fmep.org/resource/clinton-parameters/; for the Arab Peace Initiative, see "The Arab Peace Initiative,

NOTES

2002," Al-Bab, al-bab.com/albab-orig/albab/arab/docs/league/peace02.htm;
for the Roadmap, see "Roadmap for Peace in the Middle East: Israeli/
Palestinian Reciprocal Action, Quartet Support," United States Department
of State Archives, July 16, 2003, 2001-2009.state.gov/r/pa/ei/rls/22520.htm.

38. Sharon's plan for a broader withdrawal was hinted at when he declared
his policy of retaining several large settlement blocs, implying he would leave
other areas of the West Bank in order to legitimize Israel's control over these
key areas. The plan, however, was never specifically described in public
before Sharon's death, despite speculation about it. See, for example, Greg
Myre, "Sharon Promises to Retain 5 Big Settlements in West Bank," New
York Times, April 13, 2004, www.nytimes.com/2004/04/13/world/sharon
-promises-to-retain-5-big-settlements-in-west-bank.html.

39. Former State Department negotiator Aaron David Miller, who worked
extensively on Israel-Palestine issues for many years, characterized U.S. involvement in the Clinton years as having "acted as Israel's attorney, catering
and coordinating with the Israelis at the expense of successful peace negotiations." See Aaron David Miller, "Israel's Lawyer," Washington Post, May 23,
2005, www.washingtonpost.com/archive/opinions/2005/05/23/israels-lawyer
/7ab0416c-9761-4d4a-80a9-82b7e15e5d22/. Miller expanded on this idea at
length in his book The Much Too Promised Land: America's Elusive Search for
Arab-Israeli Peace (New York: Bantam Books, March 2008).

40. See "The Israeli-Palestinian Interim Agreement," Article XXXI
Clause 7, Israeli Ministry of Foreign Affairs, September 28, 1995, mfa.gov.il
/mfa/foreignpolicy/peace/guide/pages/the%20israeli-palestinian%20interim
%20agreement.aspx.

41. "The Israeli-Palestinian Interim Agreement," Article XI, Clause 1.

42. For the full Israeli case for Sharon's "Disengagement Plan," see "Israel's
Disengagement Plan: Renewing the Peace Process," Israel Ministry of Foreign Affairs, April 2005, mfa.gov.il/MFA_Graphics/MFA%20Gallery/Docu
ments/disengagement2.pdf.

43. For more on the Palestinian response to the Israeli "disengagement
plan," see Filiu, Gaza: A History, 279–89.

44. Mitchell Plitnick, "Gaza Withdrawal Backgrounder," ZNet, August 17,
2005, zcomm.org/znetarticle/gaza-withdrawal-backgrounder-by-mitchell
-plitnick/.

45. Abbas had long been recognized as the number-two figure in the PLO
behind Arafat and was expected to be his successor, yet his actual election
was controversial. The vote was held during the Intifada, and Palestinian
freedom of movement was thus restricted more than usual, limiting the ability of many Palestinians to vote. Additionally, since Fatah dominated the

Palestinian Authority and endorsed Abbas, his campaign message dominated Palestinian media. Finally, Hamas decided to boycott the election, so Abbas's election was assured, but the legitimacy was open to debate, despite the fact that few questioned that he had sufficient support to win.

46. See Mark Oliver and Agencies, "Sharon and Abbas Agree Ceasefire," *The Guardian*, February 8, 2005, www.theguardian.com/world/2005/feb/08 /israel4.

47. For background on the Bush administration pushing Abbas on this point, as well as an important example of how the issue was presented in mainstream American media, see Steven R. Weisman, "Bush Presses Abbas to Confront Armed Gangs," *New York Times*, October 21, 2005, www.nytimes .com/2005/10/21/politics/bush-presses-abbas-to-confront-armed-gangs.html.

48. See World Bank, *Stagnation or Revival? Israeli Disengagement and Palestinian Economic Prospects: Overview* (Washington: World Bank, 2004), 25 and World Bank, *Disengagement, the Palestinian Economy and the Settlements*, cited in Khaled Elgindy, *Blind Spot: America and the Palestinians, from Balfour to Trump*, Brookings Institution Press, Kindle edition, 299–300; Daniel C. Kurtzer et al., *The Peace Puzzle: America's Quest for Arab-Israeli Peace, 1989–2011* (Ithaca, NY: Cornell University Press, 2012), 196, cited in Elgindy, *Blind Spot*, 300; Elgindy, *Blind Spot*, 182–83.

49. Elgindy, *Blind Spot*, 184.

50. For background on the Washington Institute (WINEP), see MJ Rosenberg, "Does PBS Know That 'The Washington Institute' Was Founded by AIPAC?," *Huffington Post*, May 25, 2011, www.huffpost.com/entry/does -pbs-know-that-washin_b_533808. For a broader overview of the organization, see "Washington Institute for Near East Policy," *Militarist Monitor*, June 30, 2015, militarist-monitor.org/profile/washington_institute_for_near _east_policy/.

51. Ben Fishman, "The Democratic Party's Platform and the Middle East," Policy Watch No. 887, Washington Institute for Near East Policy, June 27, 2004, www.washingtoninstitute.org/policy-analysis/view/the-demo cratic-partys-platform-and-the-middle-east.

52. Testimony of Amani Kamal 'Abd al-Majid Sharif given to Khaled al-'Azayzeh, fieldworker for B'Tselem: The Israeli Information Center for Human Rights in the Occupied Territories, November 15, 2016, www.btselem .org/gaza_strip/20170228_israels_policy_of_family_separation.

53. See "The Cabinet Resolution Regarding the Disengagement Plan," Israeli Ministry of Foreign Affairs, June 6, 2004, www.mfa.gov.il/mfa/foreign policy/peace/mfadocuments/pages/revised%20disengagement%20plan%20 6-june-2004.aspx.

54. For an examination of this question, see Noura Erakat, *Justice for Some: Law and the Question of Palestine* (Stanford, CA: Stanford University Press), 2019, 194–97. Also see Lisa Hajjar, "Is Gaza Still Occupied and Why Does It Matter?," Jadaliyya, July 14, 2014, www.jadaliyya.com/Details/27557. Israel maintains that it is not occupying Gaza in any sense since it withdrew in 2005. For an exposition of this argument, see Leonard Grunstein, "Gaza Is Not Occupied by Anyone Other than Gazans—the War of Words," *Times of Israel*, July 13, 2018, blogs.timesofisrael.com/gaza-is-not-occupied-by-anyone -other-than-gazans-the-war-of-words/.

55. For a comparison of Arafat and Abbas as individuals and as leaders, see, among others, Menachem Klein, *Arafat and Abbas: Portraits of Leadership in A State Postponed* (New York: Oxford University Press, 2019). For a more contemporary view, as Abbas was first taking over for Arafat, see Ziad Abu-Zayyad, "Mahmoud Abbas (Abu Mazen): The Arafat Legacy, the Challenges, the New Perspectives," *Palestine-Israel Journal* 11, no. 4 (2005), www.pij.org /articles/300/mahmoud-abbas-abu-mazen-the-arafat-legacy-the-challenges -the-new-perspectives. The Fatah party, which had dominated Palestinian politics since it became the dominant force in the PLO in the years after Israel's decisive victory in 1967, had fallen out of favor in its twelve years of leading the Palestinian Authority. Corruption, cronyism, human rights abuses, and the degradation of living conditions for Palestinians in all of the occupied territories combined to shatter the faith of many Palestinians in Fatah's leadership. The 2004 death of Yasser Arafat—who, for all his flaws as leader of the PA, was still widely seen as the historic leader of the modern Palestinian resistance—further diminished Fatah's standing, as Mahmoud Abbas could not command the same respect as his predecessor.

56. Elgindy, *Blind Spot*, 186.

57. For an in-depth exploration of the decline of the Palestinian economy under Oslo, see Fadle M. Naqib, "Economic Aspects of the Palestinian-Israeli Conflict: The Collapse of the Oslo Accord," Discussion Paper No. 2002/100, United Nations University, World Institute for Development Economics Research, October 2002, www.peacepalacelibrary.nl/ebooks /files/dp2002-100.pdf.

58. For an analysis of Hamas's stunning victory, see Mitchell Plitnick, "Hamas Victory Q/A," ZNet, February 1, 2006, zcomm.org/znetarticle/hamas -victory-q-a-by-mitchell-plitnick.

59. MSNBC News Services, "Olmert: Israel Won't Negotiate with Hamas," NBC, January 27, 2006, www.nbcnews.com/id/11009552/ns/world_news -mideast_n_africa/t/olmert-israel-wont-negotiate-hamas.

60. For the effects of the withholding of taxes, see "'Twenty-Seven Months—Intifada, Closures and Palestinian Economic Crisis, An Assessment," World Bank, May 2003, documents.worldbank.org/curated/en /616581468765333893/pdf/263141270months0Intifada10Closures.pdf, particularly p. xi. Since 2000, Israel has increasingly used the withholding of value-added taxes (VAT) as a tool to penalize the Palestinians. VAT is, in most years, the biggest source of income for the Palestinian economy, and it's a far more stable source of income than international aid, which is not part of a larger economic system that helps the Palestinian economy, as the production and sale of goods are. The advantages for Israel are clear. As a punitive measure, it is not directly violent, like military action, so it tends to garner less international criticism. There is also the ease with which Israelis opposed to whatever government is in power can portray the disbursement of taxes as the provision of aid to the Palestinians. For a full description of the deleterious effects of withholding these taxes, as well as the argument for why it is an illegitimate tool for Israel to use, see Al-Haq, "The Unlawful Seizure of Palestinian Taxes: A War Crime to Punish Palestinian ICC Membership," April 1, 2015, www.alhaq.org/cached_uploads/download /alhaq_files/publications/The.Unlawful.Seizure.of.Palestinian.Taxes.Report .pdf. Israel has responded in different ways to defend its actions depending on the stated reason for withholding the funds. For example, in recent years, Israel has withheld the funds because of its objections to the PA's disbursement of money from the Palestinian Martyrs' Fund, which supports the families of those killed or imprisoned for acts of violence against Israelis. Other times, it has withheld funds because of unpaid bills for Palestinian utilities, which are supplied by Israel. But other times, when it has been much more blatantly political, as was the case when the PA went to the International Criminal Court to request an investigation of Israel, it has simply pointed to something the Palestinians did, as if withholding the tax money is an inherently legitimate act. For more on this, see Zvi Bar'el, "The Illusion of Withholding the Palestinians' Tax Money," *Haaretz*, February 12, 2019, www.haaretz.com/opinion/.premium-the-illusion-of-withholding-the-pales tinians-tax-money-1.6933594.

61. See "Quartet: Hamas Must Change Policy," CNN, January 31, 2006, www.cnn.com/2006/WORLD/meast/01/30/hamas.funding/.

62. The UN was not so constrained, as its fundamental peacemaking purpose dictates that it not close off, a priori, the possibility of negotiations with anyone. In addition, the UN and Russia disagreed with the U.S. position of unrelenting and uncompromising pressure unless Hamas accepted the three

Quartet conditions, although practically there was really nothing they could do about it.

63. See Martin S. Indyk and Tamara Coffman-Wittes, "Dual Dilemmas: U.S. Policy Options for the Israeli-Palestinian Predicament," Brookings Institute, May 19, 2006, www.brookings.edu/research/dual-dilemmas-u-s-policy -options-for-the-israeli-palestinian-predicament. Crucially, the authors, both very influential in Washington among Middle East policy circles in the Democratic Party, firmly believed Hamas would never diverge from the goal of Israel's total destruction. Yet, they argued, it was important to give Hamas the opportunity to do so. Ultimately, Coffman-Wittes and Indyk supported efforts to undermine the duly elected Palestinian government, although they felt that the manner in which the Bush administration was going about it needed some major refinement.

64. See Smith, *Palestine and the Arab-Israeli Conflict*, 510–11.

65. Smith, *Palestine and the Arab-Israeli Conflict*.

66. It is worth noting that, from the outset, the United States insisted that Hamas, not the Palestinian Authority, affirm the "Quartet conditions." This is a most unusual stance. As a general rule, a functioning democracy allows for a wide range of views, while, in the international arena, governments are expected to keep faith with their agreements and abide by diplomatic norms and expectations, some of which are universal, while others are context-specific. Israel, for example, has never faced a demand to reaffirm its acceptance of a two-state solution, despite the fact that one of its major parties, the Likud, stated in its 1999 party platform that "the Government of Israel [which, at that time, Likud led] flatly rejects the establishment of a Palestinian Arab state west of the Jordan river." See "Likud—Platform," web .archive.org/web/20070930181442/www.knesset.gov.il/elections/knesset15 /elikud_m.htm. Yet this has never been deemed disqualifying. Instead, when Likud leader Benjamin Netanyahu publicly affirmed support for a two-state solution, it was simply understood that, whatever the platform of his party may have been, the commitment was made by the government of Israel, not a specific party. For his affirmation, see "Full Text of Netanyahu's Foreign Policy Speech at Bar Ilan," *Haaretz*, June 14, 2009, www.haaretz.com/1.5064276. Similarly, the Republican National Committee, in 2012, resolved "that the members of this body support Israel in their natural and God-given right of self-governance and self-defense upon their own lands, recognizing that Israel is neither an attacking force nor an occupier of the lands of others; and that peace can be afforded the region only through a united Israel governed under one law for all people." This was a clear affirmation of a single Israeli state dominating all the territory under Israeli control. Yet, no one demanded

that the United States, where the Republicans held one of two houses of Congress, excise Republicans from any involvement in the Israel-Palestine issue unless Republicans changed their stance. For details on this incident, see Mitchell Plitnick, "GOP Officially Endorses One-State Solution," Re-Thinking Foreign Policy, January 19, 2012, rethinkingforeignpolicy.org/2012 /01/19/gop-officially-endorses-one-state-solution/.

67. It is worth noting here that the second condition, in particular, would have been problematic for most early Israeli governments, which included figures who had been wanted for terrorism before the state came into existence. Moreover, even as this condition was imposed on the Palestinians, Israel was, itself, clandestinely funding settlements that were not only illegal under international law but under Israeli law as well. The issue became a sufficient concern to the Israeli public that Ariel Sharon commissioned a report, later informally known as the Sasson Report, after its author. Despite years of effort that produced a report over three hundred pages long, the final document could not fully trace the sources of funding for illegal "outposts" in the West Bank—hardly an example of the sort of transparency being demanded of the PA, yet certainly as much of a concern for the peace process. For the full report in Hebrew, see Talia Sasson, "חוות דעת (ביניים)בנושא מאחזים בלתי מורשים" (Interim Report on Illegal Outposts), Israeli Prime Minister's Office, March 8, 2005, www.pmo.gov.il /SiteCollectionDocuments /PMO /Commu nication/Spokesman/sason2.pdf. For a summary of the report in English, see "Summary of the Opinion Concerning Unauthorized Outposts-Talya Sason, Adv.," Israeli Ministry of Foreign Affairs, March 10, 2005, www.mfa.gov.il /mfa/aboutisrael/state/law/pages/summary%20of%20opinion%20concerning %20unauthorized%20outposts%20-%20talya%20sason%20adv.aspx.

68. For a clear explanation of the inability for any Palestinian government, whether Hamas was involved or not, to accept the conditions in the Anti-Terrorism Act, see Stephen Zunes, "Punishing the Palestinians," Mother Jones, June 15, 2006, www.motherjones.com/politics/2006/06/punishing -palestinians. On Hamas's growing flexibility, see Fawaz A. Gerges, "The Transformation of Hamas," The Nation, January 7, 2010, www.thenation.com /article/archive/transformation-hamas.

69. For the full text of McCollum's letter, see Betty McCollum, "A Letter to AIPAC," New York Review of Books, June 8, 2006, www.nybooks.com/articles /2006/06/08/a-letter-to-aipac. See "S.2237—Palestinian Compliance Act of 2006," Congress.gov, February 1, 2006, www.congress.gov/bill/109th-congress /senate-bill/2237/text.

70. For a fuller examination of this double standard, see Mitchell Plitnick, "The Hamas-Likud Double Standard," ReThinking Foreign Policy,

June 2, 2014, rethinkingforeignpolicy.org/2014/06/02/the-hamas-likud-dou ble-standard/.

71. For the Likud's stance, see Mitchell Plitnick, "Who's Afraid of a Palestinian State?," ReThinking Foreign Policy, April 14, 2014, rethinkingforeign policy.org/2011/04/14/whos-afraid-of-a-palestinian-state/.

72. See "Full Text of Netanyahu's Foreign Policy Speech at Bar Ilan," *Haaretz*, June 14, 2009, www.haaretz.com/1.5064276.

73. See Helena Cobban, "My Talk with Hamas About Peace with Israel," *Christian Science Monitor*, June 24, 2009, www.csmonitor.com/Commentary /Opinion/2009/0624/p09s01-coop.html.

74. Smith, *Palestine and the Arab-Israeli Conflict*, 511–12. Shalit would remain captive in Gaza for more than five years, becoming a national rallying cry for Israelis, until he was freed in exchange for one thousand Palestinian prisoners in October 2011.

75. David Rose, "The Gaza Bombshell," *Vanity Fair*, March 3, 2008, www .vanityfair.com/news/2008/04/gaza200804?prin.

76. Rose, "The Gaza Bombshell."

77. Rose, "The Gaza Bombshell."

78. See "Ruling Palestine I: Gaza Under Hamas," International Crisis Group, March 19, 2008, web.archive.org/web/20160520071006/www.cri sisgroup.org/~/media/Files/Middle%20East%20North%20Africa/Israel%20 Palestine/73_ruling_palestine_gaza_under_hamas.pdf. The report notes that, "As a general matter, Israel justified its siege by pointing to the 'absurd position whereby we are allowing goods to come into an entity whose rulers are continually firing rockets at our civilians, and sometimes even using those goods—such as fuel and electricity—to carry on these attacks.'"

79. For a deep analysis of the effects of Israel's designating Gaza a hostile territory, see Omar Jabary Salamanca, "Unplug and Play: Manufacturing Collapse in Gaza," *Human Geography* 4, no. 1 (2011), journals.sagepub.com /doi/pdf/10.1177/194277861100400103.

80. See, for example, Avi Issacharoff, Barak Ravid, and Shlomo Shamir, "Cabinet Declares Gaza 'Hostile Territory,'" *Haaretz*, September 20, 2007, www.haaretz.com/1.4976309. Israel contended that its withdrawal of settlements and military from Gaza means that it was no longer an occupying power and, thus, had no special responsibilities for the people of Gaza. For a brief examination of both sides of the argument, see Ruth Eglash, "Does Israel Actually Occupy the Gaza Strip?," *Washington Post*, July 2, 2015, www.washing tonpost.com/news/worldviews/wp/2015/07/02/does-israel-actually-occupy -the-gaza-strip. However, the weight of international law does not support the Israeli position. Well after the Israeli withdrawal from Gaza, the United

Nations and even the United States called Gaza "occupied territory." See Josh Levs, "Is Gaza 'Occupied Territory'?," CNN, January 6, 2009, www.cnn.com /2009/WORLD/meast/01/06/israel.gaza.occupation.question/index.html. The legal argument holds that Israel is responsible for the people of Gaza to the extent that it maintains control over them. Thus, Israel cannot be held responsible for internal security, policing, and similar matters over which it exerts no control in Gaza. But since Israel does control most of the supply of electricity and water into Gaza, controls the crossings into and out of Gaza, controls the shoreline and the airspace, including the electronic space for broadcasting and communications, it is responsible for these things under international law. The case for that responsibility is made in detail by the Israeli human rights group Gisha. See Sari Bashi and Tamar Feldman, *Scale of Control: Israel's Continued Responsibility in the Gaza Strip*, Gisha, November 2011, gisha.org/UserFiles/File/scaleofcontrol/scaleofcontrol_en.pdf.

81. See, for example, Rashid Khalidi, "Collective Punishment in Gaza," *New Yorker*, July 29, 2014, www.newyorker.com/news/news-desk/collective -punishment-gaza.

82. See "Rocket and Mortar Shell Fire During the Lull Period Compared with the First Half of 2008," Meir Amit Intelligence and Terrorism Information Center, June 11, 2008, www.terrorism-info.org.il/en/18395/. According to their data, the first six months of 2008 saw 1,199 rockets fired between January 1 and June 18, 2008. From June 19 until November 4, there were only 66 rockets fired. Similarly, 1,072 mortars were fired before June 18, only 33 after. Israeli government spokesman Mark Regev acknowledged that Hamas was doing all it could to stop the firing of projectiles into Israel.

83. For details of these incidents, see "Chronological Review of Events Relating to the Question of Palestine: Monthly Media Monitoring Review, United Nations Division for Palestinian Rights, July 2008," unispal.un.org/DPA/DPR /unispal.nsf/0/D33DD4A30C6FBE77852574C8006B6400. For a broader view of the overall situation in Israel and Palestine during this period, see Michele K. Esposito, "Quarterly Update on Conflict and Diplomacy, 16 August–15 November 2008," *Journal of Palestine Studies* 38, no. 2 (2009): 128–59.

84. See Al-Haq, "Operation Cast Lead: A Statistical Analysis," Al-Haq, August 2009,

85. Josh Ruebner, *Shattered Hopes: Obama's Failure to Broker Israeli-Palestinian Peace* (New York: Verso Books, 2013), 40–41. Citing "Operation Cast Lead: A Statistical Analysis," Al-Haq, August 2009, www.alhaq.org/at tachments/article/252/gaza-operation-cast-Lead-statistical-analysis%20.pdf; and "B'Tselem's Investigation of Fatalities in Operation Cast Lead," B'Tselem, www.btselem.org/download/20090909_cast_lead_fatalities_eng.pdf.

86. Israel has a long history of contending that it encounters bias at the United Nations, and the issue is a contentious one. But in the case of the UNHRC, there is substantial evidence of actual bias. Ironically, the UNHRC was created in 2006 to replace the UN Commission on Human Rights because that body had become discredited for having obvious human rights abusers as members, as well as for allegations of bias against Israel, but both of those issues have dogged the UNHRC just as much. As early as 2006, UN Secretary-General Kofi Annan stated, "I am worried by [the UNHRC's] disproportionate focus on violations by Israel. Not that Israel should be given a free pass. Absolutely not. But the Council should give the same attention to grave violations committed by other states as well." See "Secretary-General's Address to Mark International Human Rights Day," UN Secretary-General's Office, December 8, 2006, www.un.org/sg/en/content/sg/statement/2006 -12-08/secretary-generals-address-mark-international-human-rights-day. His successor, Ban Ki-Moon, said, referring again to bias against Israel, "The Secretary-General is disappointed at the council's decision to single out only one specific regional item given the range and scope of allegations of human rights violations throughout the world." See "UN's Ban Faults Rights Council over Israel," Ynet, June 21, 2007, www.ynetnews.com/arti cles/0,7340,L-3415619,00.html. Israel is the only country to merit a permanent space on then UNHRC agenda, and it has been condemned more often by the UNHRC than all other countries combined. See Eliezer Sherman, "Report: Since Inception, UNHRC Condemned Israel More Than Rest of World's Countries Combined," *The Algemeiner*, June 25, 2015, www.alge meiner.com/2015/06/25/report-since-inception-unhrc-condemned-israel -more-than-rest-of-worlds-countries-combined/. Apologists often use these facts for Israel in a self-serving manner, but this does not diminish their reality. Israel's human rights violations are well documented, in this work and many others, but it is impossible to argue that the country is somehow unique in its violations. Singling out Israel in this manner not only undermines the credibility of the UNHRC, but it provides cover for Israel's denial of its very real culpability. The Goldstone Report was a clear example of a thorough investigation that was undermined by the fact that it was the UNHRC that undertook it. If justice is to be done for the Palestinians, it must be done under a system in which all countries are treated equally. That is a more than adequate standard to address Palestinian rights.

87. "Report of the United Nations Fact-Finding Mission on the Gaza Conflict," Human Rights Council, A/HRC/12/48, September 25, 2009, p. 423, www2.ohchr.org/english/bodies/hrcouncil/docs/12session/A-HRC-12-48.pdf.

88. See, for example, "Israel PM Denounces UN Gaza Report," Al Jazeera, October 12, 2009, www.aljazeera.com/news/middleeast/2009/10/20091013 0301874824.html.

89. Wikileaks, "A/S Posner Discusses Cast Lead Investigations with IDF," January 27, 2010, wikileaks.org/plusd/cables/10TELAVIV182_a.html.

90. See Aviel Magnezi, "Report: Goldstone Banned from Grandson's Bar-Mitzvah," Ynet, April 15, 2010, www.ynetnews.com/articles/0,7340, L-3876529,00.html.

91. See Richard Goldstone, "Reconsidering the Goldstone Report on Israel and War Crimes," *Washington Post*, April 1, 2011, www.washingtonpost.com /opinions/reconsidering-the-goldstone-report-on-israel-and-war-crimes/2011 /04/01/AFg111JC_story.html.

92. Roi Maor, "Does Israel Intentionally Target Civilians?," +972 *Magazine*, April 22, 2011, www.972mag.com/does-israel-intentionally-target-civilians/.

93. Eisenkot quoted in Maor, "Does Israel Intentionally Target Civilians?"

94. Mitchell Plitnick, "Rethinking Goldstone?," *Tikkun Magazine*, April 2, 2011, www.tikkun.org/rethinking-goldstone.

95. The report of the UN committee stated, "The information available to the Committee suggests that not all allegations of violations identified in the [Goldstone] report have been adequately investigated. These include allegations related to higher level decisions about the design and implementation of the Gaza operation, including those related to the nature, objectives, and targets of the Israeli military in that conflict. The Committee has no new information leading it to change its view that Israel does not appear to have conducted a general review of doctrine regarding military targets. However, it has been informed of media reports suggesting that . . . it is possible that there will be deliberations on the broader question of the rules of engagement that obtained during Operation Cast Lead." See "Report of the Committee of independent experts in international humanitarian and human rights law established pursuant to Council resolution13/9," United Nations Human Rights Council, Sixteenth Session, Agenda Item 7, March 18, 2011, https: //www2.ohchr.org/english/bodies/hrcouncil/docs/16session/A.HRC.16.24 _AUV.pdf.

96. See for example, reports from Human Rights Watch: "Deprived and Endangered: Humanitarian Crisis in the Gaza Strip," January 13, 2009, www hrw.org/news/2009/01/13/deprived-and-endangered-humanitarian-crisis -gaza-strip'"Rain of Fire: Israel's Unlawful Use of White Phosphorus in Gaza," March 25, 2009, www.hrw.org/report/2009/03/25/rain-fire/israels-unlawful -use-white-phosphorus-gaza; "Israel: Soldiers' Punishment for Using Boy

as 'Human Shield' Inadequate," November 26, 2010, www.hrw.org/news
/2010/11/26/israel-soldiers-punishment-using-boy-human-shield-inadequate;
"White Flag Deaths: Killings of Palestinian Civilians During Operation Cast
Lead," August 13, 2009, www.hrw.org/report/2009/08/13/white-flag-deaths
/killings-palestinian-civilians-during-operation-cast-lead. Also see, from the
Israeli human rights group, B'Tselem, "Three Years Since Operation Cast
Lead: Israeli Military Utterly Failed to Investigate Itself," January 18, 2012,
www.btselem.org/gaza_strip/20120118_3_years_after_cast_lead; "B'Tselem:
Cover-Up of Phosphorus Shelling in Gaza Proves Army Cannot Investigate
Itself," February 1, 2010, www.btselem.org/press_releases/20100201. And
from the Palestinian human rights group Al-Haq, see, among others, "Im-
peding Medical Relief in the Gaza Strip: Israel's War Crimes Against the
Injured," October 12, 2010, www.alhaq.org/advocacy/7230.html; "Operation
Cast Lead and the Distortion of International Law," April 6, 2009, www
.alhaq.org/advocacy/7218.html; "Forgotten: Gaza two years after Operation
Cast Lead," June 6, 2011.

97. See Elgindy, *Blind Spot*, 199–200.

98. See B'Tselem, "Explanation of Statistics on Fatalities," www.btselem
.org/statistics/casualties_clarifications.

99. For different definitions of a legitimate target, where combatants
would more likely be during an attack, see "Human Rights Violations During
Operation Pillar of Defense, 14–21 November 2012," B'Tselem: The Israeli
Information Center for Human Rights in the Occupied Territories, p. 38,
May 2013, www.btselem.org/download/201305_pillar_of_defense_operation
_eng.pdf.

100. "50 Days: More Than 500 Children: Facts and Figures on Fatalities
in Gaza, Summer 2014," B'Tselem, July 20, 2016, www.btselem.org/press
_releases/20160720_fatalities_in_gaza_conflict_2014.

101. See "Israel's Protection and Hamas' Exploitation of Civilians in Operation Protective Edge," Israeli Ministry of Foreign Affairs, July 24, 2014, mfa
.gov.il/MFA/ForeignPolicy/Issues/Pages/Israel-protection-and-Hamas-ex
ploitation-of-civilians-in-Operation-Protective-Edge-July-2014.aspx.

102. For video of Kerry's hot mic moment, and further context and reporting on the incident, see Shannon Travis, "Kerry Caught on Hot Mic: Was He
Criticizing Israel?," CNN, July 21, 2014, www.cnn.com/2014/07/20/politics
/mideast-kerry-hot-mic/index.html.

103. See Herb Keinon, "Obama Reaffirms Israel's Right to Defend Itself,"
Jerusalem Post, July 19, 2014, www.jpost.com/Operation-Protective-Edge
/Netanyahu-speaks-with-UN-chief-over-phone-363479. Obama urged re-
straint, while other Western nations expressed somewhat greater concern

over Israel's decision to launch a ground operation in Gaza, but there were few calls for Israel to cease its overall operations or many statements that considered Israel's actions excessive.

104. For a list of various statements and legislation from Congress in support of Israel's operation in Gaza, see "Support Israel's Right to Self-Defense," American-Israel Public Action Committee, www.aipac.org/learn/legislative -agenda/agenda-display?agendaid=%7B570C7179-9618-4DAC-A0C6-E5E 35E1FA5CB%7D.

105. The Senate approved the aid by unanimous consent. In the House, the vote was 395–8 in favor of the additional aid, with the "nay" votes evenly split 4–4 between Republicans and Democrats. See "Congress Passes $225 Million in Extra Military Aid to Israel. Which 8 Had the Courage to Vote No?," *Daily Kos*, August 2, 2014, www.dailykos.com/stories/2014/8/2/1318523 /-Congress-Passes-225-Million-in-Extra-Military-Aid-to-Israel-Which-8 -Had-the-Courage-to-Vote-No.

106. See *Report on UNCTAD Assistance to the Palestinian People: Developments in the Economy of the Occupied Palestinian Territory*, United Nations Conference on Trade and Development (UNCTAD), July 6, 2015, unctad.org /en/PublicationsLibrary/tdb62d3_en.pdf.

107. See Khaled Abu Toameh, "Hamas: Israel Ready to Help, But PA Blocking Fuel to Gaza Power Plant," *Jerusalem Post*, October 6, 2018, www.jpost .com/Israel-News/Hamas-Israel-ready-to-help-but-PA-blocking-fuel-to-Gaza -power-plant-568778. See Jack Khoury and Yaniv Kubovich, "Defying Abbas, Israel Allows Qatari-Funded Fuel into Gaza Strip," *Haaretz*, October 9, 2018, www.haaretz.com/middle-east-news/palestinians/defying-abbas-israel-al lows-qatari-funded-fuel-into-gaza-strip-1.6545230.

108. For details, see Shira Rubin, "Palestinians Have Spent Decades Battling Israel. Now They're Battling Each Other," Vox, August 22, 2017, www.vox.com/world/2017/8/22/16114696/palestinian-hamas-israel-indepen dence-netanyahu-abbas-trump. See also Entsar Abu Jahal, "What Are Real Motives for PA Government Visit to Egypt?," Al-Monitor, October 28, 2019, www.al-monitor.com/pulse/originals/2019/10/palestine-visit-government -egypt-gaza-economic-blockade.html#ixzz63wvutZ9g.

109. See UN Children's Fund, "State of Palestine: Humanitarian Situation Report, July–September 2019," ReliefWeb International, September 30, 2019, reliefweb.int/report/occupied-palestinian-territory/state-palestine-hu manitarian-situation-report-july-september-2.

110. Jehad Abusalim, "The Great March of Return: An Organizer's Perspective," *Journal of Palestine Studies* 47, no. 4 (2018), 90–100, jps.ucpress .edu/content/ucpjps/47/4/90.full.pdf.

111. For an explanation of just how deeply offensive Trump's attempt to "redefine" refugee status was for Palestinians, see Noura Erakat, "Trump Has No Right to Define Who Is a Palestinian Refugee," Middle East Eye, September 5, 2018, www.middleeasteye.net/opinion/trump-has-no-right-define-who-palestinian-refugee.

112. The post originally appeared in Arabic at www.facebook.com/abur tema/posts/102108173 52613780, January 7, 2018. Translated by Jehad Abu salim and cited in "The Great March of Return."

113. The open-air prison analogy is frequently used for Gaza. See, for example, Alistair Dawber, "Tales from Gaza: What Is Life Really Like in 'the World's Largest Outdoor Prison'?," The Independent, April 13, 2013, www.independent.co.uk/news/world/middle-east/tales-from-gaza-what-is-life-really-like-in-the-worlds-largest-outdoor-prison-8567611.html. See also "David Cameron Describes Blockaded Gaza as a 'Prison,'" BBC News, July 27, 2010, www.bbc.com/news/world-middle-east-10778110 among many others.

114. See Mitchell Plitnick, "Trump's Endgame in Palestine," LobeLog, September 6, 2018, lobelog.com/trumps-endgame-in-palestine.

115. See, for example, Ali Abunimah, "Gaza Medic Killed by Israel as She Rescued Injured," Electronic Intifada, June 2, 2018, electronicintifada.net/blogs/ali-abunimah/gaza-medic-killed-israel-she-rescued-injured; see also video and transcript, "Meet Tarek Loubani, the Canadian Doctor Shot by Israeli Forces Monday While Treating Gaza's Wounded," Democracy Now!, May 17, 2018, www.democracynow.org/2018/5/17/meet_tarek_loubani_the_canadian_doctor. On journalist casualties, see Loveday Morris, "He Was Wearing a Vest Marked 'PRESS.' He Was Shot Dead Covering a Protest in Gaza," Washington Post, April 7, 2018, www.washingtonpost.com/world/palestinian-journalist-in-vest-marked-press-shot-dead-by-israeli-troops-in-gaza/2018/04/07/ac57b524-3a30-11e8-8fd2-49fe3c675a89_story.html.

116. Tareq Baconi, "One Year of Gaza Protests. A New Era of Palestinian Struggle?," New York Review of Books, March 29, 2019, www.nybooks.com/daily/2019/03/29/one-year-of-gaza-protests-a-new-era-of-palestinian-struggle. No Palestinian demand causes more consternation in Israel than the demand to return. The violence with which the GMR has been met is largely explained by this fact.

117. For more on the role the schism played in the GMR and in the march's goals, see Abusalim, "The Great March of Return." For the relative importance of the Fatah-Hamas split in the GMR and its lesser stature than that of the Israeli occupation, see the comments of Diana Buttu in Huthifa Fayyad, "Gaza's Great March of Return Protests Explained," Al Jazeera, March 30,

2019, www.aljazeera.com/news/2019/03/gaza-great-march-return-protests-ex
plained-190330074116079.html.

118. "The Gaza March of Return: What You Need to Know," Anti-Defamation League (ADL), www.adl.org/resources/reports/the-gaza-march
-of-return-what-you-need-to-know. The alarmist language, which portrayed
the GMR as a very large and violent mob bearing down on Israel, elides the
fact that the gathering of protesters occurred inside Gaza, which naturally
invites the question of why Israel felt it was entitled to police that action in
the first place, particularly as it claims to have no powers or responsibilities
as an occupier in Gaza.

119. "The Gaza March of Return," ADL.

120. For photos comparing the two events, see Kainaz Amaria and Alexia
Underwood, "Photos: US Jerusalem Embassy Opening and Gaza Border
Protests," Vox, May 16, 2018, www.vox.com/2018/5/14/17353298/jerusalem
-embassy-palestinian-protests-gaza-israel.

121. Debra J. Saunders, "Did Democrats Skip Embassy Opening to Snub
Trump?," RealClearPolitics, May 20, 2018, www.realclearpolitics.com/arti
cles/2018/05/20/did_democrats_skip_embassy_opening_to_snub_trump
_137072.html.

122. See, for instance, Noam Chomsky, "My Visit to Gaza, the World's
Largest Open-Air Prison," Truthout, November 9, 2012, truthout.org/articles
/noam-chomsky-my-visit-to-gaza-the-worlds-largest-open-air-prison. Also see
Editorial, "Gaza Goes from 'World's Biggest Prison' to 'World's Biggest Solitary
Confinement Cell,'" Haaretz, July 11, 2018, www.haaretz.com/opinion/edito
rial/gaza-from-biggest-prison-to-biggest-solitary-confinement-cell-1.6265661.

123. Khalidi, "Collective Punishment in Gaza."

124. See "Practice Relating to Rule 103. Collective Punishments," International Committee of the Red Cross, Customary International Law, ihl-data
bases.icrc.org/customary-ihl/eng/docs/v2_rul_rule103.

Conclusion: Beyond the Limits

1. "Transcript: Democratic Presidential Debate in Brooklyn," New York
Times, April 15, 2016, www.nytimes.com/2016/04/15/us/politics/tran
script-democratic-presidential-debate.html.

2. This stood in marked contrast to the incumbent losses by both
George H. W. Bush and Jimmy Carter. Both president's defeats were attributed by many, to one degree or another, to their stances on Israel and
the Palestinians. See, for example, "Did the First President Bush Lose His
Job to the Israel Lobby?" Observer, July 17 2006, observer.com/2006/07

/did-the-first-president-bush-lose-his-job-to-the-israel-lobby/, also Richard H. Curtiss, "President George H.W. Bush Stood up to the Israel Lobby—and Paid the Price," Washington Report on Middle East Affairs, January/February 2019, www.wrmea.org/2019-january-february/president-george-hw-bush-stood -up-to-the-israel-lobby-and-paid-the-price.html. On Carter, see Philip Weiss, "Jimmy Carter Believed He Lost a Second Term Because He Opposed Settlements, Alienating Jews—Eizenstat," Mondoweiss, February 7, 2019, mondoweiss.net/2019/02/settlements-alienated-eizenstat/ also Kenneth W. Stein, "My Problem with Jimmy Carter's Book," Middle East Forum, Spring 2007, pp. 3–15, www.meforum.org/1633/my-problem-with-jimmy-carters-book. For a progressive perspective which offers a different perspective on the influence of Israel in American electoral politics, see Mitchell Plitnick, "The Cold Realities of US Policy in Israel-Palestine," *Middle East Report Online*, October 15, 2014." merip.org/2014/10/the-cold-realities-of-us-policy-in-israel -palestine/.

3. Greg Jaffe and Souad Mekhennet, "Ilhan Omar's American Story: It's Complicated," *Washington Post*, July 6, 2019, www.washingtonpost.com/pol itics/2019/07/06/ilhan-omar-is-unlike-anyone-who-has-served-congress-this -is-her-complicated-american-story/?arc404=true.

4. Catie Edmondson, "A New Wave of Democrats Tests the Party's Blanket Support for Israel," *New York Times*, October 7, 2018, www.nytimes.com /2018/10/07/us/politics/democrats-israel-palestinians.html.

5. Shibley Telhami and Stella Rouse, "American Views of the Israeli-Palestinian Conflict," University of Maryland/Nielsen Scarborough, December 2018, sadat.umd.edu/sites/sadat.umd.edu/files/UMCIP%20Ques tionnaire%20Sep%20to%20Oct%202018.pdf.

6. Carol Morello and Ruth Eglash, "Kerry Harshly Condemns Israeli Settler Activity as an Obstacle to Peace," *Washington Post*, December 28, 2016, www.washingtonpost.com/world/national-security/kerry-address-middle -east-peace-process-amid-deep-us-israel-strains/2016/12/28/d656e5fa-cd0a -11e6-b8a2-8c2a61b0436f_story.html. This stance was based on a State Department legal finding that held that settlements were, in fact, in contravention of international law. While presidents since Ronald Reagan had, as we discuss later in this chapter and extensively in chapter 3, blurred this fact, none had clearly contradicted that ruling until the Trump administration. In November 2019, however, Secretary of State Mike Pompeo explicitly stated that "the establishment of Israeli civilian settlements in the West Bank is not per se inconsistent with international law." See Yaakov Katz, "West Bank Settlements Not Illegal, Pompeo Announces in Historic Shift," *Jerusalem Post*,

November 18, 2019, www.jpost.com/israel-news/west-bank-settlements-not -illegal-us-decides-in-historic-us-policy-shift-608222.

7. See "Democrats About as Likely to Sympathize with Palestinians as with Israel," Pew Research Center, January 22, 2018, www.people-press.org/2018 /01/23/republicans-and-democrats-grow-even-further-apart-in-views-of-is rael-palestinians/012318_2.

8. See Mitchell Plitnick, "GOP Officially Endorses One-State Solution," ReThinking Foreign Policy, January 19, 2012, rethinkingforeignpolicy.org /2012/01/19/gop-officially-endorses-one-state-solution.

9. See Jacob Kornbluh, "Republicans Unanimously Vote to Drop Support for Two-State Solution in Platform," *Haaretz/Jewish Insider*, July 12, 2016, www.haaretz.com/world-news/republicans-unanimously-vote-to-drop-sup port-for-two-state-solution-1.5409429.

10. See, for example, Felicia Schwartz and Rory Jones, "U.S. Drops In sistence on Two-State Solution to Israeli-Palestinian Conflict," *Wall Street Journal*, February 15, 2017, www.wsj.com/articles/u-s-drops-insistence-on -two-state-solution-to-israeli-palestinian-conflict-1487140809.

11. See, for example, Mitchell Plitnick, "Pompeo Buries the Two-State Solution with New U.S. Policy on Israeli Settlements," *LobeLog*, November 19, 2019, lobelog.com/pompeo-buries-the-two-state-solution-with-new-u-s-pol icy-on-israeli-settlements. For a review of the argument and the consensus that settlements are, in fact, illegal under international law, see Marty Lederman, "Assessing the New U.S. 'View' on the Legality of Israeli Settlements in the West Bank," Just Security, November 19, 2019, www.justsecurity.org/67343/assess ing-the-new-u-s-view-on-the-legality-of-israeli-settlements-in-the-west-bank.

12. Emma Green, "Trump Has Enabled Israel's Antidemocratic Tenden cies at Every Turn," *The Atlantic*, August 15, 2019, www.theatlantic.com/pol itics/archive/2019/08/israel-bans-omar-tlaib/596167.

13. Shimon Rolnitzky, "The Hasidic Jews of Monsey Must Ignore the Out siders Who Want Us to Take Up Arms and Politicize Our Tragedy," Jewish Telegraphic Agency, December 31, 2019, www.jta.org/2019/12/31/opinion /we-hasidic-jews-of-monsey-must-ignore-the-outsiders-who-want-us-to-take -up-arms-and-politicize-our-tragedy#.XgwHFUEa9sA.facebook.

14. Linda Sarsour, Twitter, December 31, 2019, twitter.com/lsarsour/sta tus/1212417350290608129.

Index

About the Authors

Marc Lamont Hill is an award-winning journalist and the Steve Charles Professor of Media, Cities, and Solutions at Temple University. He is the author of multiple books, including the *New York Times* bestselling *Nobody*. He lives in Philadelphia.

Mitchell Plitnick, the president of ReThinking Foreign Policy, is a political analyst and a frequent writer on the Middle East and U.S. foreign policy. His past roles include vice president of the Foundation for Middle East Peace, director of the U.S. Office of B'Tselem, and co-director of Jewish Voice for Peace. He lives in Maryland.

Printed in the USA
CPSIA information can be obtained
at www.ICGtesting.com
JSHW022342251223
54313JS00012B/55